WORKING FOR THE WORLD

THE EVOLUTION OF Australian Volunteers International

Peter Britton was on the staff of the Overseas Service Bureau (Australian Volunteers International) for 32 years from 1984, serving for most of that time in its Executive Team. In 1983–84, as a volunteer in Jakarta, he edited a prestigious social science journal, building on both his academic writing and community activism especially in development education.

Peter's earlier background in political science and history is represented in journal articles and book chapters since the 1970s. His book on the Indonesian army published in 1996 continues to be widely read and referenced today.

WORKING FOR THE WORLD

THE EVOLUTION OF Australian Volunteers International

PETER BRITTON

AUSTRALIAN SCHOLARLY

First published 2019 by
Australian Scholarly Publishing Pty Ltd
7 Lt Lothian St Nth, North Melbourne, Vic 3051
Tel: 03 9329 6963 / Fax: 03 9329 5452
enquiry@scholarly.info / www.scholarly.info

ISBN 978-1-925801-62-0

Cover design: Wayne Saunders

Contents

Contents

Foreword

*BY THE HON. MICHAEL KIRBY AC CMG**

This is an institutional history. It is not a record of all of the forms of youthful volunteerism, in Australia or elsewhere. It is not a chronicle of all those who felt a moral imperative to render skilled assistance without fee or financial reward to fellow human beings. It is not the general story of Australia's helpful relationships with its overseas neighbours or foreign aid, which stretches back to colonial times. Such relationships were often fuelled by political or missionary zeal, sometimes 'voluntary' only in a broad sense.

Instead, this is the story of the emergence, after the middle of the 20th century, of a succession of organisations in Australia, established to channel the desire of many young, educated citizens to reach out to, and engage with, needy people beyond our shores. This particular form of voluntary endeavour arose at roughly the same time in other English-speaking democracies. In the United Kingdom, Voluntary Service Overseas (VSO) was formed in 1958 as a feature of the political changes that led, through decolonisation, to the comparatively rapid dismantlement of the British Empire. Australia had been a key participant in that Empire. To some extent, it was sometimes a surrogate in Asia and the Pacific for the United Kingdom. Inevitably, it got caught up in the mental and political adjustments that independence movements demanded from their former colonial 'masters'.

In the United States of America, at much the same time, the Peace Corps was established (in March 1961) as a volunteer program created by

* Justice of the High Court of Australia (1996–2009); Co-Chair of the Human Rights Institute of the International Bar Association (from 2018); Honorary Life Member of NUAUS, 1966; Patron of Australian Volunteers International.

President John F. Kennedy. It was later authorised by Act of Congress. Its program was declared in that Act to be "to promote world peace and friendship through the service abroad of young men and women under conditions of hardship if necessary", to help the peoples of countries "in meeting their needs for trained manpower". As this book demonstrates Australia had begun similar initiatives before those of Britain and America.

The Australian initiatives occurred in three phases. The first was the Volunteer Graduate Scheme (VGS). This was a body that had its roots in the international deliberations of student organisations, specifically in the argument developed at the 1950 World University Congress in Bombay that they should emphasize efforts to increase international understanding over being involved in the material aid being directed to nations that were coping with the immediate aftermath of war and the advent of political independence. In Australia, initially in Melbourne, university undergraduates became engaged in small initiatives to offer their newly acquired professional skills to needy people.

The focus of VGS was Indonesia. This new nation, Australia's closest neighbour, presented huge needs after the end of Japanese rule. These needs become most obvious following the failed attempt of The Netherlands, in a "police action", to restore colonial governance. The enormous challenge had to be faced of creating a new nation out of thousands of disparate islands linked substantially only by considerations of geography and 400 years of Netherlands' rule. It is important to appreciate how far idealism arose out of the ashes of 1945. The War had finished with the advent of the atomic age; but also, with the adoption of the Charter of the United Nations. That instrument asserted the global imperative of universal human rights and justice. People at the time took this seriously.

The adoption of the Universal Declaration of Human Rights (UDHR) in 1948, supported by Australia, planted the seeds of idealism that influenced the thinking of many Australian university students of that era. One of those students, who had been elected President of the Melbourne University Students' Representative Council, was James Bawtree Webb (1929–2009). Raised with a strong Wesleyan Methodist commitment to social justice, Jim Webb by chance won a United Nations' essay competition. This fact changed his life. It took him to New York where he met youth leaders. But also, the chairperson of the committee that had adopted the UDHR, Eleanor Roosevelt.

When Jim Webb returned to Australia in 1953, he became honorary secretary to the Volunteer Graduate Scheme. Its objective was to translate the ideals and principles of the newly created United Nations into practical voluntary assistance and to foster support by young Australian volunteers for communities in Indonesia. Thus was born the Australian notion that young citizens (mostly university graduates) would spend part of their early lives, when their tolerance of 'roughing it' was greater than it would later be, helping willing overseas communities, public agencies and private initiatives in the urgent challenges of post-war reconstruction and self-determination. Jim Webb was not alone in these initiatives. But he became an important link to what was to follow.

There were several parallel developments amongst socially engaged university students in Australia at the same time. I know this, because these were the years when I was undertaking my own legal studies at the University of Sydney. The Colombo Plan (established in 1950) brought significant numbers of young undergraduates from Asian countries to Australia's universities to study side by side with Australian students. Slowly but surely, young Aboriginal Australian students, including Charlie Perkins, began, with their supporters, playing a leading role in student affairs in Australia. They were participating in bus rides promoting equal freedoms. They were also establishing Abscol to provide university places for Aboriginal Australians whose tertiary education had been shockingly neglected by Australia. Increasingly, through the National Union of Australian University Students (NUAUS), these causes became national initiatives in consequence of more regular meetings of the previously isolated students' representative councils. VGS operated under the auspices of NUAUS and, through the agency of Jim Webb, in due course it gave birth to the Overseas Service Bureau (OSB). This book is mainly the story of that body: its creation, objectives, methods of work, achievements and occasional failures. But it grew seamlessly out of the VGS and there was much overlap in the participating personnel.

Peter Britton has done a great service by rescuing the memories of the activities and objectives of OSB. In consequence of his academic involvement with Indonesian studies in Melbourne, he met many of the early VGS participants who had retained their interest in Indonesia and would gather for meetings at the newly created Monash University. He was initially supervised by Herb Feith, an early key actor in engagement with volunteer graduates placed in Indonesia. Later, Peter Britton came to know Jim Webb who, by then, had become the Director of Community Aid Abroad.

As is often the way in civil society organisations (most especially when they are organised by students and other amateurs) many of the records of the early years are lost or variable, if they were kept at all. The memories of the participants have faded and many have died. Yet the initiatives on the part of OSB gradually became larger and better organised. In part, this was the result of greater participation in such work by agencies and officers of the Australian Government. The government offered a measure of financial support because it could see the favourable impression that most of the volunteers earned concerning Australia. But government was sometimes needed to establish firm guidelines and to enforce consistent principles in order to ensure that high standards of conduct were observed, and proper balances struck, between the adventurous spirit of the volunteers and the commonly urgent and practical needs of the recipients of their labours.

In 1999, OSB was rebranded as Australian Volunteers International (AVI). However, essentially AVI was a continuation of OSB. Peter Britton accompanied this transition. He worked with Bill Armstrong in AVI for 18 years and subsequently became its Head of Programs for many years. His service lasted, in all, 32 years. During that long-term managerial experience, he witnessed the never-ending challenges of a volunteer civil society organisation.

The challenges were particularly demanding as a result of changing governmental attitudes to funding and support as well as the never-ending stream of participants of varying skills, utility and engagement. Jim Webb often said that the value derived by the Australian volunteers in the successive Australian organisations for volunteer services was usually much greater than the benefit derived by their hosts. This may have been a reflection of Jim Webb's politeness and the respect he encouraged all his volunteers to show to the countries and communities to whom they were assigned. However, because the projects were only accepted by OSB/AVI when the recipient host approved of them and because only those who passed the tests of expertise and good character were posted, it seems likely that substantial and worthwhile contributions were often made by the volunteers. Inevitably, their efforts would frequently leave good memories and feelings of appreciation from the foreign countries concerned for the volunteers and for Australia. Nonetheless, there was definitely an element of truth in the candid evaluation expressed by Jim Webb. This book explains why that is so.

The Australia from which the volunteers were sent to neighbouring countries in the early years of VGS, OSB and AVI, was a country with serious problems in consequence of the values held by many of its citizens – perhaps most. Despite the unequal treatment accorded to its own indigenous peoples, Australians were offering help to others when, often, their own country was failing to afford similar help to disadvantaged communities at home. Despite the assertion of a moral obligation to support people in newly independent countries, many of the earlier volunteers may have been influenced by attitudes akin to the 'while man's burden' that persisted in aid policy in Australia well into the second half of the twentieth century. Despite working with, and seeking to help, people of different ethnicity, skin colour, culture and religion, some at least of the Australian volunteers would inevitably have been influenced by attitudes engendered by the 'White Australia Policy' that survived in Australian law well into the 1970s. Whilst advocating greater equality and participation of women in neighbouring countries, many of the earlier volunteers came from an Australia that still practised widespread gender discrimination. And early Australian volunteers could scarcely advocate equality for LGBTIQ people in neighbouring countries when hostility and legal discrimination, remained toxic at home.

Notwithstanding these considerations that made Australia a sometimes dubious source for volunteers to help new and developing countries, the overall impact of the successive institutions for overseas volunteer placements was beneficial both for the volunteer and for the recipient. From the point of view of the recipients, they came to know, at close range, the generally admirable human qualities of those with whom they worked. Particularly in the matter of race, this, for Australians, was a specially beneficial experience for volunteers from White Australia. Volunteer placement opened the door to experiences often denied to the volunteers at home. This was a benefit to the volunteers. But it was also of benefit to Australia. The rapid development of safe, cheap and speedy air travel facilitated the overseas placements. OSB and AVI quickly took advantage of these and other critical technological developments.

Peter Britton is to be thanked for writing this book at a time just before it would otherwise have become impossible to reconstruct this important period in Australia's transition to a more modern, multi-cultural, multi-racial society. The book describes a number of countries in transition. But some of the biggest changes were happening in Australia itself. Peter Britton captures a moment in Australia's own evolution. So this book is as much a part of the history of the solidarity shown by Australia to newly independent countries as by those countries towards Australia. And it also shows the growth of solidarity amongst Australia's people with each other and with Australia's rapidly changing neighbours and their people.

Sydney,
7 February 2019

Acknowledgements

When I was contemplating undertaking the research for this book it was both reassuring and daunting to know that AVI held many cubic metres of archives. I am indebted to the Board of AVI and the CEO, Paul Bird for providing me with unrestricted access to these records. The records are of course the products of staff work over many decades, and in reading them, even handling some of the older files, I couldn't help but be conscious of the effort involved. My gratitude goes to all the staff who directly or indirectly contributed to the organisation's record, not just those whose handwriting or initials I recognised.

At no point did AVI's Board or CEO make any effort to direct or influence my writing. This is neither a commissioned piece of work nor an official history, so the responsibility for deciding what to include, exclude and emphasise is mine alone. Similarly, there is no one else I can blame for the book's shortcomings.

I am grateful for the assistance and encouragement from former Board members and staff who read and commented on particular chapters or episodes, or, in some cases, responded to questions in personal discussion or correspondence. My particular thanks go to Bill Armstrong and Hugh O'Neill for continuing to insist that the story was worth telling. Timely encouragement also came from Chris Fogarty and Elizabeth Britten.

Geoff Atkinson and Roger King provided information which plugged gaps in the records and ably described the atmospherics of the late 1970s which no paper record could reveal. My thanks go to Deborah Rhodes, Christopher Dureau, Christine Perkins, Kirsty Sword Gusmao, Vicky Tchong and Mike Parsons who were all able to assist in describing both operational contexts and actual events. I am especially grateful to Graham Habgood for agreeing that I could tell his story.

In accessing AVI's records, certain AVI staff were particularly helpful in finding data sets, files and images. My thanks to Tracy Pearce, Yureed Ul-Ghani, Ruth Oliphant and Jane Macdonald. My thanks too for the ongoing interest and confidence from former colleagues Ian MacDonald, who personifies AVI's history, and Jess Pietsch who never seemed to doubt that the book would eventually be completed.

I am especially indebted to Rachel Salmond for supporting me in this project. She helped prepare the manuscript for publication but, more significantly, also provided the mentoring and critical support I needed.

On the home front, Tina, Jillian and Jack have always been supportive and interested, even if they wondered why it was taking so long. Tina in particular will be pleased that other priorities can now resume their rightful position on our to-do list.

Introduction

International volunteering has for decades been a valued component of international development thinking and practice. It emerged in the post-Second World War era as a response to skill shortages in developing countries and as a vehicle to express a new internationalism. Naturally enough, each country's international volunteer organisation reflected the unique characteristics of that country. The British Voluntary Service Overseas, now known simply as VSO, began life in 1958 as a program for school leavers and was at least partially informed by a sense of obligation and opportunity as former British colonies claimed their independence. The United States Peace Corps, from its inception in 1961, was a program of the State Department and has always been an expression of American foreign policy and its interests. But, in different ways and to varying degrees, international volunteer programs all share in the dual aims of providing cost-effective know-how in places and communities where it is needed and engendering mutual understanding across cultures through respectful personal relationships.

Without suggesting that the global enterprise of volunteering owes its existence to Australia's Volunteer Graduate Scheme (VGS), it was clearly a progenitor. The success of the VGS programs in Indonesia gave rise to the establishment of the Overseas Service Bureau (OSB) in 1961. Its founders had been intimately involved in VGS and carried much of its ethos and principles into the new organisation. This book charts the path of OSB from its origins in VGS, to its rebranding as Australian Volunteers International (AVI) in 1999 and up to 2002. This was the end of a defining era with Bill Armstrong as CEO and a time when AVI's relationship with government was shifting. It is essentially a history of the organisation and of the government policies and positions that affected the directions that the organisation took as its relationship with government unfolded and changed over fifty years.

There is always a story about how books come to be written and this book is no exception. Through personal involvement I knew the organisation well. When I resigned my position in February 2016 as AVI's Deputy CEO and Head of Programs, I had worked there for 32 years, for most of that time in the Executive Management team. Before this I had worked in Jakarta as an Australian volunteer editing a social science journal for a prominent Indonesian NGO. Even before that, in the early 1970s when I was a postgraduate researcher living in Jakarta, I would often be asked to meet incoming volunteers at the airport.

I also had other less direct connections to this institution. Through my earlier academic involvement in Indonesia, and in particular the Contemporary Indonesia Study Group at Monash University, I got to know many of the early volunteer graduates to Indonesia. At Monash I worked with and was supervised by Herb Feith who pioneered international volunteering from Australia. In the mid to late 1970s when working in development education in Melbourne, I got to know Jim Webb, founder and first Director of OSB.[1] These connections provided me with an unusual perspective on the organisation. In a sense I was a link between the contemporary organisation in which I worked and the organisational philosophies and lived experiences from earlier decades. I was not the only link; Bill Armstrong, OSB's Executive Director through the 1980s and 1990s, had worked closely with Jim Webb in the first years of the Australian Volunteers Abroad (AVA) program. OSB Committee members Frank Engel and Hugh O'Neill embodied the organisation's experiences and values from its very beginnings and other committee members had vivid recollections of their own volunteer experiences in the 1970s. Their voices ensured that OSB maintained a strong sense of its history and identity.

Inevitably when so much of an institution's history is an oral history it takes on a life of its own. Attachment to the past can lead to exaggeration and individuals' experiences are easily generalised. Misconceptions have arisen and persist, such as the notion that Herb Feith was the founder of the organisation or that the Australian government gave no support to international volunteering until the late 1960s or, paradoxically, that Menzies had been a great supporter of the program. Setting the record straight is a strong motivation for writing this book, which will be of interest to people who supported the organisation, worked for it and participated in its programs. A wider readership will find in it a contribution to the social and political history of Australia's engagement with the Asia-Pacific region and beyond, and to debates about international aid and development. It will also complement the growing body of academic literature concerning international volunteering.[2]

On hearing that this book was in preparation, many commented on the rich material that would be available in the stories of the volunteers. After all, in the imagination of most, volunteers are altruistic and adventurous. To the extent this may be so, it is equally true that in an infinite variety of ways self-interest drives volunteers as they pursue personal agendas of learning and growth, seeking the satisfaction of making a contribution and building substance into their curricula vitae. Bringing altruism and self-interest together is the genius of volunteer programs. There is already a wealth of material published about volunteers, their personalities, their stories and their achievements. Many Australian stories were brought together and illustrated with stunning photographs in the 2007 publication *A Place in the World*.[3] Volunteer lives and achievements have also featured in the regular publications of OSB/AVI. The story that hasn't yet been told is the story of the organisation, and that is the focus of this book. It traces the origins of OSB and documents, its growth and its setbacks, taking into account the constraints, opportunities and dilemmas it faced and the choices it made.

The principles of the organisation were determined fairly early and for the most part remained relatively constant over time. The domestic and international contexts in which OSB operated have, however, changed dramatically and keep on changing. An overriding and ever-present concern has been OSB's relations with the Australian Government. Here was an organisation established by a group of individuals acting to provide structure and strength to ideas with proven community support, but which became dependent on government funding from early in its life. Despite this, it remained resolutely independent and maintained a strong identity as it navigated changes of government and the widely differing outlooks of successive Ministers for Foreign Affairs and public servants.

OSB also needed to respond to events that unfolded around the globe as decolonisation gathered pace and entered new phases, creating demand in new countries for the services of volunteers and changing the conditions under which they could be mobilised and supported. As the environment in which it operated became more complex, the organisation learnt to manage its programs astutely, always taking into account the risks that volunteers might face, but not totally avoiding risk as this was intrinsic to its work.

Structure

Part I of the book is concerned with how OSB established its defining principles, its values and identity. The intellectual origins of the Volunteer Graduate Scheme to Indonesia and the enabling environment of the Student Christian Movement (SCM) at the University of Melbourne immediately after the Second World War are analysed. VGS was an expression of post-colonial solidarity and was run by a voluntary committee operating with the formal agreement of and financial support of the Australian and Indonesian governments, as well as with widespread support from the Australian community. The Scheme asserted the validity and moral superiority of racial and financial equality as the basis for Westerners engaging in Asia. This was a radical and minority position amongst expatriates and strongly influenced early Australian thinking about international aid.

The success of VGS encouraged Jim Webb to establish OSB in 1961 to promote work opportunities in a broad range of developing countries in Asia, Africa and the Pacific Islands. From this base the Australian

Volunteers Abroad (AVA) program was launched, with Australians taking on assignments in Papua and New Guinea, Solomon Islands, Nigeria and Tanganyika (now Tanzania). The new program enjoyed immediate community support, but, realising that government support would also be needed eventually, Webb embarked on a strategy to demonstrate OSB's worth. He assembled a Committee to function as a board of well-connected supporters and a panel of patrons drawn from the great and the good. Rather than seek government funding immediately they sought to impress with the quality of the programs and their ability to garner community and business support. The strategy succeeded and the Government offered funding support to OSB for its programs, bringing a certainty that outweighed the few conditions attached to the funding. This began a lasting relationship between OSB and government ministers, their advisers and departmental officers.

Through the 1970s, the organisation marked time, attempting to preserve established practices, resisting innovation and becoming inward-looking. Everyday management was erratic, lacked transparency and became increasingly defensive in dealing with its most important constituencies – former and current volunteers, supporters in the community and public servants. A divided Committee protected the Director and his controlling hand until those who advocated change prevailed in instituting an internal review of OSB's management, which fed into an external review requested by the Minister for Foreign Affairs.

With a new Director and renewal within the Committee, OSB instituted internal reform and rebuilt its relationships with community supporters and with government from the early 1980s. Part II of the book captures the changes wrought by an open, participatory and consultative approach to management and a relationship with the federal government characterised by mutual respect. OSB rapidly expanded the scale and scope of its programs and strengthened its identity, all the while upholding the foundational principles that defined its approach to development.

OSB continued through the 1990s confident in its own identity and values and active in international fora and in Australian debate about development, development assistance and international relations. It nurtured its relations with the Australian government and won significant financial support for expanded programs, responding as it did so to changes in the way that support was provided as government funding and contracting policy and practice changed. There was a shift in this era in the ways the government related to NGOs and this also impacted on OSB. In the mid-1990s, the Australian International Development Assistance Bureau (AIDAB) continued to show its appreciation of OSB's non-government status, impressed in particular by the strength of its engagement with the Australian community and its ability to enter international operational milieus not accessible to the government. Discussions over funding and efficiency led OSB to realise that its hitherto protected status might not always be a given, but it was not until late 1996 that the Australian Agency for International Development (AusAID) was encouraged to develop a policy on its support for volunteer programs. Until this time volunteer programs had been relatively unaffected by neoliberalism, but by 1998 AusAID's language and practice had shifted to describing OSB as a service provider to government. The volunteer program was also increasingly tied to the objectives of Australia's official aid program.

It is not possible to portray or analyse the full extent of all OSB's country programs in every era in this book. Part III details selected programs in five parts of the world – Indochina, Africa, Indonesia, Papua New Guinea and the Pacific Islands, and East Timor. The first three of these accounts are largely set in the 1980s. In Indochina this was the era when the programs began. There had been programs since the 1960s in Indonesia and Africa, but the 1980s was a time of new complexity and intensity. The Pacific Islands and Papua New Guinea had also welcomed Australian volunteers in the 1960s, but the accounts in this volume focus on the 1990s as this decade required greater scale and more innovation. AVI's East Timor story, of course, began only in the late 1990s. Selecting particular country and regional programs has meant excluding others, such as those in South Asia, the Middle East, Latin America and China. There is, however, both narrative and evaluative material available on these programs in AVI's own publications for readers interested in these areas.[4]

OSB programs in Indochina were dominated by the development of a relationship with Cambodia from the mid-1980s, by which time the true nature of the Khmer Rouge and the atrocities committed by Pol Pot had become known to the outside world. The Australian government continued to recognise Pol Pot's regime and condemned the Vietnamese invasion of Cambodia, expressing this by suspending Australian official aid to Vietnam. In this context, OSB was central to the work of a small group of NGOs who channelled government funding into an unofficial program of cooperation and established and kept open communications at the highest level, especially in Cambodia and Vietnam.

During the 1970s, opposition to apartheid galvanised church-goers, unionists, students and politicians across Australia. OSB eschewed making public statements on apartheid in favour of providing practical support to opponents of apartheid and those who suffered as a result of it in Africa's Frontline States. Departing volunteers, whatever their destination, had the opportunity to hear from representatives in Australia of the African National Congress (ANC) and the South West African People's Organisation (SWAPO). A select group of volunteers destined for Africa were assigned to work in educational institutions established for the exiled children of freedom fighters by ANC and SWAPO in Tanzania and Congo.

In Indonesia, by contrast, OSB played a leading role amongst Australian NGOs in building layered relationships with Indonesian civil society by placing volunteers in Indonesian NGOs both at the national and provincial level. This enabled OSB to build personal relationships with the leaders of Indonesian NGOs and to develop an understanding of the constraints under which they worked. It also laid the foundation for introducing Indonesian colleagues to a broader range of Australian NGOs and establishing ongoing fora for confidence-building and cooperation.

Cooperation programs with the island nations of the South Pacific were intrinsic to OSB's work since its first program and continued into the 1990s. As well as providing skilled personnel to government and non-government service providers, OSB pursued its characteristic activities, namely building relationships and networks among civil society organisations. The sense of the Pacific Islands as "Australia's responsibility", together with the features of decolonisation, made OSB's focus on people as the subject of development particularly relevant. The small island nations and larger countries like PNG and Fiji faced many of the same fundamental questions about the kind of development that would actually benefit their people the most.

The same questions arose when the East Timorese had to build a new state structure independent of Indonesia. OSB was well positioned to play an active role in supporting East Timorese independence and had been active on the issue of self-determination in Australian Council for Overseas Aid (ACFOA) circles. Given the significance of East Timorese independence as the dominant human rights issue in the Australian community, it is not surprising that many AVI staff members were deeply committed to supporting East Timor, enabling the organisation to act swiftly once circumstances permitted. AVI volunteers were quickly mobilised to work with the United Nations in conducting the independence referendum in 1999, and then contributed to transitional arrangements for the new Timorese government and NGOs in the following years.

Sources

As the organisation grew and its management styles changed, its information management practices also varied. As a result the unfolding story of OSB/AVI was supported in different eras by different sources and research methods. A number of secondary sources, including the recent publication of Betty Feith's Masters thesis by Monash University Press,[5] add insight into the intellectual origins of VGS and its development. An abundance of the original records of VGS and the early years of OSB informed the first two chapters. They are currently held in storage by AVI but will eventually be transferred to the National Library of Australia in Canberra.

A different approach was necessary in writing Chapter 3 as the records held by AVI for the period 1969–81 are sparse. For this period neither management records nor even systematic records of Committee meetings are extant. Fortunately, some correspondence files of individual Committee members containing carbon copies of memos and minutes survived. For these years the research was supplemented by examination of the reports and correspondence held in records at the National Archives of Australia which reveal the context and content of the relationship between OSB and the federal government at the time. Further records were located in a former volunteer's attic, and I have also been able to check my understanding of the period in personal discussions with key people involved with OSB at the time.

From 1982 onwards the archives of the OSB are reliably complete, so I had access to a full record of all Committee and management meetings and reports. It is important to note that from the middle of 1984 I was a staff member of the organisation and therefore a participant in or witness to much that happened in the organisation thereafter. It follows that in some episodes the writer is also a protagonist.

PART I

Establishing and Defending the Principles

CHAPTER 1

Volunteer Graduate Scheme to Indonesia (1951–69)

The Volunteer Graduate Scheme to Indonesia (VGS), the progenitor of international volunteering schemes, had an enduring influence on the many programs that followed it in Australia and other parts of the world. VGS was an employment scheme for Australian graduates who volunteered for employment in Indonesian government agencies under the same conditions that their Indonesian colleagues were employed. It was firmly grounded in an ethic of equality of living and working with local people. Its distinctive characteristics were never to be fully replicated in subsequent similar schemes. They arose from the social and intellectual environment of the time and place of the initiation of the Scheme, the nature of its co-creation with Indonesian partners determining its parameters, a particular philosophy grounded in post-colonial solidarity, and its underpinning by an intergovernmental agreement.

There is probably nothing like war to stimulate international awareness among students, and it was students at the University of Melbourne in the social milieu immediately after the Second World War who were the initiators of VGS. Furthermore, students who had recently returned from active service injected their personal experiences of the world at war into campus life. Because the War had delayed the entry of many to higher education, the presence of these older students with wider experience of a troubled world had the effect of narrowing the gap between students and their lecturers. On the campus of the University of Melbourne there was spirited debate of issues of substance in the Melbourne University Labour Club and the Student Christian Movement.

Two people stood out in this lively academic environment as having a major influence on the student initiators of VGS – Professor William Macmahon Ball, inaugural Professor of Political Science at the University of Melbourne from 1949 to 1968, and the Reverend Frank Engel, General Secretary of the Australian Student Christian Movement (ASCM) from 1949 to 1958. Both were men of intellect and integrity whose thinking was well in advance of the times.

Macmahon Ball and understanding Asia

In the 1930s Macmahon Ball had been a lone voice in arguing that Australia needed independent sources of information about Asia to develop its own knowledge base because the interests of the British Empire would not always coincide with Australia's. Macmahon Ball's outlook, then and later, was framed by an Australian nationalism and an enlightened liberalism. Behind his liberalism was a strong humanitarian inclination, consistent with his active membership in the Australasian Student Christian Union (later ASCM) in the 1920s.[1]

Macmahon Ball served the government in a number of capacities, including as organiser of Australia's wartime shortwave service, Radio Australia's precursor. He undertook several high-level diplomatic tasks for the Australian government immediately after the Second World War, including leading Australia's goodwill mission to East and Southeast Asia in 1948, which required him, as a representative of the Australian government, to defend the White Australia policy – a position completely at odds with his personal views. Nonetheless, leading the mission's tour of Asia enabled him to further cultivate his relationships with East and Southeast Asian leaders. The mission was to assess the aid needs of East and Southeast Asian governments, and Ball recommended a broad range of support for international agencies in the region and direct support from

Australia in both material aid and technical assistance. He was surprised by the breadth of anti-colonial revolutions across Asia and the depth of nationalist sentiment but understood it to be an irrevocable trend and a new reality for Australia to deal with, stating in his report on the mission that "goodwill towards these people must become a national habit, built on respect for the racial sensibilities and national aims of our neighbours".[2]

From the end of 1948 Macmahon Ball had a deep and immediate impact on his students. He combined academic pursuits with hands-on experience of diplomacy and the provision of policy advice at the highest levels. He had witnessed the collapse of empire and had personally come to know leaders across East and Southeast Asia. He understood their aspirations and thought their anti-colonial stance reasonable and supportable. In 1949 and 1950 he taught a course on nationalism and communism, focusing on Asia. One of his students was Herb Feith who pioneered VGS and later volunteered in Indonesia on several occasions. Feith built on Ball's teaching and his experience in Indonesia to become one of the world's foremost political scientists focusing on Indonesia.[3]

Looking back on Macmahon Ball's lectures, Feith was later to remark that Ball "had no illusions about communism but his main interest was Asia, and he had the nous to realise that the central problem in Asia wasn't communism at all, it was nationalism and ... decolonisation"; his challenge to his students was, "Would Australia associate itself with the insurgent nationalist forces or ... stick its head in the sand and look to London?"[4] In this course, Ball did not teach abstractions or political theory; he shared anecdotes about political leaders he had met in the region. He also explored the opportunities and challenges in establishing post-colonial systems that would respond to people's aspirations and include at least some features of liberal democracy. Other students reacted similarly. Jamie Mackie returned from service with the Australian Navy in the Asia-Pacific region and became Feith's close personal and professional colleague. Mackie's academic career also had an Indonesia focus. Much later, reflecting on his introduction to Indonesia, he too pointed to Ball's course on Asian nationalism as providing a framework for them to begin to understand the appeal of nationalism, communism and democratic concepts such as self-government.[5]

Feith formed a close bond with Macmahon Ball, who agreed to support Feith in his wish to undertake research for his Master's degree in Indonesia. Ball also provided the grant that enabled Feith to travel to Indonesia in June 1951, at the age of 20, to take up a role in Indonesia's Department of Information.

Frank Engel and the Student Christian Movement

The Australian Student Christian Movement (ASCM) was a large and influential national organisation of students, but its branches on Australia's university campuses had different characteristics. In Sydney the SCM tended to have a conservative and evangelical approach; in Melbourne it was particularly ecumenical and outward-looking and attracted students who were searching for ways to put their talents to good use and wanted to work towards lasting peace. Its large membership was spread across all faculties at the University of Melbourne where it had such an impact that it has been described as a "university within a university … through it literature, politics, religion and science came alive".[6] SCM members together grappled with the big issues of the time: the scientific challenge to religious faith; the rise and impact of communism and fascism; war and justice; and world peace.

Frank Engel, General Secretary of ASCM from the end of 1949 to 1958, was, even in the enlightened circles of SCM leadership, considered a luminary. He was well ahead of most in ASCM in recognising the significance of Australia's location in the Asia-Pacific region. He thought Australia should be involved in the region and, in particular, should support the struggle of Asian countries for democracy and independence. He became a leading campaigner against the White Australia policy and for Aboriginal land rights. Engel was a key adviser in the establishment of VGS and went on to play a key role in the Committee of the Overseas

Service Bureau as the ethical touchstone in the organisation's governing bodies.

ASCM's support and involvement in the formation of VGS was significant, leading some to characterise it as a Christian program. Herb Feith was to reject this later, insisting that groups with no SCM connection at all were also significant in founding VGS. He did, however, acknowledge that, while most of the initial participants had some connection with SCM, it was the National Union of Australian University Students (NUAUS) that was the formal and actual sponsor of VGS, describing it as "a secular enterprise which people with a particular kind of Christian inclination were attracted to".[7] Significantly, it was Frank Engel, born in Korea to missionary parents and a full-time clergyman, who had been particularly insistent that the Scheme from its inception needed to be wholly secular. Engel located the commencement of VGS "as part of a long heritage of young Australians going abroad to help other people and to build bridges between nations",[8] referring to missionaries who were mostly lay professionals. He argued that there was a body of people who supported overseas missions and, at a new stage in world history, were now ready to support a different kind of secular program. That body was ASCM, which had encouraged students to volunteer for service abroad for over 50 years. Its members responded readily to the opportunities presented by VGS to live out their principles and work in ways that would advance peace and justice in Australia and beyond.

ASCM played a vital role in helping students arrive at these principles, which were derived from their religious belief and practice. Organised religion was an important pillar of Australian society in the 1950s and 1960s when church and church activities played a key role in the lives of many. It was important socially whether people identified as Anglican, Methodist, Presbyterian, Roman Catholic or of other Christian denominations, as religion was an important part of people's identity. ASCM played an important role in bringing people from across the spectrum of denominations together, breaking down sectarian divisions by challenging students to take account of what was happening in the world.

At the University of Melbourne it had a healthy cooperation with the Melbourne University Newman Society, the Catholic student association, which shared and paralleled many of SCM's priorities.

Perhaps the most defining characteristic of VGS is the way it was co-created by Indonesians and Australians. The idea surfaced in 1950 at a conference in Bombay of the International Student Service (later World University Service), a secular organisation but one with which ASCM had maintained an active relationship. Alan Hunt, a law student, and John Bayly, an architecture student, both SCM members at Melbourne University, attended from Australia. On the sidelines of this conference an Indonesian student delegate, Abu Bakar Lubis, invited skilled Australians to work alongside Indonesians, to live amongst them, and work under their direction.

VGS – developing the concept

John Bayly's report on the conference was heard by a small group of students at the University of Melbourne who went on to develop the concept of a volunteer graduate scheme. As Betty Feith (née Evans) relates:

> This concept of equality and sharing; ... of sharing work skills and work experience on the same rates of pay as local Indonesian government servants, became the basis of the Scheme. This concept was seen quite deliberately and self-consciously as a 'New Direction' for a relationship between Australians and people of non-Western societies who had recently won political independence, and who … [rejected becoming] … objects of paternalistic planning.[9]

At the end of the year, Herb Feith and Betty Evans sought to enlist ASCM interest in their proposal. They did not ask ASCM to take it on, as they were going to ask the national union of students to do that.[10] Engel advised them to present the idea at the national conferences of NUAUS and ASCM in December 1950 and January 1951 respectively. With the constraints of wartime lifted, these national student conferences were big events and well attended. Both conferences embraced the VGS concept enthusiastically, to the extent that seven students offered their services to a scheme that did not exist yet. A VGS Committee was established under the auspices of NUAUS, comprising Herb Feith, Betty Evans, Alan Hunt, John Bayly and SCM member and medical student Vern Bailey. They realised that the idea would best be progressed by having one of their number go to Indonesia as soon as possible. Feith turned to Molly Bondan,* with whom he had been corresponding for nearly a year. She agreed to sponsor him and he made plans to leave for Indonesia in the middle of 1951.[11]

The Committee sought support for the concept and advice from academics, community leaders, civil servants and politicians. Macmahon Ball advised that for the scheme to succeed it would require explicit and enthusiastic support from the Indonesian government and that to secure this support it was important not to present it as Western benevolence as this would offend nationalist sensitivities. It should instead be presented as a supplement to the technical and administrative assistance already coming from others and as a form of cooperation designed to bring mutual benefit to Indonesia and Australia.[12] They acted on his advice and within a few months the Committee had received indications of in-principle support from both the Australian and Indonesian governments.

In December 1951, the World Student Christian Movement organised a leadership training conference in Indonesia for SCMs in East Asia. An SCM leader at the University of Melbourne, Don Anderson, travelled to Jakarta for the meeting. Feith had been in Jakarta for six months by this time, which was long enough to have established some useful contacts. He found that doors opened for him in leadership circles once it was known he

* Molly Bondan (née Warner) was a Sydney writer, artist and broadcaster who married an Indonesian nationalist in exile in Australia. After returning to Indonesia to support the new Republic, she passionately supported the nationalist cause. As an Indonesian citizen with English as her first language, she had a significant role in the Department of Information. She was highly respected and well connected to the emerging political elite in Indonesia at the time.

had the support of Molly Bondan. For Anderson's visit, he organised a hectic round of meetings with key people whose support would be needed for the scheme to take off. Meetings were conducted with Australian Embassy officials, heads of departments, politicians and Ministers and student groups, including Indonesia's SCM counterpart, Gerakan Mahasiswa Kristen Indonesia (GMKI).[13] Anderson returned to Australia in time for the ASCM national conference in January 1952 in Canberra and, given his recent experiences in newly independent Indonesia, he was invited to give a major public address which the Prime Minister, Robert Menzies, attended with his Solicitor General, Kenneth Bailey. At the meeting Menzies asked about the cost of the proposed scheme and not long after the Australian Government agreed to cooperate with their plans.[14]

Formal agreement

An intergovernmental agreement for the Scheme was signed in November 1952, based on a formal request from the Indonesian Government for more volunteers. As the request met Colombo Plan criteria, funding was made available through the Plan's mechanism. The intergovernmental agreement was exceptional in that it provided for operational costs to be shared between the Australian and Indonesian governments. Australia was to pay for the volunteers' travel to Indonesia and a bicycle for local transport; Indonesia would provide government employment at local rates of pay. The liaison, publicity, coordination and administration were left to the honorary organisers in the VGS Committee. By the time the agreement was signed there were three volunteers in Indonesia and they took on the work of the Committee in Jakarta.

The Melbourne-based Committee was strengthened with Don Anderson taking on the role of Chairman and, late in 1952, Jim Webb becoming Secretary and effectively the national coordinator of VGS. Jim Webb was Warden of the Student Union at University of Melbourne (a significant role in the 1950s), a member of ASCM's National Executive and

Vice-President of NUAUS. He was an old friend of Herb Feith and Betty Evans, having been at Melbourne High School with Feith. As teenagers they had been active in a campaign operating through local churches, under the aspirational name of Save Europe Now, which collected tinned food and old clothing for war ravaged Europe.[15] Since that time a variety of local and international study and work experiences had equipped Webb with significant administrative, business and organisational skills. If Macmahon Ball and Engel provided the intellectual inspiration for VGS, and Herb and Betty Feith were its pioneers, then Jim Webb brought the required organisational nous.

Webb had no experience of Indonesia, but remedied this by visiting Indonesia from December 1952 to February 1953 when he spent time with the volunteers, developed a closer understanding of their lives and work, and met the Indonesians who were key to the Scheme's operations. In 1955 he spent nine weeks in Indonesia at the invitation of the Indonesian government.

VGS – in operation

The details of the agreement between the governments of Indonesia and Australia were spelled out in promotional circulars issued by NUAUS. Volunteer graduates would receive return fares, a tropical clothing and equipment allowance, a grant for Indonesian language study (in Australia), the use of a bicycle, and the right to draw on an emergency fund at the discretion of the Head of Mission at the Australian Embassy. Salaries were payable at Indonesian civil service rates. Assignments were for between two and three years, but there were no contracts fixing the length of assignment. It was expected that the Australian government would provide sufficient funding for between 10 and 15 volunteer graduates each year. Applications could be made at any time directly to the Embassy of Indonesia in Canberra. The circular clarified that "volunteers are selected by the Indonesian Government on the basis of Indonesia's need for qualified personnel … in the light of the candidate's qualifications, experience and character, subject to the approval of the Australian Government".[16]

In practice, the Melbourne Committee had extensive contact with applicants through correspondence and conversation before the formal selection and approval process. It was not until Committee members were satisfied with an applicant's suitability and aware of a possible placement that details of that applicant were passed to the volunteer graduates in Jakarta. They would then liaise directly with the Indonesian employing agency and work with them on securing budgets and approvals. This ensured a high level of certainty that the Indonesian employer would fully support the candidate volunteer. The Jakarta liaison work was a substantial undertaking for the volunteers in addition to their ongoing work and could only be conducted on an in-principle basis pending the formal approval of the Indonesian and Australian governments.

Another NUAUS circular that helped volunteers prepare for their departure spelled out some of the practicalities, such as what to include in their luggage. It also gave details of the Australian government's contribution to the Scheme and explained that volunteers would first hear of their acceptance through informal contact with volunteers already in Jakarta, followed by the first official notification,

> perhaps a month later … [by] a request from the Department of External Affairs in Canberra that he should fly there for a day to be interviewed at the Government's expense … As well as chatting generally with External Affairs officers he may use this opportunity to discuss with them the details of Commonwealth Government assistance to be given. He should also visit the Indonesian Embassy … The Government makes a booking shortly after the volunteer has been to Canberra and informs External Affairs of the boat on which he wants to travel. It is wise to have made some initial investigations from the shipping companies in advance.[17]

The shipping lines described are the Italian Flotta Lauro ("somewhat 2nd class") and Lloyd Triestino ("rather high class") lines, and the Dutch Royal Interocean Lines ("considered high class"). The Government normally paid first-class boat fares, although it would consider paying air fares if necessary.

It was a busy time for the voluntary committee, as indicated by the numbers of departing volunteers. Because the agreement was signed so late in 1952, work to select applicants and arrange placements intensified, resulting in a group of four volunteers leaving in 1954. Twenty-seven volunteers took up placements organised for them between 1954 and 1958. While the aspirational figure of 15 volunteer graduates per year was never achieved, the 1950s were clearly the heyday of VGS. The Melbourne committee met at least monthly; the Jakarta-based volunteers met frequently, often every week, to feed back to supporters in Australia the news and views of the volunteers. They also reported on progress with Indonesian authorities, including the long periods of informal inquiry that preceded the official request and formal approval for each placement. There was a constant supply of information about the challenges and rewards of living and working in Indonesia on civil servant salaries. From 1957 it was presented to the wider group of subscribers through *Djembatan* (Bridge), the quarterly bulletin of the Volunteer Graduate Association (VGA),[18] edited mostly by Ailsa Zainu'ddin (née Thomson), a volunteer in 1954–55 with Betty Feith in the Education Department in Jakarta.

Anti-colonial cohesion

There was a strong bond among the volunteers and a common adherence to the fundamental philosophy of identification with Indonesian society. This was absolutely in line with the sentiment expressed by Indonesians in Bombay and brought back to Australia by John Bayly; they were to be technical experts in "underdeveloped lands" entering the whole life of the society, identifying with its problems and committing to solutions.[19]

Although the volunteers were clearly proud of having a role in building the new nation of Indonesia, they were careful not to overstate their contribution. Indonesians who had close contact with the Scheme appreciated that it was quite different from other ways of deploying expatriate expertise, and their appreciation helped strengthen the VGS ethos by influencing the thinking and behaviour of the volunteer graduates. Jo Kurnianingrat, a senior member of staff in the Ministry of Education in 1954, when Ailsa Zainu'ddin and Betty Feith worked there as volunteer graduates, expressed this clearly in an essay first published in *Djembatan* in 1959 and, more recently, in *Bridges of Friendship.*[20]

Kurnianingrat's memoirs are invaluable in explaining the post-colonial mentality of professional Indonesians. She reveals her lived experience as an aristocratic girl in late colonial times, a young professional woman in the Japanese occupation and a participant in the revolution and its aftermath. Her stories, even the humorous anecdotes, serve to bring the dramas of colonialism and liberation into clear light, particularly her experience of social division and the impact of her awareness of not belonging to "the ruling race". As a professional and a nationalist this translated into an understandable sensitivity to and a determination to avoid paternalism of all kinds. On the basis of her story, it is easy to see why she would have been initially cautious, if not reluctant, to take on the services of volunteer graduates in her workplace.[21]

In the straitened circumstances of Indonesia in the 1950s the Indonesian civil servants who were the colleagues, mentors and supervisors of the volunteers necessarily lived modest lifestyles. The volunteers insisted on a moral decision to identify as far as possible with their Indonesian friends, to live in a style as close to them as possible, even to earn the same money as similarly qualified Indonesian civil servants. They were determined to demonstrate that they were not colonial in their attitudes or demeanour in the workplace, in homes or in public. Their conscious rejection of what others took as the entitlements of race meant they eschewed expatriate lifestyles and, with notable exceptions, expatriate company.

Molly Bondan offered a remarkable model of how to live modestly and avoid giving offence and she had a powerful influence on the volunteers. The volunteers' identification with Indonesia went further than issues of lifestyle and took on a distinctly political edge. It is clear that Indonesian supervisors and colleagues of the early volunteers not only talked the nationalist talk; through demonstration and collegiality they showed that nationalist pride was something one lived and the volunteers embraced this challenge. Their wholehearted support for Indonesian patriotism was very much of the era. There was a romance in identifying with the Indonesian revolution and relishing the opportunity to be part of nation building.

The volunteers fully believed in this way of thinking and behaving and they reinforced each other's enthusiasm. They proudly differentiated themselves from non-volunteer expatriates who, almost by definition, exhibited colonial behaviour. It was important to them that this culture be maintained in the group and they insisted in communications back to the Melbourne Committee that only volunteers with "the right attitude" were welcome.[22]

Political change in Indonesia

By late 1957 and 1958, the optimism and confidence of the volunteers started to take on a more defensive tone. Political events in Indonesia were a cause for alarm amongst Australian observers and journalists, so the volunteers had to explain repeatedly that these events were not a threat to their wellbeing. In 1957 Indonesia had begun its campaign to wrest back West Irian, the only part of the former Dutch colony not to have been ceded to Indonesian sovereignty. The campaign was a rallying point for Indonesian nationalism and a source of increasing anti-Dutch sentiment. From 1956 to 1958, rebellions in parts of Sumatra and Sulawesi by elements of local elites and sections of the Indonesian army demonstrated the depth and extent of hostility to the mismanagement, inefficiency and corruption of the central government in Jakarta. By mid-1958, the Indonesian government had nationalised Dutch businesses and put down the rebellions.

Political parties had become increasingly irrelevant as the elements contending for power were now the Parliament as a whole and the Army, with President Sukarno holding them in balance. Sukarno announced his concept of a Nasakom (Nasionalisme, Agama, Komunisme) Cabinet which would bring together the political forces of nationalism, religion and communism. In mid-1959, Sukarno reintroduced the 1945 Constitution to avail himself of the greater powers it provided to the President. Soon after, in his Independence Day speech on 17 August, Sukarno introduced a new broad outline of state policy, a political manifesto known as Manipol-USDEK, an acronym of five elements: the 1945 Constitution, Indonesian-style Socialism, Guided Democracy, Guided Economy and National Identity.

In 1958, there were 12 volunteer graduates in Indonesia and in 1959 there were six. To an increasingly nervous Australian public, and especially to their families and friends, they needed to provide reassurance that daily life continued as usual. They also increasingly felt a duty to explain the background to what was occurring and even to defend Indonesian policy and politics as it was changing. By and large they were still excited by their participation in the project of Indonesia. By the middle of 1959 rapidly changing political and economic circumstances in Indonesia made it difficult for the Melbourne committee to keep up to date. It became increasingly difficult to get traction with Indonesian officials in Jakarta and there was even some discussion about employing an Indonesian supporter as a liaison officer on his return to Jakarta.

VGS – a risk

Towards the end of the 1950s Australian Embassy officials in Jakarta and public servants in the Department of External Affairs sought to play down the role of the volunteers and the Department's association with them. Early in 1959, the National Committee of the Volunteer Graduate Association for Indonesia discussed a memo from the Department of External Affairs in Canberra that reminded the Committee of an August 1958 suggestion that measures be taken to reduce interaction between the volunteers and the Embassy so as to avoid "any impression that volunteer graduates are under continuing direction from the Australian government".[23] Given that Embassy approvals were required for the allocation of bicycles and use of the emergency fund and that the Embassy would continue to provide normal consular assistance, there was little that could be pulled back, apart from clarifying that Embassy assistance would not be sought in welcoming new arrivals, sourcing accommodation or in matters of the volunteers' employment.

Indonesia's move to Guided Democracy had certainly exercised the minds of officers in the Australian Embassy and the Department in Canberra and there were signs that their fulsome support of VGS was wavering. Two cases indicative of faltering support have come to light, one regarding Molly Bondan and the other a dispute between the Department and the VGA Committee regarding intermarriage. In each case, the personal outlook and behaviour of officers concerned were probably as much a factor as any shift in policy, but at least they bring to light a less supportive attitude.

Australian Embassy officials became concerned by Molly Bondan's closeness to and influence upon the volunteer graduates. In 1957, the Australian Ambassador to Indonesia, Laurence (Jim) McIntyre, in correspondence with Keith Waller of the Department of External Affairs, expressed concern about the influence on the volunteer graduates of "a somewhat sinister creature, Molly Bondan", known for her "manifestly anti-Australian and anti-white" broadcasts. McIntyre described how Bondan welcomed the volunteer graduates to her home whenever they came to Jakarta, lamented that they held her in high esteem and wondered what could be done about this. Waller asked for an ASIO report and recommended that they "go slow with the Volunteer Graduate Scheme".[24] In later years, Molly enjoyed the respect and admiration of Australian ambassadors, but in the late 1950s there was something of a binary approach to international relations, resulting in a position whereby to be pro-Indonesian was to be anti-Australian.

Thirty-five years later, Jim Webb had clear memories of the conflict in Jakarta where diplomats were irked by volunteers' local knowledge and volunteers were "disdainful of the diplomats and their ... condescension, their lack of knowledge of the country and their lack of Indonesian language". Webb saw the need at the time to "keep volunteer activities as far out of government hands as possible".[25]

This theme is repeated in a protracted dispute over Australian government approval for a volunteer graduate to return to Indonesia. Joan Minogue (later Hardjono) successfully completed 20 months, from March 1957 to November 1958, as a volunteer in Indonesia. Before returning to Australia she attended an interview with an Embassy official who asked her whether she planned to return to Indonesia to marry an Indonesian. She told him that she did, without any idea that this might be used in evidence against her. When asked by the Indonesian Embassy if they supported her application, the Committee in Melbourne had no hesitation. She was in good standing with them and they knew she intended to stay in Indonesia for at least a year. The Committee then learnt that the Department of External Affairs had refused to approve her second assignment and failed to give any reason in their letter to her for rejecting her as a volunteer. Don Anderson (VGA Committee Chairman) raised the matter with the Department of External Affairs in the course of a scheduled meeting. The Committee was understandably angry, particularly with the External Affairs position that marriage would give rise to divided loyalties, but expressed this in masterly understatement, saying that this was a "very limited view of the Scheme. We feel that divided loyalties are inherent in a Scheme such as this for graduates are at the same time Australian citizens and public servants of the Indonesian Government".[26]

The volunteer, Joan Minogue wrote directly to Richard Casey, Minister for External Affairs, demanding to know the grounds of her exclusion, and received a reply stating that her application had been rejected because of her intention to marry an Indonesian. The Committee resolved at a Special Meeting of the Committee on 9 August 1959 to persist in their efforts to have the decision reversed and to support the volunteer to return to Indonesia outside the government-funded scheme if it was not reversed. Anderson's hand-written note on the minutes of the Special Meeting confirms the Minister's reversal of the decision.[27]

Don Anderson's confidential notes on his meetings with External Affairs department officials are revealing. He concludes that while

> some officers...would say that marriage generally need not contradict the aims of the Scheme; [Mr] Truelove on the other hand feels that marriage with Indonesians is undesirable ... The discussion about marriage and divided loyalty made me feel that the officers present were very woolly on the aims of the Scheme and the reasons for the Australian Government supporting such a Scheme.[28]

Anderson took the opportunity to raise with the Department of External Affairs the nine-month delay between volunteer application and departure, which was largely due to the time it took for the Department to assess the application of and communicate its decision about each candidate:

> I was able to outline the history of External Affairs procedures and pointed out that for the first few years the External Affairs interview was, on the Solicitor General's advice, solely to inform the applicant of the Australian Government's limited responsibility to him. It is only in recent years that a second purpose, namely assessment, has been added to the interview. I asked whether this was considered necessary since it added to the delay and we were very thorough in our own assessment and briefing. There is no hope of getting this one altered; Truelove states that the Government must protect itself by making its own assessment.[29]

Anderson was highlighting a heightened awareness in the Department that the volunteers could constitute a risk to Australia's relations with Indonesia or at least to the way the Department was representing Australia.

Volunteer graduates presented a united front to the outside, reassuring friends, family and supporters that they were safe, not under threat of violence and that life was normal. Nevertheless, within the group there was a spirited debate about the nature, value and viability of the Scheme. Criticism surfaced from 1958 on, with volunteers increasingly doing it tough, as they had to pay foreign prices but did not have the income that other expatriates in Indonesia enjoyed. As an indication of the difficulties generated by Indonesia's economic decline, Ailsa Zainu'ddin commented that food prices in Jakarta in 1961 were more than ten times those of 1958.[30] Some advocated augmenting Indonesian income with an Australian-sourced supplement, while others considered this to strike at the very spirit of the Scheme. There was also a creeping doubt as to whether the volunteer graduates were truly wanted in Indonesia, or whether it was purely a matter of policy (or politeness) to accept them. Was it possible that the Scheme had served its purpose and that doors were now closing? Because of what seemed a lack of stability in Indonesia, the numbers of enquiries from Australians about the Scheme dropped.

Internal review

Recognising the fundamental criticisms of VGS that were being raised and considering that it was ten years since the Scheme was first envisaged, the Committee embarked on a review. A questionnaire distributed to all past and current volunteer graduates gathered a diversity of views and experiences. Some questioned whether adequate nutrition was possible on Indonesian salaries. They were divided in their opinion of whether financial supplements from Australia would distort the character and intention of the Scheme. There was discussion about the impact of the freeze in appointments to the Indonesian public service, and of the rights and wrongs of trying to seek an exemption from this or to work around it. Some reported ambivalence, if not antagonism, towards the Scheme from high-level officials, recognising that official Indonesian policy was opposed to foreign assistance. Others recorded the warm appreciation of them by their immediate superiors and colleagues. The feeling was that the increasingly difficult political situation and the hostile press in Australia gave added importance to the Scheme's role in keeping a door between the two countries open.[31]

In the early 1960s much of the Jakarta liaison work fell to Lance Castles, a volunteer graduate at the University of Indonesia. He described the dilemma cogently in a letter to the Melbourne group in 1960:

> The Manipol-USDEK pressure on aspects of the nation's life and contact with foreigners is growing ... While one feels that these uncooperative officials ... need reminding that this is after all an intergovernmental agreement which it is their duty to carry out, it is also true that if the scheme were brought under review some crackpot would probably allege that it too is not in in accord with Manipol-USDEK, and no-one would dare to contradict him. I am not suggesting that on this account we should dissolve ourselves to avoid being dissolved; I don't think bangs have any advantage over whimpers. On the contrary I think we have the responsibility to hang on as long as we can, (1) so that other Australians can have the opportunity that I am having to know and love the Indonesia behind the political façade, (2) for the sake of those who personally or intellectually have a foot in both countries or worlds, and (3) because at any moment should the regime feel the need to change the basis of its support we may have the opportunity to expand again.[32]

In October 1961, Webb wrote to the Department of External Affairs requesting funds to travel to Indonesia for a month. He pointed out that the Department had supported his travel in 1956 to Java and Sumatra, where he had been able to explain the nature of the Scheme to Indonesian officials, investigate placement possibilities and become more familiar with the situations in which volunteers live and work. He pointed out that while recently returned volunteers had assisted the Scheme in the past, they had not continued do so to the same extent as several of them had travelled overseas for further study or employment.

On the advice of the Australian Embassy in Jakarta, the Department declined the request, so Webb travelled at his own expense. During his visit he successfully argued for greater support for the volunteers and the Scheme. A letter dated 14 August 1962 from the Acting Secretary, External Affairs, referred to Webb's report on his visit and confirmed that the Minister had approved the use of Colombo Plan funds for modest increases in resettlement and clothing/equipment allowances and for an annual visit to Jakarta by volunteer graduates placed in the provinces. As to whether it would provide motorcycles or scooters for the volunteers, the Department was still to make a decision.[33] The Department eventually confirmed in July 1963 that five Vespa 125 scooters would be acquired for use by volunteers.[34]

Management and governance

Administration of the Scheme in Australia and Indonesia became more difficult as the load fell on fewer people, particularly on Jim Webb. The daily costs of stationery, postage and communications were considerable. Webb and colleagues had already established a new organisation by this time, the Overseas Service Bureau (OSB), to bring a full-time professional approach to providing services to overseas employers in a broader range of countries. Nevertheless, Webb maintained his central coordinating role as VGA Secretary. At its meeting on 10 July 1963, VGA noted with satisfaction that the Committee of OSB had agreed that routine administration costs of VGS – postage, stationery, newsletters etc. – would be met from OSB funds, that VGA could propose each year a budget for special activities such as publicity and retain its existing, albeit limited, assets. There was further discussion of how arrangements could work with OSB playing a greater role as the trustee of funds received from the Department of External Affairs for VGS, which VGA would continue to run, independently of the Department.[35]

Governance and management issues did not go away. In anticipation of the VGA Committee Meeting on 11 November 1964, Don Anderson wrote to Hugh O'Neill, who had served as an architect with VGS from 1958 to 1960 and, after working in London for two years, had returned to Melbourne and become involved in VGA. Anderson wrote that, in spite of the Scheme's successes, VGA had not been so successful in assisting with its administration, noting communication with the volunteers and briefing of applicants as two examples of how the burden of administration fell on Jim Webb.[36]

The VGA Committee had swollen as former volunteer graduates had been automatically co-opted as members, leading to a large and unmanageable team. Don Anderson proposed that the Committee elect a Chairman, Vice-Chairman and up to three members, who together with the Director of OSB, as Secretary of the Committee, the President of NUAUS and up to two co-opted members would meet every two months. Day-to-day management would rest with an Executive, comprising the Chairman, Vice-Chairman and Secretary. Anderson took the opportunity to inform Hugh O'Neill that, because of changes in his circumstances, he would not be available for nomination.[37] Anderson's proposed arrangements were accepted at the VGA Committee meeting on 11 November and O'Neill was elected its Chairman.

Difficult times

Events in Indonesia caused the relationship between Australia and Indonesia to continue to falter. In 1963 the two countries were on opposite sides over Sukarno's Konfrontasi campaign to resist the creation of Malaysia through the federation of Britain's former colonies, Malaya, Singapore, Sarawak and Sabah. In 1965 and 1966 Australian military forces along the Sarawak border were even engaged in sporadic gun battles with Indonesian forces.[38]

The political temperature continued to rise and Australia contemplated the possibility of a communist-dominated Indonesia as its northern neighbour, until October 1965 when political upheaval led to the destruction of the Indonesian Communist Party and an anti-communist backlash that enabled the military under General Suharto's command to remove Sukarno from power and seize control of politics, national ideology, community life and much of the economy. The country Suharto's New Order took hold of was traumatised by the killing of hundreds of thousands of people and the detention of many others.

No new volunteer graduates were mobilised in 1964 or 1965, and between 1966 and 1968 only five went to Indonesia – three in 1967. Remarkably, in spite of Indonesia's political upheaval, a constant, if minimal, presence of volunteer graduates persisted through this period. In 1967, Webb received official notification that the Indonesian Government was postponing the recruitment and acceptance of volunteer graduates until better conditions prevailed, prompting Webb to ponder whether the time had come for an exchange program that was financed entirely with Australian funding. Options for funding volunteer graduates became the subject of ongoing debate.

Salary or allowance

Volunteers had long become accustomed to finding additional sources of income to make ends meet, most often through private English tutoring. As a Jakarta-based volunteer graduate, the last one to be sent under the Scheme (from January 1968 to December 1969), Harold Crouch was heavily involved in liaison work for VGS but found that this ate into the time he needed to earn money. He was offered $10 a month so that he would not have to teach English and could spend more time on VGS matters. Crouch knocked back the offer, maintaining that the only way to overcome the time-consuming bureaucratic hurdles and obstacles was to pay for volunteer salaries, allowances and scholarships with Australian funding. A precedent had been set, as other international organisations were placing volunteers in Indonesia without hindrance, and paying for them from outside the country.[39]

OSB made it known to VGA that it could pay $10 a month as a supplementary allowance. This quickly led to the question, that if $120 a year was available, why not $500, which would remove the financial risk from volunteers and attract a wider range of people. The counterview was that $500 paid from Australia would rob the Scheme of some of its central virtues; in particular, it would remove the necessity for volunteers to take second jobs, which was the reality of their local colleagues' lives. The issue remained unresolved.[40]

David Mitchell, a serving volunteer, provided a clear view in May 1969, commenting that VGS remained a useful means to put Australians into places in Indonesia where they were needed. He believed there were opportunities to increase numbers, but only if the idea of working on the same terms as Indonesian civil servants was dropped. He explained that this was a very worthwhile stance in the 1950s, when it was important to state and act out the idea that we were the same sort of people as Indonesians and to reject anything that seemed to put us on a higher level than Indonesians. He noted that he had "lived in a funny sort of symbolic poverty for the last couple of years, in a (compromised) attempt to identify … with Indonesian public servants" and that he would have been much more useful and happier if he had a reasonable income. David argued that, although he wanted to jettison the civil service equality principle, he continued to envisage Australian volunteers living in the midst of Indonesian communities, amongst the middle class.[41]

These big issues went to the heart of the VGS mode of operations and its philosophy, and required discussion beyond VGA's executive group. David Scott, Director of Community Aid Abroad (CAA), had suggested that CAA might be able to assist with allowances if funding was not available from OSB or the Department of External Affairs. Some volunteer graduates again raised the question of the continuing usefulness of VGS and, once again, the predominant view was that it was still appropriate. Advice was sought from Mick Shann, Assistant Secretary in the Department of External Affairs in charge of aid, who was well placed to advise on the basis of his remarkably successful spell as Australian Ambassador to Indonesia from 1962 to 1966, the particularly difficult period of political upheaval. Shann saw no problems in paying salary or allowances to volunteers from Australia and did not think this would require high-level renegotiation of the Scheme. He agreed that administrative control of the Scheme should transfer from the Department of External Affairs to OSB and that the Bureau would have "the same combination of government subsidy and administrative autonomy in relation to the Indonesian scheme as it has with regard to AVA".[42] Shann proposed that an officer from the Department should come to Melbourne to negotiate details when appropriate and that the Australian Embassy in Jakarta would assist with visa issues.[43]

VGS – the legacy

Over the two decades of its operation in Indonesia, 50 Australian graduates participated in VGS. At no point did it ever get close to placing 10 to 15 people each year, as first envisaged when the Department of External Affairs allocated Colombo Plan funds to the Scheme. Nevertheless, the Scheme had an impact far beyond what the numbers would suggest. Among the 50 were many who, through personal and professional choices, were able to multiply the impact of their experience. Marriage and the creation of truly bicultural families was one example. So too was academic expertise across several disciplines which enabled former volunteer graduates to teach generations of Australian (and sometimes Indonesian) students about Indonesia and to influence policy-makers and journalists.

Another impact that is just as far reaching is that VGS directly led to the establishment of the Overseas Service Bureau in 1961.[44] OSB developed a professional approach to the management of international volunteer programs, providing services to employers in Africa, the Pacific Islands and several Asian countries. VGS continued to exist as a scheme, separately funded by the Australian government, to the end of 1969, albeit at a scaled-back level. From January 1970 it was absorbed into OSB's global Australian Volunteers Abroad (AVA) program.

The continuities from VGS to the AVA program were crucially important. One volunteer lived and symbolised the ethos of volunteering through both VGS and AVA probably more than any other. Mary Johnston went to Solo, Central Java in 1963 at a difficult point in Australia–Indonesia relations. Sukarno had declared his intention to crush Malaysia. The Australian media were describing Indonesia as a chaotic country whose leaders were attempting to distract their people with anti-Western adventurism. In preparing volunteer graduates for their departure, VGS provided them with the most complete and up-to-date information possible, but Mary Johnston was determined to go. As a social worker for a rehabilitation centre, she quickly won the respect and admiration of her colleagues, but in late 1965 the aftermath of Indonesia's political upheaval made it impossible for her to continue. She was reluctant to leave her friends and colleagues, but they persuaded her to return to Australia in December of that year. Communities throughout Central Java were experiencing a traumatic time; with massacres in both villages and urban centres, circumstances were not conducive for effective volunteering. On her return to Melbourne, Jim Webb engaged Mary Johnston in the OSB office, where she undertook promotional work and responded to volunteer correspondence.

Johnston returned to work in Central Java through the AVA program in early 1970, this time in community development with a public health foundation in Solo. In July 1974, she took on a new assignment in an organisation she had helped found, Yayasan Indonesia Sejahtera (YIS: Indonesia Welfare Foundation), which is today one of the largest and most respected NGOs in Indonesia. Johnston's community development work achieved international acclaim and she became sought after to advise and consult in many countries, always ensuring that anything she earned in international consultancy were passed on to YIS to support its work with village people, sometimes to the embarrassment of her Australian and Indonesian colleagues.[45] Declining health forced her to return to Australia in 1988. For over 20 years as a volunteer Mary Johnston was a role model, valued mentor and an inspirational friend to generations of Australian volunteers in Indonesia in both the VGS and AVA programs, as well as being a hero to her community development colleagues in Indonesia.

Those who established OSB and designed its programs had been intimately involved in running VGS, most notably Jim Webb, Frank Engel, Herb Feith and Hugh O'Neill. Their close connection with VGS enabled a continuity that was a determining influence on OSB. They ensured that much of the ethos, principles and the values first enunciated and put into practice by VGS were preserved in the DNA of the new organisation.

Herb Feith with his adopted village family, Ibu Kromodiharjo (seated left) and Bapak Kromodiharjo, in Pendoworejo near Yogyakarta, Indonesia, 1953. Courtesy AVI

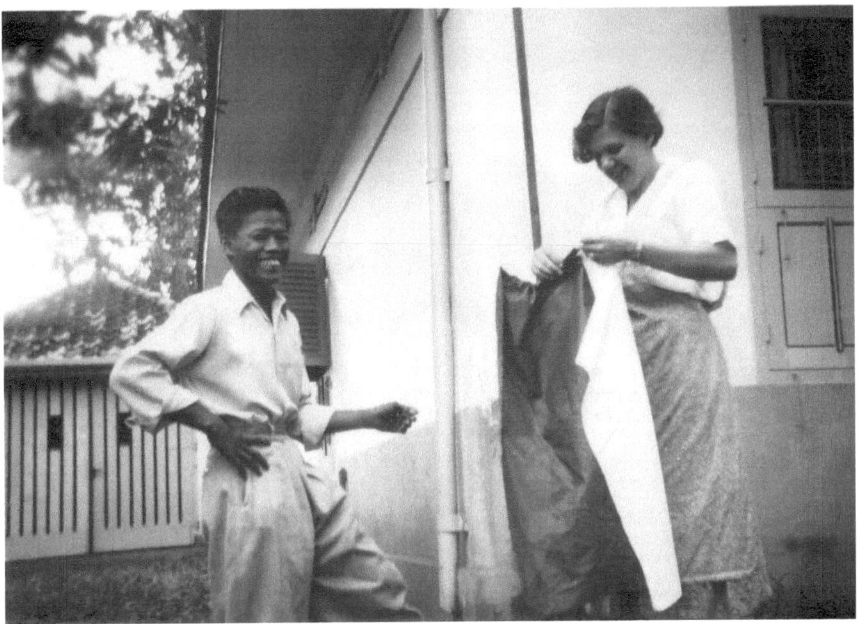

Betty Feith, with Djaelani (interpreter), prepares to raise the Indonesian flag on Independence Day, Jakarta, 17 August 1954. Photo Ailsa Thomson Zainuddin. Courtesy AVI

1957 brochure promoting membership of Friends of the Volunteer Graduate Association for Indonesia. ("Pegawai" is the Indonesian word for public servant and an abbreviation of "Plan for the Employment of Graduates from Australia to Work as Indonesians".) Courtesy AVI

Hugh O'Neill, architect with Department of Public Works and lecturer, Bandung and Jakarta, with Junus, a cousin of his Indonesian host family, c.1959. Courtesy AVI

Left

Australian volunteers disembark in Jakarta, c.1963. Courtesy AVI

Below

Mary Johnston in discussion with a village leader, c.1963. Courtesy AVI

CHAPTER 2

Overseas Service Bureau: The Early Years (1961–68)

The success of the Volunteer Graduate Scheme to Indonesia led to suggestions to develop similar programs in other countries. Burma was mentioned in the mid-1950s as a possibility as it presented many of the same issues as Indonesia. VGA Committee members and Burmese officials met and corresponded enthusiastically from 1954, but a program of cooperation with Burma did not take shape, as the Australian government showed absolutely no interest. Proposals involving Thailand and Malaya were also put forward, but Jim Webb, who had been working for VGS virtually full-time and unpaid since 1953, thought it unrealistic to act on any of them. In his view, ambitious new schemes could not be countenanced until the money and resources were available to do so. As a new decade began he thought the time had come for a fully professional, full-time position to be established and he saw himself in such a role.[1]

Webb had been exploring the idea of a register of available overseas positions with Doug Hobson (Engel's successor at ASCM), Mary Tait (World University Service) and Lois Griffith (Australian Christian Youth Council). In September 1961, Webb, Tait, Griffith and Geoff Lacey (Melbourne University Newman Society)[2] began to collate information from all available sources about employment opportunities in Asia, Africa and the Pacific.

At the same time Webb was trying to gauge the likelihood of any Australian government support and sought a meeting with an official in the Department of External Affairs with whom he had had dealings on VGS matters. He was hoping to spark interest in a broader range of activities, but was also intent on making the point that the government should not assume that the work of VGS would continue without funding. Webb explained to Herb Feith that he was cautious about building a new organisation without some indication of support from the Department:

> if External Affairs shows some real interest and indicates potential support, then an effort should be made to get the Bureau well underway as soon as possible. Frankly, at present, I cannot see how enough resources could be obtained to develop the total project, unless Government finance is provided.[3]

Launching the Bureau

The Department of External Affairs made it quite clear to Webb that the government had no interest in the establishment of a new organisation and that there was no prospect of government financial support for it. There was, however, definite interest among community and faith-based organisations, as well as certain business leaders. The idea of publishing lists of overseas vacancies and assisting people to apply for them was seen as a useful avenue to encourage the participation of more Australians in supporting developing communities. Before long there was sufficient moral and financial support for Webb and his friends to establish the Overseas Service Bureau (OSB) on a permanent basis.

In February 1962, the first of many OSB bulletins was issued, with a foreword that announced that this was only the beginning. The Bureau was founded on the belief that "Australians have not as yet responded adequately to the challenge to assist developing societies, and to bridge barriers of race and nation".[4] Accordingly, the new organisation would encourage Australians to serve in the developing countries of Asia, Africa and the Pacific. It saw itself as providing services in the field of international employment, namely:

- an advisory service to help interested people choose between employment alternatives;
- a selection service to act on behalf of overseas agencies and employers not represented in Australia;
- the development and administration of employment schemes, such as VGS, to create new opportunities for overseas service; and
- a training service to run introductory courses for people going to work in developing nations.

The vacancies listed were quite diverse in both location and profession. In Africa, most were university teaching positions in Bechuanaland (now Botswana), Ghana, Kenya, Nigeria, Rhodesia (now Zimbabwe), Nyasaland (now Malawi), and Sierra Leone. Positions were also available for medical officers and Grade 1 secretaries/stenographers for the governments of Tanganyika (later part of Tanzania) and Uganda. In Asia, there were teaching posts in schools and universities and positions for doctors and nurses in Hong Kong, Malaya, British North Borneo, India, Pakistan and Indonesia. A similar mixture of positions was available in Pacific Island nations: for teachers and medical staff in the New Hebrides (now Vanuatu) and the Solomon Islands, for teachers in church schools in Fiji, Tonga and Samoa, and in the public service and hospitals and clinics of Papua and New Guinea.

Strengthening the Committee

The OSB Committee (Webb, Hobson, Tait and Lacey) was expanded to include VGS stalwarts Herb Feith and Frank Engel, along with R.W.T. Cowan (Warden of Trinity College at the University of Melbourne) who was elected Chairman in November 1962. They discussed a draft constitution, determining that membership of the Bureau should not exceed membership of the Committee and decided to invite two new members to join them, Bernard Callinan and T.R. Garnett. Callinan was an engineer who had served with Sparrow Force in Timor in 1941 and led the commandos' campaign there and, later, Australian forces in the Bougainville Campaign. Working as a consulting engineer in Melbourne after the war, Callinan was appointed to many boards and committees and went on to chair the Federal Parliament House Construction Authority and the Melbourne Cricket Club. Garnett, who had served with British forces in India and Burma during the Second World War, settled in Australia when he took up the position of Principal of Geelong Grammar in 1961. He had been involved with Alec and Moira Dickson in establishing the Volunteer Service Overseas for British school leavers in the years immediately before his move to Australia.[5]

The Committee immediately sought support from organisational sponsors and individual contributors. They were confident that the Department of External Affairs had no plans to establish a program like the very newly established American Peace Corps and would eventually consider assisting schemes for overseas service that grew out of the Australian community. The Committee's strategy was not to approach the Department for support until the Bureau was well established and had widespread community backing.[6]

The funding issue was revisited at the Committee's December 1962 meeting at which Garnett, attending his first meeting, urged an early approach to the Commonwealth government. Jim Webb reiterated that, when the Department of External Affairs had been informed of the Bureau's formation in 1961, Robert Menzies, then Minister for External Affairs, had made it clear that Commonwealth government assistance would not be provided.[7] The Department knew of the Bureau's existence; there was no likely competitor and the Bureau would be advised if there were any changes in the government's attitude to providing funding support. The Committee reaffirmed its November decision to wait until OSB was better organised as a stronger autonomous body with more visible community support before it approached the government again.

Community funding and interest

Funding was clearly a significant issue for OSB, so the Committee was pleased to hear that one supporter, Martin Clemens,* had raised £1,800 for the Bureau – enough to set up its first office (in the Majorca Building, 260 Flinders Lane, Melbourne) and pay the first year's rent, while leaving £200 for operating costs. At Clemens' request the donation was not publicised.[8] The funding contributed by Clemens was one outstanding example of donations made to OSB by individuals, community organisations and trusts.

Although there had been little publicity, in just over a year the Bureau received 420 enquiries from people interested in service overseas and was attracting support for its work from organisations in the community. Many of these were Christian and/or student organisations that had been part of the supportive milieu of VGS, such as the Australian Council of Churches, Friends Service Council, National Missionary Council, National Youth Council, Student Christian Movement, Australian Catholic Federation, World University Service, and Association of Apex Clubs.

The OSB *Bulletin* of May 1963 presented a copious digest of employment opportunities, principally in education and health services. In Asia, most teaching opportunities were in secondary schools with expatriate links or in church-run institutions. There were no opportunities in the government education systems in which local languages were the medium of instruction, thus requiring the employment of local teachers. In Africa, by contrast, English was the dominant language of instruction and there were severe shortages of qualified staff, which meant there was a huge and immediate demand for foreign teachers. Many of the opportunities were quite attractive: Nigeria was paying salaries, housing and airfares; Northern and Southern Rhodesia were offering bursaries and a Post Graduate Certificate of Education after three years' service.

* Clemens settled in Australia in 1961 after a distinguished career as a British colonial administrator. He was sent to the British Solomon Islands Protectorate in 1938, where in 1941, as a District Officer, he helped prepare for eventual resistance against the Japanese. As a coastwatcher he alerted the Allied forces to Japanese plans to build an airstrip on Guadalcanal, which led to the landing of US forces and their invasion of Guadalcanal.

The Committee had plenty of evidence of the depth of shortages of trained people in developing countries and were convinced of the importance for Australians to gain "personal experience of the post-colonial issues of nationalism, race-relationships and economic development" and to learn "more about the new shape of the international community and about our neighbours, so that we may conduct ourselves appropriately as a nation".[9] They also perceived very strong indicators of the breadth of interest in OSB's work amongst Australian individuals and community organisations.

Proliferation of programs

Jim Webb's travels to Southeast Asia, London and East Africa and his correspondence networks made him acutely conscious of a supreme irony. Although Australia had initiated the first international volunteer program soon after the end of the Second World War and had by 1963 supported 40 volunteer graduates in Indonesia, it was being left behind by world events.[10] There were three agencies in the United Kingdom, one of which, Voluntary Service Overseas (VSO), was planning to mobilise 250 school leavers and apprentices for one-year terms around the world, including to New Guinea and the Pacific Islands. The Canadian University Service Overseas (CUSO), established in 1961, had 100 volunteers in Asia and Africa by 1963. From 1959 New Zealand also had a VGS for Indonesia (assisted by the Melbourne VGA Committee) and by 1963 the newly formed Volunteer Service Abroad (VSA) had sent its first volunteers to the Pacific Islands with New Zealand government support. In the Netherlands a joint government and non-government foundation was established in March 1963 and was planning for a corps of 200 volunteers aged between 25 and 32.

The most influential development was, of course, the establishment of the United States Peace Corps. The American government had considered the idea of volunteering during the Eisenhower administration (1953–61), seeing it as a defensive Cold War activity; in 1959 it had consulted in Washington with Herb Feith and Jim Webb about Australia's experience in Indonesia. The Kennedy administration also invited Don Anderson to Washington in 1961 for discussions when the Peace Corps was being designed.[11] The formation of the Peace Corps, illuminated by President John F. Kennedy's charisma and propelled by cover stories in *Time Magazine*, announced to the world that volunteers were a good thing.[12] In Australia it led to countless calls in the 1960s (and in subsequent decades), mainly by people with no knowledge of the role and function of OSB, for the formation of an Australian Peace Corps.

Australian Volunteers Abroad plan gains support

Webb told the Committee that he hoped that by January 1964 the Bureau would have volunteers in the field under a new scheme. By early July 1963 he had drafted a proposal for a pilot scheme for young people on one-year assignments in North Borneo, New Guinea and the Pacific Islands where he knew placements were available. The employing authority in each country would provide accommodation, medical care and pocket money, with the possibility of an additional modest payment for longer-term volunteers with professional skills. OSB would be responsible for their transportation and insurance. Volunteers would be 18 years or over with matriculation or a completed apprenticeship as their minimum qualification. Publicity for the program would be limited and applications would be sought from Headmasters' and Headmistresses' Associations, Education Directors, Mission Boards, NUAUS and the National Youth Council. Webb was keenly aware that the proliferation of volunteer schemes had created a competitive environment in the potential host countries. To ensure the best quality of volunteers, the interviewing process would be rigorous. In his view it was essential that a high standard be set from the outset in the selection and placement of candidates, as, inevitably, they would be compared with volunteers from other countries.[13] The plan was to recruit at least 12 candidates to be sent on assignment in January 1964 in a program that was to be known as Australian Volunteers Abroad (AVA).

The Bureau had reason to approach a new program with confidence. After circulating the last *Bulletin*, there had been 50 enquiries in one month and more funds had become available, principally through the agency of Martin Clemens once again, who guaranteed £5,000 for 1963 and for each of the next 4 years. Clemens declined an invitation to join the Committee, preferring to spend his efforts establishing his Forelanders Trust more broadly, but he agreed to be listed as a Patron.[14]

The Minister for External Affairs, Sir Garfield Barwick, also emerged as a keen supporter of the Bureau. Cowan, as OSB Chairman, had written to the Minister to bring him up to date and request a meeting. The Minister met with Cowan, Webb, and several others on 22 July 1963. The next day Major General Sir Walter Cawthorn (Head of the Australian Secret Intelligence Service) conveyed a sense of the meeting in a letter of thanks to Barwick for the informal discussion of the previous night: "All those present appreciated the time you devoted to us and the patience with which you listened to what we had to say about the project we have in hand".[15] He forwarded a copy of one of the papers Webb had presented that night. Described by Cawthorn as a "star gazing forecast" rather than a plan, it envisaged a volunteer program expanding in stages to reach 84 placements each year by 1967. There would be two-year assignments for professionals and one-year assignments for matriculants and apprentices, in Africa, Asia, the Pacific Islands and in Aboriginal communities. There was also a proposal to hold a three-day national consultation on overseas service in August 1964 in Sydney. Webb's estimate of what would be required to set up the program, establish a branch office in Sydney and provide travel grants for professional appointees in Africa and India was £52,750.

Barwick was supportive of the idea and conveyed his encouragement to Webb:

> The success of the Australian Volunteer Graduate Scheme in Indonesia is known to me and has evoked my warm admiration. Consequently the Bureau's plans for further endeavours by Australian Volunteers Abroad and its role

> in assisting other like projects encourage me to express the hope that the Bureau will receive wide personal and financial support. For my part, I will be pleased if my Department can assist in any way and would be grateful for any suggestions as to how such assistance might be given.[16]

Although he made his interest clear, Barwick had a strong view that this kind of work would best be conducted apart from government. As Webb reported to the Committee, "The Minister did not rule out the idea of Government aid to the Bureau, but appeared keen that it should develop its work as far as possible as an independent agency, free from External Affairs supervision and control".[17] The Committee still held the view that detailed approaches to the Minister should wait until the Bureau had firm proposals for 1964.

Recruitment and employment services

The work of making known overseas employment opportunities and providing a recruitment service to overseas employers was proceeding well. OSB was conducting interviews in Canberra on behalf of the Tanganyika Education Trust. Nigeria had asked OSB to recruit secondary teachers for whom the Nigerian government would provide airfares as well as a local salary, but the fares they would provide were from London to Nigeria and needed to be supplemented. In the British Solomon Islands, Methodist, Anglican and Catholic educational institutions all wanted teachers.

The British VSO was already providing six volunteers to the Solomon Islands, which exhausted the funds that country's administration had budgeted for volunteers. In April 1964 OSB planned to request the Solomon Islands administration to make budgetary provision for some AVA volunteers in 1965. Burns Philp had been sourcing about 25 people a year in Australia for the British Solomon Islands Protectorate and OSB was now asked to be the recruitment agency to fill vacancies for professionals such as agricultural officers, hospital matrons and education officers, while Burns Philp continued to handle lower level clerical appointments in the Solomon Islands.[18]

At the same time, Webb became involved in moves, orchestrated in Canberra, to coordinate NGOs involved in overseas aid.[19] He was one of three invited by Sir John Crawford[20] to a lunch meeting in Canberra on 15 October 1963 to discuss a proposal Crawford was preparing to put to the Minister for a way of coordinating NGOs involved in overseas aid. Crawford held that a much larger aid effort was needed, that present activities were a mere fraction of the potential support from Australia and that, without coordination, the sector would become competitive and fragmented as it grew. Crawford invited Jim Webb and David Scott (Director of Community Aid Abroad (CAA)) because of their strong connections in the voluntary sector and he wanted them to encourage the participation of NGOs in a seminar to be held in March 1964 at which NGOs were to present their work and plans according to an agenda he was to draw up. The third person invited to the meeting was Alan Manning, representing the Australian Institute for International Affairs (NSW), who presented his vision of an Australian Peace Corps involving thousands of volunteers each year and requiring several million pounds from the government. In response, Webb gave an account of how OSB was developing as quickly as possible, that it had not set an upper limit on the number of volunteers, and envisaged a program of several hundred volunteers at a cost of some tens of thousands of pounds.

The issue of government funding for OSB was raised again, this time by Mr Arnott of the Department of External Affairs, who sought Webb out during his Canberra visit to ask if OSB would accept an invitation from the Minister to submit a proposal for assistance. He pointed out that any proposal would need to be submitted without delay for it to be considered in the next budget cycle. He gave Webb the impression that he was in favour of some government support and intimated that it might be possible to be given as a direct grant to OSB, thus avoiding the complexities inherent in the program-specific assistance given to VGS.

For Webb, the Canberra meetings emphasised the need to speed up OSB's development with additional staff in order to stay ahead of ideas likely to come from people in or close to government. He wondered whether OSB should ask the Department for support on the basis of the work in hand and OSB's intentions for the future, rather than on the basis of incomplete detailed plans. As an interim measure, OSB approached the Forelanders Trust to see if they would underwrite the Bureau to the extent necessary to engage more professional staff.[21] By December 1963, with an understanding that the Trust was sympathetic to the idea, OSB had advertised a position, to which Bill Armstrong, a youth worker with Young Christian Workers (YCW) Movement since 1958, was appointed.

Preparations for the AVA program were proceeding – 62 had applied for assignments, 30 were interviewed, 18 were selected, and five withdrew. Trans Australian Airlines (TAA) offered assistance with fares but asked that their assistance not be publicised.[22]

The first Australian Volunteers Abroad group

The first AVA group to set off for their assignments left Australia in mid-January 1964.[23] There were ten volunteers, aged from 18 to 27, with qualifications ranging from matriculation to completed degrees; eight went to Papua and New Guinea and two to the Solomon Islands. An eleventh volunteer went to the Solomon Islands at the end of January, only to be repatriated in February after finding the assignment too isolated. In addition to these 11, a volunteer teacher went to a secondary school in Nigeria, after 12 months in Tanganyika where he was regarded as a pioneer for OSB. Although OSB had not provided his fare to Tanganyika, he had been invited to consider himself a member of AVA and to avail himself of its accident and baggage insurance cover. The same arrangement was made for another volunteer who took up an assignment in Tanganyika in March 1964.

By the meeting of the OSB Committee in April 1964, OSB's Constitution, after many amendments and alterations, was finally ready. In accordance with its provisions, the Foundation Members (Webb, Hobson, Lacey, Feith, Engel, Cowan, Callinan and Garnett) became the first Committee, with Cowan elected as Chairman and Lacey as Honorary

Treasurer. Many members of that first Committee had played significant roles in the formation of both VGS and OSB and would continue to do so in the following years. From June 1964 Jim Webb became the Bureau's full-time director. At its July meeting the Committee decided to invite two others to join them. L.J. Dooling (Victorian Manager of the Commonwealth Banking Corporation) became Honorary Treasurer following Lacey's departure for Pakistan and K. Travers (lawyer and member of the Melbourne University Newman Society) joined as a regular member.

OSB put together a draft plan for AVA for 1964/65, alongside VGS, which was separately funded by the Commonwealth government. The plan proposed 57 new volunteers. Thirty-five were to be one-year assignments, with volunteers receiving pocket money from local sources; 20 were intended for Papua and New Guinea, eight for the Solomon Islands, four for other Pacific Islands, and three for Sabah. Twenty-two two-year assignments were proposed for more experienced volunteers who would be paid salaries or allowances at local rates from local sources; four were allocated to Papua and New Guinea, four (including trade teachers) to Sabah, four secondary teachers to Nigeria, four teachers to Tanganyika church schools, and the remaining six to Malaya, Thailand, India and Pakistan.

An initial draft budget for 1964/65 showed that £5,000 of OSB's total income of £14,000 would come from the Forelanders Trust, nearly £5,000 from other trusts, organisations and individuals, with the remaining £4,000 envisaged as coming from the Commonwealth government as support for administration costs.[24] In its submission to Government OSB requested a further £15,000 from the Department of External Affairs toward the cost of the AVA program.[25]

This plan was put to Arnott in the Department of External Affairs, who in spite of his indications that it was a very modest proposal, proceeded to ask quite detailed questions about activities to date and the plans for 1964/5. Dealing with the world of government officials was becoming more problematic. At this point it became clear that no assistance from External Affairs could be used for any operations in the Territory of Papua and New Guinea, for which funding would have to come from the Department of

Territories. It also emerged that the Department of Treasury didn't approve of grants to community organisations from multiple departments.

NGO coordination and the funding context

Following on from his October 1963 lunch meeting, Sir John Crawford was pushing for a clearinghouse or a standing committee/conference as a mechanism for consultation and cooperation among NGOs. Webb told the OSB Committee that he saw very little advantage in having such a coordinating body, but that a seminar to be held in March or April 1964 was likely to recommend one. The Committee's advice was that OSB should position itself to be the sole channel for overseas service and should try to minimise other forms of coordination.[26] Although other organisations also had reservations about the need for a central organisation, it was agreed that some sort of informal association would be maintained. OSB was asked to convene a further meeting, which it was hoped that the Minister for External Affairs might attend, to discuss the role of the agencies and Government's relationship to them.[27]

Proposals for an Australian Peace Corps were once again seen off as participants in the April seminar were quite unimpressed with ideas beyond what OSB was already attempting. It was clear, however, that the idea of coordination had definite support amongst the Department's officers, who wanted an umbrella organisation to advise them and to become a single coordinating agency for the Commonwealth government to deal with. This presented a conundrum for Webb. On the one hand, he could see inherent problems in any coordination or machinery for cooperation, but that there would be an advantage if OSB could receive Commonwealth funding through that machinery rather than directly from the Department of External Affairs which would probably impose too many conditions. On the other hand, he could see that there was "something to gain from sheltering within a community of interested agencies".[28] Webb's position now was that, if OSB were to receive Commonwealth government assistance, he would prefer to delay receiving it until the principles of the coordinating mechanism were sorted out. In the meantime it was vital to maximise the organisation's income so that, if a base line were to be used to establish a comparative scale of grants, the Bureau's position would not be too modest.

Barwick's influence on Webb

The influence of Sir Garfield Barwick in Webb's strategic thinking is clear. Barwick was a strong supporter of OSB because it fitted so well with his multi-dimensional understanding of foreign policy. He was interested in the totality of relationships between countries at all levels, not just in formal foreign policy. His interest was not shared by officials in the Department of External Affairs, who also had no interest in dealing with a host of NGOs. It was because Barwick was not getting any useful response from officials in his own department that he had turned to Sir John Crawford, economist and aid expert at the Australian National University.[29]

Barwick came very close to securing untied funding for OSB during his time as Minister for External Affairs (1961–64). He had received a draft proposal from his department to fund volunteers, had made a correction and sent it back to be changed, but it was never finalised because, on 24 April 1964, he was removed from Cabinet and installed as Chief Justice of the High Court of Australia. Barwick had expected that his transition from Cabinet to High Court would occur in the fullness of time, but Cabinet made the decision effective immediately. Barwick had been battling with Prime Minister Menzies and others in Cabinet for years on a number of issues in his Attorney-General and External Affairs portfolios.

The disputes that arose in his External Affairs portfolio concerned Indonesia. Although Barwick had a reputation as a particularly conservative Attorney-General, as Minister for External Affairs he was anything but conservative. One of the first challenges he faced in his ministerial role had been to shift Menzies from his support for the Dutch against Indonesia in their sovereignty dispute over West Irian. He managed to convince Menzies that his position was supported by no other country and was unsustainable. When it came to Malaysia, however, Menzies was intractable. Menzies' instinct was to provide the fullest possible support to Britain in its sponsorship of the new federation and he had vocal support for this stance from pro-British forces in Cabinet and in parliament. Barwick's position was that Australia's support should be tacit at best, thus allowing a mediating role. He was very active in this diplomacy, meeting with his Indonesian counterpart Subandrio and essentially offering to bring Malaya to a negotiation if Subandrio could bring Sukarno. Menzies' position hardened during a visit to the United Kingdom and, on his return, his voice was the only voice for Australia's position on this issue. Although he had been unsuccessful politically, Barwick had brought a new approach to Australia's foreign policy. He was the first Australian External Affairs Minister to introduce to the Australian community the realities of post-colonial Asia and he was able to recognise that people's fears were largely the result of unfamiliarity created by their lack of contact with emerging Asian nations. Through his meetings with Indonesian leaders, Barwick had developed a genuine understanding of the political culture he had encountered, which he attempted to explain:

> Men who have gained their freedom as a result of revolution or of a war of independence are less likely to be tight lipped than those who have come to power in a system which is a result of centuries old constitutional process and who are answerable to a ballot box. I can myself understand them even coming to think that revolution is an intrinsically good thing ... in judging what our neighbours say we try to place their words in their historical and local setting ... it will reduce the risk of an erroneous reaction whose consequences may not be limited or easily reversible.[30]

Intrinsic to Barwick's approach was that he valued contact between Australians and people in neighbouring countries to establish familiarity and to build knowledge. Paul Hasluck, Barwick's successor as Minister for

External Affairs, shared neither Barwick's approach to foreign affairs nor his interest in OSB.

Barwick maintained a close and respectful relationship with Webb, going out of his way to support OSB and provide advice, often at short notice, including on how to approach his ministerial successors.[31] Barwick remained of the view that, if possible, OSB should be financed from community effort and not become dependent on government grants. He was quite sure dependence on government funding would give rise to undesirable problems at home and abroad. To that end he actively sponsored fundraising events for OSB amongst corporate leaders.

Building community support

In July 1964, the Bureau issued a fundraising prospectus detailing its achievements to date. OSB's Melbourne office had functioned for over a year on a full-time basis and there were OSB representatives in the capital cities of each Australian state. It had sponsorship from over 80 youth, church and community organisations. It had published six *Bulletin*s listing overseas vacancies and handled 900 enquiries. Its recruitment work on behalf of overseas employers had resulted in professionals working in Nigeria, Tanganyika, Sarawak, and the British Solomon Islands. OSB continued to assist the VGS for Indonesia and had launched a wider program called Australian Volunteers Abroad. By July 1964 the Bureau was responsible for 21 volunteers on overseas assignments and needed funds to expand the program. The average cost for a one-year placement in New Guinea or the Pacific Islands was £250; for a two-year assignment in Asia or Africa the average cost was £800. In the previous year the Bureau had received £9,324 in donations from individuals, sponsoring organisations and trusts.

OSB always presented to the public the full suite of its activities. Its *Bulletin*s showcased international employment opportunities and the recruitment work undertaken on behalf of foreign governments and agencies. Webb and his Committee realised full well that these activities were never going to result in large numbers of Australians working overseas, but they had strategic significance. In some cases recruited individuals played a pioneering role in feeding back information about the country they were assigned to, as was clearly the case in Nigeria and Tanganyika. A more significant benefit of providing these services and making them known through the *Bulletins* was building the profile of the organisation and attracting support.

Reflecting on this aspect of the Bureau's work 30 years later, Webb commented:

> We didn't have the funds to send more volunteers but we could put out a quarterly bulletin of vacancies saying here are all these opportunities and partly they were dressed up opportunities ... What I'm trying to say is [it] was partly an organisational move to create some window dressing. There was a big field here and a big opportunity but in fact not many people would find a job but on the basis of that we could recruit support from patrons and sponsors and organisations to give us money.[32]

From its inception, OSB had prioritised a strategy to demonstrate the moral support it had from distinguished members of the community as a way of attracting financial support from organisations, individuals, trusts and companies. Central to this strategy was assembling a list of the most prestigious patrons it could. As early as 1962 the Committee had decided to secure about 20 patrons and developed an initial list of 27 to approach, most of whom agreed quite quickly. Even though it was less than a year old, the organisation could project a remarkable depth and breadth of well-placed patronage.

The list of patrons, featured prominently on OSB letterhead and every publication, was a compendium of the great and the good in early 1960s Australia.[33] Among the patrons were leading churchmen (Anglican, Catholic and Protestant), academics and educationalists, writers and artists, colonial administrators, company directors, philanthropists, politicians and judges. Knights of the realm were well represented, but women were not. There were only three women, and two of these were titled. As a group, the list was representative of authority in the Australian community.

Prospect of government funding

The proposal that the Department of External Affairs had sent to the Minister just before Barwick had been moved out of the Cabinet in April 1964 resurfaced. This time it encompassed the involvement of NGOs in overseas aid and the Crawford-initiated meetings. It also included a section on volunteers, the Peace Corps model and the Australian experience. The submission recommended that OSB receive £21,000 towards AVA fares and allowances and OSB administration costs. This was envisaged as a grant with no strings attached, so the Bureau would not be required to work through the Department or through Australian posts overseas.[34] The Minister neither approved nor rejected the proposal, but sent the document back to the Department with a few critical notes and called for further material. Apparently Hasluck thought that any assistance to voluntary agencies would need Cabinet approval.

Webb arranged to meet Barwick in Sydney, whose advice was that OSB should urgently settle the question of a new Chairman (vacant following the death of Mr Cowan in June) and only then consider an approach to Hasluck. Barwick revealed his plan to write a memo about AVA and to approach the Prime Minister privately with it in August. In the meantime, he intended to discuss the Bureau's immediate need for several thousand pounds with several influential persons known to him.

The Committee acted quickly and invited Professor D.P. Derham to become Chairman of OSB. David Derham, who happened to be a nephew of Macmahon Ball, was Professor of Jurisprudence at Melbourne University and had just accepted a position as Foundation Dean of Law at Monash University. The Committee discussed the most appropriate way to approach Derham and secure his participation, deciding to ask Barwick to indicate to Derham that an invitation from the OSB Committee would be forthcoming and that it had his support. Derham agreed in August 1964 to take up the position of Chairman, bringing additional prestige to OSB and perpetuating the connection with Melbourne University and the social and intellectual origins of VGS.

NGO coordination agenda progressed

To follow up the April seminar, OSB convened a further meeting of NGOs in Canberra on 27 July 1964. Representatives of 15 organisations attended the meeting, chaired by Sir John Crawford. Most favoured a cautious approach to maintaining some kind of continuing relationship. They recognised a common need to improve public opinion on aid and appreciated the value of cooperation in public relations, research and training for overseas service. Hasluck attended but admitted his ignorance of the field, adding that he saw value in coordinated liaison with his department. The meeting adopted a resolution favouring in principle the formation of an ongoing body in the foreign aid field. Crawford was invited to prepare three papers: a summary of cooperative arrangements in place in Canada, the United Kingdom and elsewhere; a draft of possible aims and structure for a coordinating body; and a note on the implications for member organisations. The meeting appointed an ad-hoc executive, with Webb as convener and six other members, including David Scott (CAA), to consider the detail of the drafts and arrange a full conference.[35]

Meanwhile OSB had continued with its organisational and operational planning and had arranged for volunteers to be sent in January 1965 on one-year assignments to Papua and New Guinea and the Pacific Islands and for two years to Sabah, India, Tanganyika and Nigeria. Although OSB had selected 30 volunteers, it only had funds for 15. All were requested to raise funds and contribute what money they could to the costs of getting to their assignments and, in the end, all 30 departed.

In his Director's Report for the October 1964 Committee Meeting, Webb again reported on developments in Canberra. A few months earlier he had been advised by Mr McDonald of the Department of External

Affairs of a fresh attempt to get approval for a grant for AVA. Senior Department officials had kept the matter alive and several Liberal MPs had also approached the Minister. Because of the questions directed at Webb regarding how volunteers and projects were selected he was wary that a grant might come with unwelcome strings attached. In any case, in July 1964, Webb was advised that the Minister had not approved a grant for AVA. Barwick repeated his advice to Webb, expressing his belief that it would be better to build up the Bureau independently of government as he was "fearful of the public service interference that might follow Government money – 'The further away from the Government and the less control by Government the better'".[36]

Despite the Committee's decision to raise money from the public and then seek a meeting with the Minister early in 1965, Webb successfully asked the Committee to change its position. In November 1964 he put the case in a carefully argued memo on Bureau finance.[37] He argued that the earlier decision had been taken because the Committee felt it had no option other than to seek Government assistance, despite realising that the Minister was not committed to the volunteer idea and that any government funding would entail unwelcome administrative obligations and policy restraints. He presented his analysis of the current situation:

- The Australian Freedom from Hunger Campaign (AFFHC) was planning to launch a public appeal in 1965 for £1.5 m and OSB had been invited to be associated with the appeal and propose projects.
- Crawford's documents regarding coordination of NGOs were now ready – they had been drafted mostly within the Department of External Affairs – and it was now likely that a Council for Voluntary Aid Overseas would be formed early in 1965.[38] This would strengthen the Bureau's dealings with government, as the other NGOs would support government funding for OSB without strings.

- On 9 November 1964 the Forelanders Trust held a successful function attended by Lord Casey and about 60 leading Melbourne businessmen, including the Myer brothers, Mr Reginald Ansett and Mr Jones of BHP. The Trust presented OSB as its main beneficiary to date and attendees were generally encouraging in their response. The Trust was planning similar approaches to the Sydney business community.
- More than ten volunteers had departed in January 1964. About 30, some 15 of whom were allocated to Papua and New Guinea and the Solomon Islands, were due to set off in January 1965, bringing the number in the field up to 39. There would probably be sufficient funds from non-government sources to send another 30 in January 1966.
- A case would be put to the Myer Foundation and the Howard Norman Trust for adequate underwriting over the next year. Shortage of suitable senior staff was noted as another constraint, which meant that, if substantial funds were suddenly available, OSB would not have the capacity to expand its activity and it would take time to recruit staff with the right combination of necessary skills and experience.
- If the organisation continued to progress, it was likely that the government would approach OSB to offer help, rather than OSB being in "the weaker position of begging for official support". The Committee could decide to approach the Minister again if it was necessary to do so, but it would improve OSB's standing with government if it could demonstrate reasonable achievement and steady expansion with independent funding.[39]

Webb's analysis and recommendations were all accepted by the Committee, which undertook to review the situation in mid-1965 and revisit the question of approaching the Commonwealth government for funding.[40]

Public relations intensified

Webb captured the atmosphere in the first half of 1965 in a letter to Derham in which he asked him to immediately issue a press release in support of a recruitment drive. The urgency was to get the attention of the press before the Australian International Cooperation Year Convention in Canberra in May and because he had decided to mention the Peace Corps:

> I'll be most surprised if 4 days of discussion by these good people doesn't produce a Peace Corps proposal! … I'm afraid we must be bold and cash in on press and publicity interest in the Peace Corps. This may give the news angle which will lead to good coverage. Although I've rather resisted this easy way to fame in the past, in recent months I've weakened and am afraid we must be willing to fall in behind known titles and slogans. In any case we are sufficiently ahead of any other Australian efforts to be able to make some bold claims about ourselves, even though we have no plans for a huge programme.[41]

In 1965 OSB began producing an AVA newsletter for circulation to all volunteers. About three quarters of the content was news of volunteers arriving, settling in and being at work, much of it quoting from letters that volunteers had sent. The remainder was thoughtful summaries of press coverage of events in Papua and New Guinea.[42] The newsletters proved to be a useful channel to inform volunteers of staff travel and to share volunteer news. Reviews of relevant articles published in a wide range of media, including the *Pacific Islands Monthly*, were included and Webb used the newsletter to let the volunteer community know what he was thinking and about opportunities he had identified. He provided a brief report on his seven-week trip to the United Kingdom, Africa and Asia, where he met with VSO and the United Kingdom government and had exploratory meetings in Kuala Lumpur, Bangkok and New Delhi. He also reported on his discussions in Nigeria, Tanzania and Zambia, noting that

> there are many opportunities in all these countries for volunteers and it seems that Australians are particularly acceptable. We have no colonial past in Asia and Africa, as a small power we are not seen as a threat and Australians are viewed generally as being adaptable, relaxed and friendly people. So the opportunities are there. It remains for us to find the money and the people.[43]

The June newsletter reported that, following Webb's visit to New Guinea, there were interesting opportunities for volunteers to work with indigenous organisations such as local government councils and co-operatives. It was also reported that the Minister for Territories, Charles Barnes, was considering a proposal for a "Peace Corps" in New Guinea and that OSB had been in touch with him. Webb expressed enthusiasm about the opportunities likely to open up in New Guinea, stressing the value of friendly people-to-people relationships independent of government involvement, but that OSB and its AVA program had "no desire to develop into a huge and impersonal peace corps".[44]

Government sees advantages in funding volunteers

Barnes' consideration of a proposal for a peace corps was a response to two developments, both of which were to be important for OSB. One was a World Bank report on Papua and New Guinea recommending the use of more volunteers. The other was lobbying in the Department of External Affairs by senior Australian diplomat David Hay, who had been High Commissioner in Canada and then Ambassador to the United

Nations when the United States Peace Corps was launched and developed; he had been to enough international conferences to recognise the great value of volunteers. On his return from Canada the position he held in the Department was the most senior role overseeing technical assistance. Hay went on to become the Administrator of Papua and New Guinea from December 1966.[45]

Because both the Department of External Affairs and the Department of Territories were being pushed, at the same time and from different quarters, to get serious about enabling and providing more volunteers, a new discussion about support for OSB opened up. This time there was an urgency in the government side of the discussion. OSB's strategy of pushing ahead without government support and waiting for the government to approach them with offers to assist had succeeded. It had been a high-risk strategy that was saved by fortuitous developments totally beyond OSB's influence. The approach from government was also extremely timely because, although it had not disclosed the fact, the Bureau was close to bankrupt.[46]

Derham reported how events had transpired to the Committee. David Hay, First Assistant Secretary Department of External Affairs, and Mr R. Swift, First Assistant Secretary of the Department of Territories, met with Derham and Webb at Monash University on 11 August 1965 and made three main points to OSB about the government's position:

1. The government had no desire to operate a peace corps, but would be prepared to support an organisation already managing volunteer programs, provided it was national in character and set up for the purpose.
2. They were looking for a formula and their preferred option was to provide funding for AVA operations, with OSB raising the funds necessary to cover its administration costs.
3. They flagged the idea that the government would seek something in return for financially supporting OSB, such

> as the right to exercise some control over the selection of volunteers and placements and to have placements negotiated at a government-to-government level.

In the circumstances the Committee's response was naturally supportive of the government's overtures, but they made it clear that they would agree to nothing that prejudiced the organisation's independence and integrity.[47]

The government required a detailed written submission from OSB, and the Committee quickly agreed to the content of the draft. The submission began by presenting the nature of the organisation's governance and its relationships with other organisations, specifically with ACFOA, CAA, AFFHC, ACC and the Protestant Mission Boards, Catholic Overseas Relief, Catholic Mission Offices, the major youth and student organisations, community service organisations, welfare organisations, the Royal Commonwealth Society and the English Speaking Union.

In the submission they argued that it was essential for the funding formula to accommodate paying for some of the administration costs directly generated by expanding the AVA program, at least by 1967. For the January 1966 program, £26,000 would be required: £5,000 in December 1965 and £10,000 in January 1966 to mobilise the volunteers, and £4,000 in December 1966 and £7,000 in December 1967 to bring them home again. OSB indicated its willingness to provide annual budgets and operational plans, audited annual accounts and lists of volunteers selected, giving the name, date and place of birth, address and occupation of each, and to engage in an annual discussion of program parameters. Although OSB stated its preference to continue negotiating directly with overseas employers, it was willing, if requested, to inform the government of these negotiations and to seek the government's assistance in any negotiations that would benefit from government involvement.[48]

The Bureau expected to cooperate closely and fully with the government in working out some general policies for the program, including the countries and sectors of work. It showed its understanding that in the case of the Territory of Papua and New Guinea there would be detailed examination of particular assignments. In new program areas, such as local government councils and cooperative societies, OSB wanted volunteer relationships and responsibilities, including to the Administration of the Territory, clearly defined in advance. Volunteers would be employees of the organisation with which they were working and not subject to oversight by officers of the Administration.

Proposed agreement

By late October 1965 Webb was able to inform the Committee that Department of External Affairs officers had let him know that the Ministers had reached agreement and that a proposal would go to Cabinet within days, a draft of which Derham and Webb had been able to comment on.[49] The terms of agreement were outlined in a letter from the Minister of External Affairs to the Chairman of OSB on 5 November 1965, much of which had already been conveyed by telephone. In essence, the proposal was that OSB would cover its own administrative costs and the Commonwealth government would provide funding for the AVA program's operational costs, as agreed annually. It was a triumph for the original VGS vision, as the government embraced the notion of volunteers being employed within the country of their assignment, specifying that "volunteers would be subject to direction regarding their employment only by the authorities with whom they are employed in host countries. They would have the same responsibilities and obligations in respect of that employment as other persons employed by the same authorities".[50]

The terms also included the beginnings of the controls Barwick had warned of and which Webb had sought to avoid. OSB had to agree to follow certain procedures that would enable the Commonwealth government to exercise such control as the government thought necessary. OSB and government officials were to meet annually to discuss the next year's programs and this annual meeting would be the forum that ensured the government's views were taken into account. The government explicitly acknowledged the value in preserving as much as possible the voluntary character of the Bureau's activities. Within the Department, it was recognised that its independence had been important in the success of VGS and that Australia's diplomatic posts did not want a peace-corps type program.[51] The question remained, however, about what degree of control government should have and how it was to exercise its control. Government representation on the organisation's directorate was thought to be unwise and it was decided that that sufficient control could be exercised by other means.[52]

The subtler understatement of most of Hasluck's letter about the terms of agreement was abandoned in its discussion of selection of volunteers:

> It will be necessary for these Departments to be informed of persons whom it is proposed to select for service in the Government assisted programme and to have full opportunities to state their views on them before selection is notified to those persons. Normally the Bureau would be expected to exercise its discretion to exclude any candidate whom the Department would not wish to be selected, and in a way that would not attract public comment or make it apparent to the candidate that he had not been selected because of a Government objection.[53]

Because they had not yet received the letter and, therefore, could not yet reply to it, the Committee communicated its acceptance of the terms, as had been outlined in phone conversations, in a telegram to the Minister. They had to complete this interim formality, because the first "annual meeting" required by the agreement had in fact occurred on 4 November, the day before the formal letter was written and before it could be formally agreed to. At the meeting were Hay (Department of External Affairs), Swift (Department of Territories), D. Hunter (Department of Treasury), Webb and other departmental officials, who had convened in advance of receipt of the Minister's letter because of the urgent need to confirm the January 1966 program.[54]

Webb clarified in the meeting that it would be difficult to raise sufficient funds to cover the administration costs for the year but, rather than cut back on numbers of volunteers for 1965–66 just to meet administration expenses, OSB would go ahead with its plans and carry over the deficit to next year. Funds held in reserve for operational costs, such as the £2,000 per annum recently agreed to by the Leverhulme Trust in London, would be released for administration. It was now imperative that OSB have additional staff. A small office was to be opened in Sydney, while voluntary agents would be assisted by local committees representing sponsors and interested groups in the capital cities of other states.

In his response, Hay indicated that the Department of External Affairs would need to consult overseas posts about all future programs, citing the example of Thailand where the Thai government had expressed the wish that placements in Thailand should be discussed at an inter-governmental level. It was agreed that the government would contribute up to the amount of AVA operational costs for the year and OSB would raise its administration costs at least. The departmental representatives conceded it would be wise for OSB to accumulate a modest reserve. If, at any point in the future, the government thought the reserves had become excessive it would raise the matter with OSB at one of their scheduled meetings.

For the 1966 program, the country allocations, the choice of institutions as employers and the spread of skills sought were all approved, subject to the view of the Administrator in Papua and New Guinea. Given the unusual and urgent circumstances of this meeting, the departmental representatives did not object to any of the candidates OSB submitted as potential volunteers, although the Department of Territories reserved its right to object.

It was confirmed that, for the 1966 AVA departure group, the government would pay £27,400, with £15,300 in the 1965/66 financial year, of which £7,500 was to be used for volunteers to Papua and New Guinea, which matched what OSB had requested in August. The next annual discussion was scheduled for March 1966.

Left

Jim Webb peruses *Bulletin* No. 3, October 1962. Photo C. Bottomley, Australian News and Information Bureau (NAA: A1200, L44221)

Below

The first group of Australian Volunteers Abroad with Jim Webb prepare to depart in January 1964. Photo C. Bottomley, Australian News and information Bureau (NAA: A1200, L46221)

Volunteers at pre-departure briefing before leaving for Papua and New Guinea in January 1965. L to r: Barbara Johnson and Liz Cogan, nurses, with teacher Lois Elkin. Courtesy AVI

David Fowler and Richard Refshauge, teachers in Papua and New Guinea, 1965, admire taro. Courtesy AVI

Bob Meyenn, secondary teacher, collects the weekly mail with a student, Solomon Islands, 1966. Courtesy AVI

Jan Ho, hostel supervisor with Papua Ekelesia, Papua and New Guinea, 1966–67.
Courtesy AVI

Left

Elizabeth Layton, library assistant at Goroka Local Government Council, Papua and New Guinea, 1966–67. Courtesy AVI

Below

David Derham with the "AVA Flying Squad", 1968. L to r: Mary Considine, Field Officer (previously volunteer in Papua and New Guinea), Derham, Liz Cogan (PNG), Margaret Noonan (India), Neville Christie (Malaysia). Courtesy AVI

Margaret Gibson and her assistant Heli travel by canoe to conduct maternal and child health clinics Papua and New Guinea, 1968–69. Courtesy AVI

The tone of OSB's fifth newsletter for the year was jubilant, as the Bureau explained the arrangement to its volunteers, quoting from the government's press release and spelling out what it meant in practical terms:

> The Government believed that the work being done by the Bureau was important in the national interest and that it should therefore provide assistance for the expansion of the Bureau's volunteer activities ... the government hoped that its support would encourage continued and expanded support from private sources for the Bureau's work, thus permitting a significant increase in the number of Australian volunteers going to Asia, Africa and the Pacific, as well as to Papua and New Guinea.[55]

In practical terms, government funding meant fares and expenses for a greater number of volunteers could be covered, thus ending the need for some volunteers to contribute substantially to their costs and for employers to contribute fares.

Planning with newfound confidence

With the new agreement in place, OSB would still need to raise £17,000 from private sources – more than they had raised in the past. The audited accounts for the year ending 31 December 1965 showed a total income of £17,750 (trusts: £6,400; sponsors: £3,008; contributors: £1,620; and the first instalment from the government: £6,413). Total income in 1964 had been £12,031 (trusts: £9,000; sponsors: £1,655 and contributors: £911). The additional funds made it possible to send 61 new volunteers, which gave OSB a sense that it had entered a new era. Although it would need to raise more money, it was free from anxiety about its existence. For the first time definite AVA plans could be made months in advance.[56]

The second newsletter for 1966, not issued until August, detailed a particularly busy six months, with extensive staff travel to state capitals and overseas. Although the newsletter had been delayed, there had been three separate mailings to volunteers and supporters: a new AVA leaflet on "Australia's External Aid"; reviews of new books on New Guinea (*The New Guinea Villager* by C.D. Rowley and *Green Armour* by Osmar White and reviews of articles; and the OSB *Bulletin* No 8. Recruitment drives had been supported by publicity that included feature articles in daily newspapers, *The Bulletin*, *Readers Digest* and *Walkabout*.[57]

The target for 1967 was 100 new volunteers; in the event 80 were deployed. Following established practice the ten-day residential briefing course was held at the University of Melbourne and featured several speakers, including Dr Victor Prescott, a geographer at the University who spoke about Africa, and Dr John Gunther, Vice-Chancellor of the University of Papua New and New Guinea. Lord Casey, the Governor-General, addressed volunteers and guests at the farewell function at the end of the course.[58]

Fundraising and the publicity to support it were major preoccupations for the organisation and everyone was involved. Returned volunteers were actively engaged, particularly those in the "AVA Flying Squad" which visited state capital cities and regional centres in the first half of 1968. Barwick, Callinan and Webb also met at the Melbourne Club to discuss fundraising strategies, and soon after Webb could inform Derham that the Howard Norman Trust had agreed to contribute $1,000 each year for the next five years. In June 1968, recognising that a wider call for funding was needed, Derham prepared a letter to send to private companies. He pointed out that the OSB budget for 1968 needed an additional $15,000 and that the organisation had not yet received significant support from industrial and commercial organisations. He appealed to companies with growing interests in the Southeast Asia and Pacific area to commit to giving OSB $2,000 each year for five years.[59] A frustrated Webb chided Derham, suggesting that he should ask for $5,000–10,000 per year. One of the more sustaining avenues for fundraising at the time was the Volunteer Adoption Scheme, in which community organisations adopted individual volunteers, contributed funds and established a connection through ongoing correspondence.

By the start of 1968 the number of volunteers serving overseas had increased four-fold, rising from 31 in 1965 to 124 in 1967. Of these 63 were in New Guinea, 38 in Asia, 14 in Africa and nine in the Pacific Islands. Newsletters continued to share snippets of news and views from volunteers and to document staff travel. In the first half of 1967, three staff had visited 92 volunteers. While not all volunteers were visited, the extensive travel had helped staff develop a closer and more realistic understanding of the realities of volunteer life and its challenges:

> There have been some ups and downs in AVA experiences in recent months. Most new volunteers have settled into a fairly busy routine, a few being over-busy. One or two have found that they aren't as occupied as they would wish. Although most AVA teachers find their pupils to be attentive and co-operative, in some spots in Papua-New Guinea schoolboys have resented and made things difficult for female staff. Health has been a problem for some, while in Nigeria political events* have sadly overshadowed all else.[60]

Controversy: volunteering and Papua and New Guinea

The AVA program was not without controversy. Ron Crocombe, an academic with extensive hands-on experience in Papua and New Guinea and elsewhere in the Pacific and head of the Australian National University's New Guinea Research Unit in Port Moresby from 1962 to 1969, published an article arguing for much greater use of volunteers in New Guinea. The article appeared in the January 1968 issue of the quarterly publication of the influential Council on New Guinea Affairs. Crocombe wrote appreciatively

* The "political events" were the impact of the Nigerian Civil War, which began in July 1967 following Biafra's secession in May and continued for three years.

of the value of volunteers from many angles, including race relations: "By creating better relationships at the contact level they reduce inter-racial friction, and by working at local rates of pay and conditions they reduce the resentments due to the common assumption that all Europeans are rich and privileged while all indigenes are poor and underprivileged".[61] He argued that volunteers were better value than expatriate workers, being substantially cheaper and often better educated. Noting that the Peace Corps had expressed interest in New Guinea but had been rebuffed by the Minister who wanted to see if more volunteers could be sourced from Australia and the United Kingdom, Crocombe asked why there were not more Australian volunteers:

> AVA selection procedures are highly effective, and the field record of its volunteers very creditable. The two main reasons for its not having recruited more people are, I believe, firstly that it has not got its message across to the youth of Australia sufficiently loud and clear, and secondly that it is too cautious, too conservative, in its conception of what constitutes a volunteer service.[62]

OSB viewed Crocombe's writing of the article as a hostile act, unnecessarily critical and likely to add impetus to calls for an Australian Peace Corps – a serial threat. OSB responded with a letter to the Editor of *New Guinea and Australia, the Pacific and South-East Asia.*[63] Although apparently from Derham, the level of programmatic detail in the letter suggests that Webb had drafted it. It sought to correct the record, pointing out that, unlike Peace Corps volunteers, AVAs were fully qualified and directly employed within the country of their assignment. The letter explained that the modest scale of the program was partly attributable to the difficulties in raising funds from private sources to sustain the administration required and to its adherence to a set of basic principles to "ensure success":

(a) The employer of a volunteer must need the volunteer's assistance for financial and substantive work reasons;

(b) The volunteer must not be regarded merely as a source of cheap labour and must not feel he is being exploited;

(c) The volunteer must be fully, effectively, and usefully employed;

(d) The employer must have the capacity to make full use of the volunteer's skills and capacity …;

(e) To maintain and improve public interest in, and support for, volunteer activities in Australia, it is essential that volunteers should not become disillusioned or discontented – volunteering must not become discredited;

(f) A correlative to (e) is the principle that the work done by volunteers must be such as to maintain an appreciation of their value and a demand for their work in the local areas concerned.[64]

OSB also argued that, because Papua and New Guinea was administered by Australia and received strong financial support from Australia, it was inappropriate to consider a volunteer program that was comparable to those in other (independent) countries.

Instead of appreciating Crocombe as an ally in advocating for volunteers and AVA and seeing both challenge and opportunity in his critique, OSB had responded preciously and defensively. For the most part the principles outlined in Derham's letter were drawn from VGS and early AVA experience, but it read as though principles had become policy imperatives that could never be changed, as dogma that did not reflect the realities experienced by volunteers in the field and apparent to OSB staff.

Webb moves on

Webb continued to comment on the challenges faced by volunteers in the field. In July 1968 he repeated his earlier observations about some volunteers being too busy and others being underutilised. Housing for volunteers varied from the very comfortable to the quite basic. Their social circumstances also varied substantially, with some volunteers building excellent and meaningful relationships with local people, while others found themselves confined in boarding schools or mission compounds with expatriate staff. It seemed that such variation was regarded as a natural part of the volunteer experience. As Webb put it: "Certainly many volunteers have had reason to query the meaning of their AVA experience. I have no doubt that such questioning will continue to the end of many assignments – and beyond!"[65] Webb had clearly been asking questions of himself and made it known that he had decided to leave the Bureau in April 1969. In May, Webb moved to Seoul, Korea, to take up a post with the Asian and Pacific Council's Cultural and Social Centre for the Asia-Pacific Region.[66]

Webb's achievements were extraordinary. He had become Secretary of VGS in late 1952, had envisaged the Overseas Service Bureau and founded it in 1961, establishing independent programming that rested on the values and principles engendered in VGS. He positioned OSB as a leading NGO and played a central role in the formation of ACFOA. With the backing of a Committee well connected to leaders of the business community, he secured private support from foundations and built a powerful and prestigious list of patrons, whom he developed as a channel for community support to the organisation. Webb succeeded in securing ongoing government support for OSB on terms that preserved organisational independence and required OSB to pursue a mixed funding model with government, corporate and community input.

By the end of 1968, OSB had 13 staff in Melbourne, and branch offices and auxiliaries in each state capital. Support from the Commonwealth government contributed $89,653, and the Volunteer Adoption Scheme had raised $37,836. Eighty new volunteers in that year brought the total number of volunteers on overseas assignments to 135. Most of them (83) were in Papua and New Guinea, ten in other Pacific Island countries, 40 in Asia, and two in Africa. AVA volunteers were working in 12 countries, and there were a further five VGS volunteers in Indonesia. The *Bulletin* was published annually and newsletters were issued regularly, routinely carrying plenty of news of volunteers, quotes from their letters, staff news, and, increasingly, details of volunteer engagements and marriages.

Faced with finding a new director to replace Webb, Committee members approached Bill Armstrong, who had been working under Webb's direction since 1964 across all aspects of the AVA program in Australia and internationally, but had been involved most intensively in organising assignments in Papua and New Guinea. Armstrong decided not to apply for the position, partly because he recognised that he wasn't ready to take on the demands of an executive role and partly because he had already decided he wanted to work in development education. The Committee appointed Allen Martin as Webb's successor. Martin was from Albury on the New South Wales–Victoria border, where he had managed a radio station and, through his membership of a service club, had come into contact with returned volunteers promoting AVA. Recognising that Martin was new to the field, the Committee asked Armstrong to stay on for a year to keep his significant expertise in managing the AVA program in OSB as Martin became familiar with his new role. Of particular importance were the expertise and contacts Armstrong had built in Papua and New Guinea, to which half of the program's volunteers were assigned. The Committee wanted him to travel to Papua and New Guinea with Martin to introduce him to the realities of volunteering overseas.

CHAPTER 3

Preservation, Defence and Crisis (1969–82)

When he took over as Director of the Overseas Service Bureau in 1969 Allen Martin inherited an organisation with strong community support and respect and a collaborative relationship with government. The operations of its Australian Volunteers Abroad program were driven by an established philosophy and Martin was determined to maintain the program's assets and attributes, making only minor changes when necessary. Martin sought neither to transform OSB's offerings nor to dramatically increase either the number of volunteers or the number of countries they went to. He wanted to preserve the operation at its current scale and to defend the philosophical principles entrusted to him. Consequently, there was little innovation or growth at OSB during his time as Director.

Martin inherited enormous goodwill and support among the Committee, volunteers, staff, community organisations, the Australian Government, and host countries. As support in each of these quarters diminished, distrust grew and, over time, materialised as opposition. When disgruntled staff, returned volunteers and Committee members came together in an internal review early in 1981 they were able to imagine a different future. The review fed into an external review instigated by the Minister of Foreign Affairs, which exposed the full extent of the Bureau's problems and provided signposts to a more progressive future.

From early in his time as Director Martin focused almost exclusively on the AVA program, finding even the Volunteer Graduate Scheme an unwelcome distraction. The VGS group were a formidable, knowledgeable and committed band, who led Martin, just a few months into his new job, to comment to the OSB Chairman: "regardless of the good intentions of Professor Feith and Co. I am not anxious to become too involved in this very big time-consuming group for some time, having my hands pretty full in running the AVA programme as it is".[1] The need for the AVA program to take over VGS in Indonesia had been thoroughly canvassed in cables between the Australian Embassy in Jakarta and the Department of External Affairs in Canberra. Martin negotiated a way for this to happen by limiting the program to the teaching of English in Indonesian universities, but in doing so he ensured that there was no transition period and that the end of VGS was a clean break.[2] He refused to take Harold Crouch, the last volunteer graduate in Jakarta (1968–69), into the AVA program, aware that Crouch had been quite vocal in explaining to the VGA Committee in Melbourne what changes would be needed for the VGS program to continue.

Australian Volunteers Abroad

The AVA program reached its high point in 1968, when 97 volunteers were selected and deployed, after which the number settled back to 76 new volunteers in 1970 and 1971, rising to 90 in the mid-1970s before declining to 67 in 1979 and 57 in 1980. In 1971 over half the volunteers went to Papua and New Guinea, with a handful to other Pacific Islands (British Solomon Islands Protectorate, Fiji and New Hebrides), less than a third went to Asia (most to Malaysia, but some to Indonesia and India), and a handful went to Botswana, Tanzania, Kenya and Nigeria.

The annual process cycle for the AVA program continued throughout the 1970s as it had previously. Mid-year volunteer selection enabled placement and matching to occur in September and October, with final numbers decided late in the year, in time for a briefing course in early January shortly before the volunteers departed. The briefing course was a week-long residential program at one or other of the colleges at the University of Melbourne. From 1970, an additional two-day course was held as a crash teacher-training course for recent graduates going to teaching placements, but it ceased in 1976 when untrained teachers were not required as more experienced and better qualified volunteers were sought. From 1976 there were no further 12-month assignments; all assignments were for two years.[3]

The briefing course was one component of the AVA program that was constantly improved in both its content and methodology while Martin was Director. Volunteers engaged in area studies with returned volunteers, nationals of the countries to which they were sent and academics. Experts and practitioners were assembled to discuss the realities of international development. Course participants were also engaged in discussions of prejudice and the nature of Australian society, focusing particularly on poverty, Aboriginal Australia, migrants and migration policy, and foreign policy. In 1973, OSB was one of the first organisations in Australia to use simulation games, developed in the United States just four years earlier and still in use today in some educational and non-profit settings, as participatory learning/training aids.[4] StarPower focused on power and the abuse of power; BaFa' BaFa' explored how culture influences behaviour.

On the last evening of the briefing course volunteers were farewelled and their families and the community organisations assisting the program were thanked. It was also an opportunity to showcase the level of political support OSB enjoyed. If the Minister for Foreign Affairs could not attend, it was not uncommon for them to send a representative or at least a message. Both sides of politics publicly supported the volunteer program and saw advantages in being associated with AVA. Early in his time as Prime Minister, Gough Whitlam sent a message of support to the departing volunteers:

> [T]he work of Australian Volunteers Abroad is a personal communication between Australians and the people of developing countries. Such a program reaches the needs of developing countries in an intimate and friendly way beyond

> the scope of official government aid. Congratulations are due to the Overseas Service Bureau for the efficient way in which it conducts its Scheme. I wish the Australian Volunteers Abroad Program every success and the 1973 volunteers a fruitful and satisfying period of overseas service.[5]

Volunteers

Once volunteers were on assignment, OSB kept in touch with them mostly through the *AVA Newsletter* (usually issued four times a year), a practice continued by Martin. The newsletters continued to carry news of staff travel and of volunteers, with much of their content comprising excerpts from letters volunteers had sent to OSB. Martin continued to include a list of the addresses of all serving volunteers in the newsletter. Sometimes it contained no more than a page of news compiled from volunteer correspondence and, usually, a section reporting on the "Overseas Marriage Bureau". What disappeared from the newsletter under Martin were the reviews and summaries of recent books and articles about international development or specific issues or political developments in places that volunteers were serving. Jim Webb, a voracious reader, had written the reviews and summaries and without his input they did not continue. From 1973, reprints of articles garnered from the *New Internationalist* and other magazines, or of United States Peace Corps material on culture shock and similar themes, were included, but without any commentary. As this practice developed, the amount of volunteer news in the newsletters was reduced, sometimes to just a few pages giving details of new arrivals, changes of address and extensions of assignments. They no longer contained anything to stimulate volunteers or supporters of the AVA program, and their lack of any intellectual content other than the reprinted articles led some volunteers to describe them later as superficial and insubstantial.[6] The newsletter was often used as a way of communicating program and organisational news and, occasionally, to flag issues with volunteers.

In August 1976 Martin included in the *Newsletter* a piece headed "Is your volunteer salary too high?" He pointed out that OSB's preferred way for volunteers to be supported was for them to be paid a salary equivalent to that of a similarly credentialed local person in a similar position. He conceded that the governments of some countries were not conforming to this practice, but in countries where they did volunteers who received a local salary could be on a high income compared to others in the community. Few local people received salaries and those who did had extensive family and community obligations. Martin contrasted the situation of local people with "the tendency of some volunteers to spend their high incomes entirely on themselves – perhaps in the form of expensive international travel during holidays, or expensive sound equipment etc." which tended to set the volunteer apart from the local community.[7]

Martin had raised a question – what was the most appropriate way for volunteers to dispose of their excess income? He explained that he was preparing new briefing material and asked volunteers to send in their views, "even if you're not in a high income situation". His generalisations and assumptions about volunteers' lifestyles were not based on field knowledge and, unsurprisingly, if he received any useful feedback from the volunteers, he included none it in subsequent newsletters. This episode is consistent with Martin's direct dealings with volunteers. He did not invest time in listening to volunteers and learning from their experiences. From very early in his time as Director he showed a tendency to put volunteers offside with his dogmatic and often conservative views and with his reluctance to engage with volunteers' realities. One informant told of how Martin would invite the volunteer he was visiting to meet him at his hotel, thus not seeing how, where, or with whom the volunteer lived or worked, and not using the opportunity to build a relationship with the organisation employing the volunteer.

The self-reliance and resilience of volunteers was not just a philosophical hallmark of the AVA program; it was a practical necessity throughout the 1970s when letters were the means of communication and airmail was only between major centres. The unavoidable delay that this built into written and mailed correspondence was exacerbated by a lack of responsiveness from Martin and his staff. A sampling of correspondence in volunteer files has revealed a pattern of response; letters from staff to volunteers would begin with an apology for the delay in responding, explain how busy the staff member had been, include some news about national events or Melbourne's weather, and make little reference to the volunteer's circumstances. Volunteers were to complain later about the fact that their letters were either inadequately answered or not answered at all.[8]

Returned volunteers

Volunteers' disapproval of Martin's management of the program did not end on their return to Australia. Many returned angry at the lack of support from OSB during their time away. While it is true that many of the issues that arose were not amenable to resolution from Melbourne, their anger was generated more by the fact that no one had visited them or, if they had been visited, they had not been listened to and issues they raised had not been addressed. Returned volunteers were given no credence for their knowledge and perspectives.

From as early as 1974 disgruntled returned volunteers expressed their disagreement, disappointment and anger with program management practices in Australia, including how the program was promoted and advertised. Roger King, a volunteer who returned from Perak in Malaysia at the end of 1972, became a key critic of OSB and its management of the AVA program and encouraged others to express their dissatisfaction. As he described it ten years later,

> [T]he Bureau was virtually impenetrable. It would blame the volunteer, or the host country, but rarely blame itself. It was happy to see volunteers going through a two year course in self-exploration but it was unmoved by the suggestion that it should perhaps examine some of its policies. It was a most thoroughly undemocratic and unimaginative organisation.[9]

When in 1974 Martin refused even to support seminars proposed by returned volunteers, they wrote in frustration to the Chairman and members of the OSB Committee, who closed ranks and rebuffed their protests.[10] Their protest hardened the organisation in its stance against any efforts by returned volunteers to establish an association which could have become a mechanism for peer support and a ginger group.

A small number of returned volunteers had a stake in the organisation's management because Martin had continued the practice, begun by Webb, of having one or two returned volunteers on the Bureau's staff. Throughout Martin's time as Director they were in a difficult position, having loyalty to the AVA program and to OSB as their employer but all the while knowing that the grievances of volunteers and returned volunteers were not without foundation.

Staff

Staff were constrained in their dealings with volunteers because they did not necessarily know what Martin's approach had been in previous dealings with them and, if they travelled to visit volunteers, they were often expected to convey messages from Martin verbally. In the OSB office very little information was shared with staff who, therefore, knew little of what Martin had communicated to Australian government officials in Canberra or in embassies and high commissions abroad. Consequently, staff had to operate with little contextual background knowledge about country programs or the policy issues peculiar to them and little knowledge of the history of OSB's engagement with particular employers.[11]

Staff also found themselves disempowered by Martin's decision-making practices, which they described as quite arbitrary. At times he would undermine staff by overturning their volunteer selection decisions, without presenting any rationale, and he routinely ignored their suggestions for improvements in policy and procedures. They had verbal employment arrangements with variable conditions. When they disagreed with Martin he tended to remind them that their ongoing employment was at his discretion. As there were no written job descriptions, so too was there no organisational chart. Thus Martin's dealings with staff have been characterised as lacking transparency, fairness and respect, so it is not surprising that staff turnover was high.[12]

The Australian community and ACFOA

Jim Webb had been fully aware of the importance of positioning OSB with the other NGOs that came together in the Australian Council for Overseas Aid (ACFOA). He had played a central role in establishing ACFOA and OSB had won respect as an organisation that did not compete in the fundraising stakes and was a worthy partner for support and collaboration. Community Aid Abroad (CAA), the Australian Freedom from Hunger Campaign (FFHC), Australians Caring for Refugees (AustCare) and church-linked aid organisations supported OSB over many years. Some of these bodies paid an annual donation to OSB as organisational support; others sponsored ("adopted") individual volunteers and their assignments or contributed to particular programs or projects.

As OSB Director, Allen Martin also became part of this world and was elected Vice President of ACFOA. At the 1976 ACFOA Council meeting, Martin was once more a candidate for Vice President. As he was not the only nomination a ballot was required and the successful candidate was Bill Armstrong, who had worked with Jim Webb in OSB's early years. He had been elected to ACFOA's Executive Committee in 1975, shortly after his return from working for the Young Christian Workers in Belgium. Because he had neglected to nominate for the Executive Committee, Martin found himself without a role in ACFOA and he did not regain one thereafter,[13] which seriously limited his opportunities to engage in the Australian NGO community.

Apart from continued support from AustCare and YMCA for specific programs with Lao refugees in Thailand in 1976–77, support to OSB from

Australia's development NGOs subsided. For example, Australian Catholic Relief (ACR) had made an annual donation, but advised Martin in 1978 that their National Committee was losing interest in OSB. As they saw it, the Australian Government claimed the credit for the volunteer program, so the Government should fully fund it. By 1979 Martin could not even get a meeting with ACR.

Once government financial support for the AVA program was in place, it had become increasingly difficult for the OSB to raise funds from the private sector. Continuing support came mostly in relatively small amounts from community organisations, such as schools and many service clubs. In dollar terms, the significant supporters were the international development organisations that were fellow members of ACFOA. With the exception of a peak in NGO support in 1977 specifically for refugee work in Thailand, the percentage of OSB's income from private sources fell from 43% in 1975 to 24% in 1978.[14]

Securing government funding

Through 1973 and 1974 Martin negotiated a new funding model with departmental officials in Canberra. Treasury had proposed a model whereby the government would provide a two-for-one subsidy for all OSB's income. Martin argued against this model, pointing out that the Treasury model would commit the government to support all OSB activities, some of which they might rather not support. Martin's proposed alternative was a service fee arrangement, which would increase government funding but limit it to the AVA program. There were also arguments about forward commitments and obligations to current volunteers, but at its core it was a negotiation about independence. There was a feeling that Treasury officials would have been quite happy to use the funding as a way of limiting OSB's activities and Martin made much of the view that the program needed to be, and be seen to be, independent of the Australian government.[15]

Martin rejected Treasury's two-for-one subsidy offer and informed the Australian Development Assistance Agency (ADAA) that OSB would have to reduce the numbers of volunteers it sent. Treasury's insistence that the subsidy would apply in its entirety from the date of its inception put OSB in an invidious position. As Martin explained to Derham, it meant that OSB had to find a third of the funding needed for keeping all those volunteers already overseas and for bringing them home, costs which the government had previously accepted for the AVA program. It would mean that most of OSB's private income for 1974 would go to meeting those costs and would leave little as the basis of a two-for-one subsidy under Treasury's new proposal.[16]

Eventually, because Treasury was prepared to honour past commitments and even to talk about a three-for-one subsidy ratio, Martin agreed to consider the subsidy further. In the meantime he worked up more arguments for Derham to take to the Minister for Foreign Affairs, Senator Willesee, in support of a fee-for-service approach.[17] At the same time, he persuaded ADAA to ask Treasury to pay for that year's commitments at least. Knowing that the current year's costs were covered made it possible for OSB to proceed with its 1974/75 program.[18] The eventual agreement was a guaranteed minimum of $200,000 per year for 3 years (1975/76 to 1977/78), with the proviso that OSB income over $100,000 would attract a two-for-one subsidy.[19] As OSB's fundraising capacity in the private and community sectors was by this time considerably eroded, the subsidy never came into play and the funding agreement was reshaped.

As the annual meeting between OSB and the government, scheduled for 31 May 1977, approached, Neville Ross, the Australian Development Assistance Bureau (ADAB) officer responsible for the relationship with OSB and other NGOs, began to strategise well ahead of the meeting. His major preoccupation was the funding model. Until 1975, any ADAB funding for OSB had been for AVA, but the funding relationship had been complicated by additional funds for the Development Worker Scheme (DWS), which was conceived as a way of utilising returned volunteers in specific projects on conditions that were more attractive than standard AVA terms. The additional payment made to these returned volunteers was not made in the host countries but in Australia and was intended to help them meet financial commitments such as mortgages, insurance and superannuation in Australia. ADAB had paid $10,000 in 1975/76 to help establish the Scheme, and operational costs of $33,000 in 1975/76 and $38,000 in 1976/77. On top of this OSB had applied for $34,000 from ADAB's (NGO) Project Subsidy Scheme for its work with refugees in Thailand. Ross proposed to his colleagues that, as DWS assignments were actually not much different from AVA assignments, it would be easier to increase OSB's funding to an agreed annual limit and to let OSB determine its own programming priorities within that envelope.[20]

At the 1977 annual meeting in Canberra on 31 May, OSB was represented by Martin and his assistant and ADAB by Jim Ingram (the agency head) and four officers. Also present were two experienced officers from Treasury. Ingram used the opportunity to quiz Martin on the shape of the program: Why were so many volunteers placed in Malaysia? Why were there no AVAs in the Solomon Islands, Tonga, Tuvalu, Philippines and Nepal? Why had AVA stopped placing people in Indonesia? Martin's answers were evasive at best.[21] Further negotiations followed and eventually, in August 1977, formal agreement was reached to proceed with annual grants to OSB determined on a calendar year basis. The Australian government agreed to be responsible for future funding obligations generated by the program, and the two-for-one subsidy of income over $100,000 was withdrawn.[22]

Issues in OSB–government relations

Although an agreement had been reached, OSB continued to be the subject of correspondence between the Australian Embassy in Jakarta and ADAB in Canberra. When issues arose concerning a particular volunteer, the Australian Embassy felt sandwiched between the Indonesian view that there had to be an official relationship between the volunteers and their Embassy which should play an active role in managing the program, and the reality of the Embassy's hands-off position in relation to AVA. As an

ADAB officer explained to the Ambassador, "It is almost a 'tenet of faith' with the Overseas Service Bureau that we do not interfere with volunteers assignments as they claim that a volunteer can only achieve a good relationship with his counterparts if he is not connected to the Embassy".[23]

The ADAB post in Jakarta had lost confidence in OSB. Their position was that the AVA scheme in Indonesia would only improve if there were more volunteers in the country supported by a dedicated officer based in Indonesia and with the ADAB post playing an active role in their placement. Even though there were only two volunteers left in Indonesia, Martin refused to make the changes requested by government officials in Jakarta and Canberra, requesting instead that volunteers be issued with Official Passports (such as were issued to staff on bilateral aid projects) in the hope that this would resolve accreditation issues. Embassy officials were quite clear in their view that without Embassy involvement "volunteers are likely to remain unplaced or misplaced". They were very aware that the British Council provided one full-time officer for 20 VSO volunteers and that an American agency was running eight volunteers with one staff member overseeing their placement. They maintained that there should be at least 12 AVAs in Indonesia with one full-time staff member to support them.[24]

ADAB also raised concerns about the AVA program in Thailand where the Thai government insisted on an umbrella agreement with the Australian government before the AVA program could be introduced there. Neville Ross noted: "Mr Martin is inclined to the view that our Post is causing the delay, however, this is definitely not the opinion conveyed to me by DTEC (Department of Technical and Economic Cooperation) on my recent visit to Thailand".[25]

Issues in relations between OSB and Australian government officials continued to accumulate. Others in Australia's diplomatic service commented that the program had very low visibility, being unusually small and thinly spread.[26] Matters relating to DWS were also unresolved. An ADAB review of DWS in Bangladesh had been highly critical of poorly supported volunteers in inadequate placements. Ross's message to his colleagues was that they would have to rethink the relationship between ADAB and OSB. Among other questions, he asked whether ADAB should continue to fund an AVA program determined and operated by OSB or whether they should seek to have greater influence on the program generally, or specifically in difficult countries like Indonesia and Thailand.[27]

ADAB funding for DWS was due to conclude in June 1978 and Martin pressed for it to continue, but Ross resisted recommending an increase in the general allocation and leaving it up to OSB to decide whether to engage returned volunteers on more favourable terms. At a meeting with ADAB officers in May 1978, Martin accepted Ross's recommendation, but said he would continue to separate DWS and AVA in his accounts. It was put to Martin again that the program would benefit from having a small number of administrative/development officers, possibly returned volunteers, in some countries, but Martin dismissed the idea, maintaining that numbers were static because recruitment was difficult in a time of high unemployment in Australia and that no one would be interested in such a position in Indonesia.[28]

Government dissatisfaction

Ross advised his Branch Head, Erik Ingevics, that ADAB had suggested to Martin that the 1979 annual meeting between ADAB and OSB be held in Melbourne so they could meet with the full Committee, raising again the need to re-examine their relationship:

> Our reservations are on several grounds. We appear to be locked into a situation where we are paying increased annual grants for a fairly static number of volunteers …
>
> At various times in past years we have made suggestions to Martin about expansion of the program into new countries or consolidation of certain country programs … Allen Martin has not responded positively to these suggestions …

> We feel it is appropriate for these matters to be taken up with the Committee of OSB at this time to ensure that our concern is fully understood. It would ensure that Allen Martin produced answers to satisfy both the Committee and ADAB about the present status of the AVA Scheme.[29]

Martin agreed to put the idea of such a meeting to his Committee and suggested that it be held in July, after, and quite separate from, the annual budget consultation. In his annual report for 1979 Martin raised for the first time as a major concern the damage being done to the AVA program by the British, Canadian and American volunteer programs which were paying the in-country costs of volunteers. OSB was under pressure from developing countries to adopt this practice. Martin outlined a stark dilemma for the organisation – to swallow its philosophical pride and match other donor countries or to disband. If it chose to continue the program, the financial costs would be high.[30]

Approaching a crossroad

Both ADAB and Martin prepared for the meeting with the OSB Committee. In material he sent out in advance of the meeting, Martin stated that AVA could maintain no more than 140 volunteers in the field without radical change. He pointed to the growing dependence on government funding and argued that because international volunteering was no longer new or different it was no longer interesting to private supporters, who increasingly saw it as an established program with all the kudos going to the government that was expected to fund it. He suggested that ADAB had to commit to higher funding levels "or else give firm notice of withdrawal from the program over a number of years", adding that this was "not a threat, but realities must be faced". He confirmed that in Papua New Guinea, Indonesia and Malaysia the trend was for international volunteers to be placed at no cost to the host government or community. By 1979 it was known that Papua New Guinea had arranged for German, Austrian and Japanese volunteers to be received in 1980 as aid contributions.[31]

In the position paper ADAB's NGO and Information Section prepared, it was acknowledged that most international volunteer programs had developed from an earlier concept of a "cultural experience/youth exchange/voluntary aid" mix to a staffing assistance type of program requiring higher levels of experience and expertise in volunteers. At the same time, many countries had moved from a method of financing in which the volunteers received a local allowance from the receiving/host organisation to a program fully funded by the volunteer agency. ADAB also acknowledged that winding up the volunteer program was not an option as it had too much political support both in the Government and the Opposition.[32]

The issue of how to structure the meeting remained. Ross suggested to Martin a two-part structure that would enable discussion of the organisation's philosophy and procedures, priorities and community support, along with current trends and issues. Ross thought it wise to forewarn his Director of what might affect the tone of the meeting. He explained that Martin had objected to the agenda and had made it quite clear that ADAB was being invited to an OSB Committee meeting, so it was their prerogative to decide what to raise with ADAB. Ross reported that Martin maintained that some of his Committee thought that OSB had been wrong to negotiate with ADAB and should have instead pressured

> politicians who would then instruct bureaucrats. Without actually saying so Mr Martin implied that these members felt that ADAB regarded the OSB as just another NGO and that somehow they had lost their unique position. Mr Martin is therefore concerned that if ADAB officers adopt a critical attitude at the meeting this view will be reinforced. It is difficult to know, not having had contact with the OSB Committee, to what degree this view is held by the

> Committee or whether Mr Martin is merely attempting to put pressure on ADAB.[33]

Putting the jostling to one side, Ross acknowledged that government funding of overseas costs was a defining issue that would move the AVA program clearly into the development assistance field as a low-cost staffing assistance/technical assistance program, and away from its original concept of community service and cultural exchange. In Martin's view, while the original concept was, in the eyes of the Committee, still the major justification for the program, governments of developing countries considered the AVA program as a development assistance program that should be fully funded by OSB. As winding up the program was not an option, OSB seemed to have come to a crossroad where the choice was between a volunteer program as traditionally understood and a staffing assistance program. In an attempt to find a middle way, Martin suggested that the government meet the costs of volunteers in the least developed countries (LDCs). Ross thought this a possibility as only five LDCs were concerned, so any additional funding required would be limited. His advice to Ingram was to resist considering funding for volunteers in countries other than the LDCs, as the considerable additional funds required would compromise the funding of other NGO programs, which should have priority over OSB programs in countries like Malaysia and PNG. Ross suggested that Ingram agree in principle to funding for AVA in LDCs and that he may want to raise the issue of ADAB representation on the OSB Committee.[34]

The meeting between ADAB and the OSB Committee in July 1979 resolved nothing, and, because it went so badly, became a strong marker in the ADAB–OSB relationship. The hubris of Derham and Martin was on full display. ADAB Director James Ingram and his staff arrived at OSB's offices in East Melbourne for their meeting at 9.30 and were told to wait until 11.00 when the Committee would see them, leaving them with a lengthy wait while the Committee conducted routine business upstairs.[35]

ADAB's view of Martin's management was not improved by his performance in the 1980 annual meeting held in May in Canberra. ADAB notes of the meeting recorded that Martin was opposed to assessing prospective placements on "philosophical grounds", claiming it "reduced local capacity to plan for and use trained manpower", although he also let it be known that his staff would support more placement assessment as it would lead to more effective placements and fewer problems arising in the field. The ADAB note-taker added a comment in parentheses about this being a rare reference to differences between the views of Martin and of his staff. As would be expected at these annual meetings, planned volunteer numbers were discussed, but there was a sense that they were not based on anything real; "In past reports, Martin's targets have borne little relation to what eventuated", the note-taker recorded. At one point, Martin reaffirmed his stance that 150 volunteers overseas was at the upper limit of the organisation's capacity, prompting the ADAB observation: "This is an important admission: the OSB is not concerned to increase beyond its present depressed level (148 in May 1980) and confirms the general theory, advanced in a previous paper, that the OSB is inhibited by its management structure to expand its numbers or scope".[36]

Committee of the Overseas Service Bureau

From the beginning of his time as Director Martin was quite pro-active in managing the Chairman and, through him, the Committee. Derham was proud to be OSB's Chairman and conscious of his role as the eminent link to OSB's origins with the small elite within the University of Melbourne who had been associated with it since its inception. He did not, however, play an active role beyond staying informed of OSB's operations and tended to act on Martin's advice when asked to do so. Martin had little direct contact with members of the Committee other than Derham, with whom he communicated frequently. He was comfortable in his relationship with Derham and, as early as May 1969, asked Derham to agree to be re-elected as Chairman in 1970.[37]

The Committee was increased in 1971 from nine members to 11, which made it possible to include prominent Melbourne businessman and sports administrator Lewis Luxton.[38] The Luxton family had prospered through their ownership of McEwan's Hardware (later Bunnings) and he held multiple directorships and was a member of the Forelanders Trust, which had been a strong supporter in OSB's early years.[39] Martin also advised Derham that the Committee should have a member with a medical background and brought in Melbourne surgeon and paediatrician Edward Durham Smith.

There were further changes to the Committee in 1972, when Kevin Travers asked to step down as Treasurer and from the Committee, although he later agreed to act as OSB's Honorary Solicitor. On Martin's suggestion, Russell Chancellor, a Senior Partner at Price Waterhouse and Co., was elected to the Committee as Honorary Treasurer.[40] In the same year, Hugh O'Neill was invited to join the Committee. O'Neill, a University of Melbourne academic and architect who had been a volunteer in Indonesia, had been elected Chairman of the VGA Committee in 1964 and had got to know Jim Webb very well. From 1969 to 1972 O'Neill was also President of the Australian Indonesian Association of Victoria.

The first woman to join the Committee, in 1975, was Elizabeth Britten, a volunteer in the second AVA group, who spent 1965 and 1966 at Popondetta in Papua and New Guinea.[41] While she was there, Tommy Garnett, OSB Committee member and Head of Geelong Grammar School, suggested that when she returned to Australia she go to Geelong where she became Principal of The Hermitage from 1968 until it was absorbed into Geelong Grammar School in 1975.[42] She became Principal of Shelford Girls' Grammar in Melbourne in 1979.

With Garnett due to end his time on the Committee, discussion arose in April 1976 about how best to fill two vacancies. Four ideas were canvassed: replace Smith, who had had to retire, with another member with a medical background; add another woman; add another returned volunteer; and add someone from outside Melbourne. In the end all four ideas materialised in the appointments of Dr Jeannine Paton,[43] Clinical Supervisor at the Royal

Melbourne Hospital Clinical School (a woman with a medical background) and Chris Fogarty, a former AVA volunteer in Papua and New Guinea who was a legal research officer in the Australian Parliament (a returned volunteer based in Canberra).[44] In July 1977, Herb Feith, having decided that 15 years of involvement was enough, resigned to make way for someone with more recent experience. He was replaced on the Committee by Mr B.B. Thorpe, former AVA in Western Samoa, then Deputy Principal of Rockhampton Grammar School and later Principal of Woodlands Church of England Girls' Grammar School in Glenelg, South Australia.[45]

The Committee met four times a year, usually for two to three hours, and followed a formal business agenda. Although Derham chaired the meetings, Martin actually ran them, preparing material that was only made available to Committee members on the day of the meeting. The major agenda items were the Director's Report and the Treasurer's financial statements, which were based on the Director's own book-keeping. The Committee received no other reports and discussed no correspondence unless it was first introduced by either the Director or the Chairman.[46] Martin was never forthcoming with details about volunteers or his travels, and issues of OSB policy or purpose were certainly never raised, leaving the Committee with very little to discuss.

Between meetings, Martin prepared any correspondence for Derham and ensured that he was aware of the context and the strategies he was pursuing. Derham never sought an alternative view or consulted other sources of information, seeing no reason to doubt Martin's approach. Neither he nor any of the Committee had any contact with staff. Derham and Martin were very comfortable with and confident in their working relationship. The atmosphere of the Committee was in part that of an exclusive men's club. O'Neill recalls how Luxton sat with his back turned to him until the day he learnt of his association with Melbourne Grammar. After the Committee meetings it was not uncommon for some of them (Derham, Luxton, Simpson, Chancellor and Martin) to adjourn to the Melbourne Club for lunch. If the Adelaide-based Simpson was in Melbourne, he would stay at the Club.[47]

Dissent leads to internal review

The 1976 appointments to the Committee of Paton and Fogarty were significant, as both went on to challenge and influence the affairs of the organisation. Chris Fogarty was the first Committee member to air a dissenting view when he wrote to Derham in January 1980 to express his concerns about the way the Committee functioned. He had a strong view that the Committee should be treated seriously as the Bureau's major policy-making body rather than as "window dressing". To achieve this, papers would need to be made available in advance of Committee meetings, which would need to be either longer or more frequent. He questioned the value of retaining Simpson on the Committee as he rarely attended, and suggested that the Committee would benefit from having a more recently returned volunteer: "Out of a Committee of eleven it is strange to have only four members [O'Neill, Britten, Thorpe and Fogarty] who have any first-hand knowledge of the OSB's major function". Fogarty let Derham know that he was not alone in his dissatisfaction and that Paton, O'Neill and Engel supported the content of his letter.[48]

The response from the Committee's Chairman and Deputy was swift. It was customary for the Committee to meet on the last day of the January briefing, before the farewell function. The Rector of Newman College invited them to sherry beforehand and Derham and Callinan took the opportunity to take Fogarty aside and berate him. They accused him of disloyalty, of being presumptuous, and of failing to understand that as a Committee member he should have nothing to do with the management of OSB.[49]

Martin found Fogarty's letter offensive and regarded it as an attack on his integrity. He vented his anger to Derham, maintaining that four meetings a year was adequate to deal with normal Committee business. Martin expressed his aversion to "loading the Committee with returned volunteers" and disputed Fogarty's claim that he had the support of other members. Martin suggested to Derham that the letter not be circulated any further and that he reply to Fogarty, with an undertaking to have papers ready in advance of the April meeting and to put Committee membership on that meeting's agenda.[50]

Fogarty had brought a fresh approach to the Committee. He was not constrained by any allegiance to the establishment core of the Committee; he identified as a returned volunteer and was aware that he was on the Committee in that capacity. He was also in contact with other returned volunteers and knew that their complaints had substance. Some OSB staff were also returned volunteers and were learning for the first time something of how the Director and Committee conducted themselves through their contact with Fogarty. The seamless Chairman–Director relationship had been absolutely effective in blocking or controlling information flows to the Committee and staff. There was now a chink in these defences as staff could go around Martin directly to a Committee member who was also in touch with other returned volunteers. Returned volunteers had become more vocal, partly because of Roger King's activism. It was also significant that Fogarty and staff members knew each other quite well from the ten days he had spent in residence at the University Women's College assisting, on Martin's invitation, with the January 1975 pre-departure briefing.[51]

One staff member, Barry Preston, reached his limit and resigned in protest. In the aftermath in September and October 1980, Roger King and a group of six others (staff, former staff and returned volunteers)[52] sent letters to the Committee, expressing their concern about the operations of the Bureau and the lack of communication between Committee and staff. A measured response from Derham assured them that their correspondence had been noted and considered and that the policy matters raised by their letters would be addressed at future Committee meetings.[53] Preston wrote to the Committee ahead of their meeting to impress upon them what he saw as the priorities: to terminate Martin as Director; to arrange for the committee to learn about OSB from sources other than the Director; to discuss how to get input from excluded groups like returned volunteers; and to organise a wide-ranging assessment of the Bureau. He also informed the Committee that he had made the Minister and the head of ADAB aware of "the appalling administrative situation at OSB".[54] The Committee discussed the situation at length and agreed in December 1980 to appoint a sub-committee (Britten (Convenor), Chancellor, Engel and Martin) to examine and report on the structure of OSB and its Committee and make suggestions for improving communications with the general public, donors and ex-volunteers and to ensure staff understanding of the Committee and sub-committee's roles.[55]

Britten embraced the task and met individually and confidentially with all senior staff, four former staff, and four others, and received five written submissions. She uncovered four main areas of concern:

- inadequate financial accountability;
- lack of input into policy deliberation by staff, returned volunteers and supporting bodies;
- low morale and tension among staff; and
- the need to ensure ongoing evaluation of policy and operation.

When she sent the completed report to Derham on 20 March 1981, Britten did not hold back from telling him that behind all the criticisms only one real problem was being enunciated – Martin's inability to treat people with any sensitivity. Because he manipulated and filtered information "... the Committee has been made to appear rather foolish at times due to decisions we were supposed to have made". She described how he had alienated numerous volunteers, staff, and people in Canberra, with the result that OSB and its Committee were considered arrogant. Information he had given to the Committee about staff had been only partly true. Staff morale was problematic and made worse by his threats of instant dismissal; there was a very real concern that staff with knowledge of the AVA program would leave if he remained Director.[56]

The Britten sub-committee made several recommendations:

- that annual bulletins (reports) include simple financial statements and a list of staff;

- that an informal group of returned volunteers be established in each major city;
- that an advisory committee of two Committee members meet regularly with the Director, consult with staff as they saw fit, arrange for Committee agendas, reports and decisions to be circulated to staff and arrange for staff to present to the Committee; and
- that the Director be supported to meet regularly with staff, plan activities and establish clear roles and responsibilities.

Foreign Minister requests investigation

In the lead up to the October 1980 federal election, the Young Liberal Movement of Australia once again proposed that Australia establish a peace corps, but their proposal was rejected quite quickly, with Liberal Party leader Malcolm Fraser making an election commitment on 30 September 1980 to increase funding for the AVA program. In the context of this commitment Foreign Minister Tony Street made inquiries of ADAB about the current state of the AVA program and OSB. ADAB's advice was that OSB had changed and had become increasingly difficult to work with. ADAB found it difficult to get accurate information from OSB and OSB was unresponsive to ADAB suggestions. Accordingly, in January 1981 Tony Street established a Committee of Review into the relationship between the government and OSB, with particular reference to the AVA program.

Before announcing the Review and introducing Senator Baden Teague as its Chairman, Street wanted to give Derham advance notice. Teague contacted Derham to introduce himself and to discuss how the Review would proceed and was invited by Derham to a meeting at the University of Melbourne. Teague made his way to the Vice-Chancellor's office to find Callinan there as well. Derham proceeded to berate Teague and told him to go back to Canberra and tell the Minister for Foreign Affairs there would be no inquiry, taking the view that OSB was a private company limited by guarantee and that the Minister had no right or basis for any inquiry. Teague gave Derham no apology and "was unmoved by Derham's bluster and protest".[57] For Derham to feel it was acceptable to send such a blunt message to Street was presumably because Street had been his student.[58]

Derham's protest was not heeded, but he was invited to propose an OSB Committee member to serve on the Committee of Review. He needed someone safe and reliable for this role and turned to Dr Jeannine Paton. He had known her for a long time; he had been a student of her father, Sir George Paton, who had also preceded him as Vice-Chancellor of the University of Melbourne. He had every reason to assume her loyalty and support, but she was anything but tame and saw her role as a member of the Committee of Review as an opportunity and a responsibility to be taken seriously. The Committee, chaired by Senator Baden Teague, comprised Dr Jeannine Paton (OSB Committee), Rev John Mavor (ACFOA) and Rosaleen McGovern (ADAB), with Laurie Engel of ADAB providing secretarial support. Once the Review was announced, Teague was quickly contacted by people who said they needed to talk with him, including Britten, Fogarty, Engel and Webb.[59]

Advertisements were placed in all major Australian newspapers, outlining the Committee's Terms of Reference and calling for submissions from interested organisations and individuals. OSB was asked to send the Terms of Reference and the invitation, without a covering letter, to all serving and former AVAs, but Martin subverted this process. He delayed sending anything out until late February and included a covering letter that was deliberately misleading on two crucial grounds and angered those who knew the facts. It referred to the idea of an Australian Peace Corps, which the government had dismissed almost as soon as it had been raised, and it implied that the Review had come about because the OSB Committee had requested it. It was mailed only to some of those it was supposed to be sent to. A second group of former OSB staff, returned volunteers and current AVAs received the letter in March, too late to respond with their submissions. A third group of those who should have received it got nothing at all.[60]

OSB was invited to make a submission to the Review and to present it at the first Melbourne hearing on 10 April 1981. Paton suggested, with Fogarty's support, a meeting early in March to determine the content and process for OSB's submission, but Martin advised Derham that, because the time required to give notice of a Committee meeting would cause an unwise delay, he would prepare the document for endorsement by the Committee at a meeting on 9 April, the day before the hearing.[61]

In the Committee meeting on 9 April, Derham argued strongly that the internal affairs of OSB were no business of the Committee of Review and that the Britten sub-committee's report was a private document and not part of the documentation OSB would provide to the Committee of Review. OSB's submission was 90 pages long and the OSB Committee was required to speak to its submission. As requested, the Committee members went to the meeting at the Commonwealth Offices in Melbourne, but Derham had determined that only he would speak. Teague later commented on the embarrassment this caused everyone present, as not only had Derham failed to master all the material in the OSB submission, but his presentation was difficult to follow.[62] Derham, however, persisted in his refusal to answer questions he deemed "matters internal to the OSB" or outside the Committee of Review's Terms of Reference.[63] He even insisted that the correspondence that constituted the agreement between OSB and the government in 1965 was highly confidential.[64]

The Britten sub-committee's report was eventually tabled and discussed at the full OSB Committee meeting on 21 May and its recommendations were accepted, including the recommendation that an Advisory Committee be established to work with the Director. The meeting was long and tense and became even more so when the Chairmanship of the Committee came up for discussion. Derham confirmed his desire to relinquish his Chairmanship of the Committee and nominated Callinan as his replacement.[65] Rather than accepting this as a *fait accompli*, the ginger group was confident of the numbers for an alternative candidate, so O'Neill nominated Britten. After a ballot Martin declared Callinan elected, but Paton demanded a recount, which revealed a tie, and insisted that if the Chairman was exercising his casting vote, he should do so formally. Callinan was elected as Chairman but never chaired a meeting. He described the nomination of Britten as a hostile act and, recognising that he did not have the confidence of the Committee, formally stepped down as Chairman.[66] Chancellor took over as Acting Chairman.

Although the OSB Committee had on 21 May 1981 passed a formal motion to send the recommendations of the Britten sub-committee to the Committee of Review, Martin did not send the document until after the Committee's meeting with the Committee of Review on 2 June. Frank Engel, who had moved the motion, was incensed and wrote to the Acting Chairman to complain about this and other moves to frustrate the Committee of Review:

> In this connection I would also express my concern at a report I have heard that Senator Teague and Mr L. Engel were refused the opportunity to meet the OSB staff when they had travelled to Melbourne for that purpose. That, if it is true, seems to me extraordinarily discourteous, and, in the circumstances, unwise.[67]

Martin loses the OSB Committee's confidence

Britten wrote as Convenor of the Advisory Committee to Chancellor to request an extraordinary meeting of the Committee without the Director, specifically to discuss Martin's handling of an ongoing issue with a female staff member who had not been sacked, had not resigned, but was, nevertheless, unable to work with him. She noted that she was no longer "prepared to sit on or even forget" confidential information she held while Martin continued to take unilateral action with no input from anyone. Britten's impatience with Martin's insistence on doing things his own way had escalated.[68]

Following the second Advisory Committee meeting, Britten again wrote to Chancellor to explain that Martin's insinuation that senior staff had connived with former staff to canvass support from current volunteers was untrue.[69] Britten let Chancellor know that the Committee was close to moving a vote of no confidence in Martin and asked if Chancellor could get him to resign before the Committee of Review report came out because otherwise it would be seen as a result of outside pressure. For Britten, it looked better for OSB to be putting its own house in order and she believed it might be possible to save the Bureau with a new Director.[70]

In a move to seek further support, Britten sent copies of all her correspondence with Chancellor over the preceding two weeks to Engel, commenting that while Martin was trying to prove that OSB could not function without him, she was determined to show that it could. She documented the reasons to support a no confidence motion in Martin which, even in summary, were quite a charge sheet: selectively informing the Committee; not accepting Committee advice; providing inaccurate and misleading information; not keeping accurate minutes of meetings; being unable to mould staff into a team; freely using threats of dismissal; destroying OSB's credibility with host country governments and with ADAB.[71]

An informal discussion was arranged on 12 August for Paton to brief Committee members about the report that would be presented to the Minister on 14 August. Paton clarified that the Committee of Review had a positive view of OSB and its capacity to expand, but that it was vital that the organisation be seen to change. For example, OSB was the only NGO that sent only its Director to ADAB for discussions and that it was important that he be accompanied by Committee members, adding that OSB must get over its fetish for secrecy.[72] Paton made it clear how important it had been for the Committee of Review to receive the recommendations of the Britten sub-committee, as they were evidence of OSB's intention to make changes. It was seen as significant that the internal review had started before the Committee of Review had been announced. Paton lamented the resignation of three dedicated staff over the last year and spoke of her own sense of failure as a Committee member, because of her inability to influence changes in policy and operations of OSB. She had revealed to Teague that when the Committee of Review had finished its work she was likely to resign from the OSB Committee. Teague, however, had counselled her that the government would be watching closely and would interpret her departure as a result of pressure from the Committee. There was also considerable discussion among Engel, Fogarty, Paton and Britten about the continuing issue of what they saw as Martin's outrageous treatment of the experienced and dedicated staff member he was in conflict with. Martin had ignored advice from both the Committee as a whole and the Advisory Committee. This issue had become one of the principal cleavages in the Committee. Fogarty's view was that, because the Director refused to change his ways of working, the Committee must take action.

With the report of the Committee of Review still to be released, ADAB Director Jim Ingram rang Martin on 24 August to seek assurances that the group of volunteers due to depart for their overseas assignments in 1982 would indeed do so. Martin did not provide any certainty; if he thought he was in a position to negotiate, Ingram clearly did not, saying that he would raise with the Minister any threats to the ongoing program, reminding Martin that OSB had "funding for the 12 months, and that's technically all you've ever had".[73]

In preparation for the Committee meeting on 9 September, Fogarty worked with Britten on a draft no-confidence motion and shared it with Paton, Thorpe, Engel and O'Neill. The assumption was that Martin would resign during the meeting after the motion was passed and, if he did not, a dismissal motion would follow. Chancellor as Acting Chairman foiled the plan by postponing the Committee meeting, claiming that he was reluctant to have more than one more meeting this year as it would be too burdensome for staff.[74] In fact, he was acting on advice from Martin who had argued that the main purpose of the meeting was to discuss the Committee of Review report which was still not available and would require at least a week to read and digest. He pointed out that Derham was due to return from abroad on 17 September, so Martin suggested to Chancellor that he schedule a meeting in mid-October. As Simpson planned to be overseas, Martin suggested that Chancellor get Simpson to sign several undated proxy authorisations.[75] In response, the Committee members involved in drafting the no-confidence motion provided Chancellor with written notice to call a meeting on 23–25 September and indicated their intention to move a no-confidence motion unless Martin resigned. Chancellor informed the committee on 22 September that Martin had resigned, giving six months' notice but that he would leave earlier if that was desirable.

A week later Chancellor revealed to the Committee that he had received the Committee of Review report from the Minister for Foreign Affairs two weeks earlier, explaining his secrecy by saying he had been asked to discuss with ADAB certain aspects of a new agreement and had been trying to see the Minister "for guidance on some aspects".[76]

Government support for AVA and OSB

The Committee of Review came out in favour of increasing government support for OSB to put the AVA program on a secure and expanded basis with enhanced features, about which the report included a raft of recommendations. It also comprehensively condemned the management of the program, the governance of the organisation and the mishandling of relationships with all key stakeholders.

For Derham, a public figure of enormous reputation and proud Chairman of OSB from 1965 to May 1981, the report was an unconscionable attack on his integrity and his long-standing colleagues. He shared his view of the report with Callinan, Luxton, Chancellor and Martin:

> I am very surprised that four adult and apparently reasonable people could manage to include so many errors in such a relatively small space. It is clear that the Committee not only misunderstood the purposes of its terms of reference, but also failed to manage properly and to check the evidence which

> apparently it received ... Its recommendations denigrate the conduct of the Bureau's affairs in the past.[77]

Such was Derham's anger with the report's content that he threatened to sue the Minister if he published the report.[78]

At the OSB Committee meeting on 13 October, Chancellor tabled a document containing his personal notes and recommendations. In his view, although the Committee of Review report was intended to be constructive, it was unnecessarily critical and should not be published. He had been in communication with both the Minister for Foreign Affairs and the Director of ADAB who thought publication should at least be deferred. Chancellor's position was that the Committee needed to vote itself out of office but should not do so until February 1982 so as not to impede the departure of volunteers in January. He proposed forming a planning group as soon as possible to liaise with ADAB and plan a restructure. The group should comprise an independent person with management expertise, an ADAB representative, Chancellor, Britten, O'Neill and the Director. His notes were merely tabled and discussion of the Committee of Review report was deferred for yet another week.

Derham and Luxton advocated delaying the January departure of volunteers. Martin informed the meeting that, although selection of volunteers had been proceeding and would soon be completed, he had held back all letters to the potential volunteers so none of the successful applicants had been informed.[79] The following day Martin proposed to defer all volunteer departures until June so that the new Director could lead their placement and briefing. He was still under pressure over his refusal to re-employ the victimised staff member and, in a bizarre twist, he managed to conflate the two key operational issues at stake into an improbable negotiating gambit. Martin's proposal was:

> Provided the Committee agrees to disband and vest ALL its powers in a Management Committee, and adopts a June 1982 departure date for the next AVA group, I am prepared

> to write to [her] and say it is likely there will be a deferral of the next AVA group and an effort to mount two programs a year starting the new cycle in June 1982. The new Director may then feel the need for new staff.[80]

Chancellor again proposed to the Committee that the affairs of the Bureau be put in the hands of a management group with full powers. He had now abandoned his view that the January departure should go ahead.[81] Britten wrote to Chancellor immediately, completely rejecting his position. Her view was that they should avoid any actions that might look like they were reacting in haste or anger to the report. She insisted the 1982 program go ahead as planned and that it would be a folly for the OSB Committee to disband at this stage, adding that a Melbourne-based management group was absolutely not what ADAB were looking for and would be disrespectful of the interstate Committee members, Thorpe, Fogarty and Engel.[82]

Over the following week O'Neill initiated a flurry of correspondence and phone calls with Chancellor and Thorpe and had a series of meetings with Britten resulting in an agreement that the two of them would work together to ensure that the January 1982 group of volunteers departed. On the basis of this agreement, Britten wrote to reassure Minister Street:

> You'll know from the Chairman that although some were against going ahead with January we have decided to do so and have appointed an Executive Committee to carry on with this operation as well as to investigate ways of improving the structure and ongoing function of the Bureau.[83]

At its meeting on 13 October, the Committee had put in place the process for selecting a new Director. A precisely balanced Selection Subcommittee (Chancellor, Britten, Luxton and O'Neill) was appointed to liaise with the external consultants and to report to the OSB Committee. Chancellor had to travel and asked Britten to convene the Selection Subcommittee in his absence, proposing that Simpson be his alternate in the group. Britten sought legal advice and informed Simpson she could not agree to Chancellor's request because the Committee had made no provision for alternates.[84]

When the position was advertised, Bill Armstrong was encouraged to apply by a number of people, including some from the NGO community, returned volunteers, former OSB staff and Jeannine Paton, who made it clear she represented the views of several people connected to OSB. Armstrong was short-listed, along with three other candidates, and subsequently offered the position. Although pressure was applied to Armstrong to start as soon as possible, he was adamant that he would take no responsibility for the January briefing program, strongly preferring that the current staff and Committee see it through.[85] That the January briefing occurred and the volunteers departed was a triumph for Elizabeth Britten and Hugh O'Neill and their interstate supporters, Chris Fogarty in Canberra, Frank Engel in Sydney, and Bruce Thorpe in Adelaide, and due to the efforts of the dedicated OSB staff. They saw the briefing through without a Director because, on 24 December, a majority of the Committee decided that Martin's rearguard actions had to cease and that he had to go.[86] O'Neill was delegated to give Martin the news in a meeting at Chancellor's home in Kew.

On 19 January 1982 the old guard played out its last act in their efforts to stop the program and bring the organisation down. Chancellor, as Acting Chair, informed the OSB Committee, the Minister for Foreign Affairs, ADAB and Armstrong that he was resigning forthwith, also submitting the resignations of Sir David Derham, Sir Bernard Callinan, Lewis Luxton and Robert Simpson.[87] Chancellor agreed to attend one more meeting of the Committee to provide a quorum for the election of office bearers. Britten was elected Chairman, Hugh O'Neill Deputy Chairman and Phillip Harris, Managing Director of the Australasian Branch of Pitman's Publishing Company came onto the Committee as Treasurer.

When he learnt of the resignations, Armstrong's immediate thought was that the five Committee members had resigned in protest at his appointment as Director, a concern that was not without foundation.

Chancellor had already told him to his face that he was the wrong person for the job. Callinan as a prominent right-wing Catholic was hostile to Armstrong's activities with Action for World Development, particularly his activism on the Indonesian invasion of East Timor. When Armstrong explained to Chancellor how the resignations might be interpreted, Chancellor put in writing, on 26 January 1982, that the resignation of the five Committee members had not been a response to Armstrong's appointment.[88]

The report of the Committee of Review provided Armstrong with a mandate to advance his vision. The report affirmed the unique strengths of the Australian approach to international volunteering and emphasised that the volunteer program's need for flexibility, responsiveness and roots in the community was best served by an NGO. This affirmation underlined the expanded support envisaged by the Committee of Review that became real in the 1980s as OSB moved beyond the stagnation of the 1970s and the crisis of 1981 into a decade of renewal and growth.

Volunteers flew TAA from Melbourne to Port Moresby on 16 January 1970.
Courtesy AVI

Robyn Kidd, lecturer in Papua and New Guinea, 1971. Courtesy AVI

Ken Rubeli, forestry lecturer in Malaysia, 1974–76. Courtesy AVI

Steve Zabarauskas, science teacher in Western Samoa, 1978–79. Courtesy AVI

Stewart Heffernan, medical statistician, records oral histories for PNG's Institute for Medical Research, 1979–80. Courtesy AVI

PART II

Renewal and Extending the Reach

CHAPTER 4

Organisational Renewal (1982–90)

By 1982 the preconditions had been met for the renewal, rebuilding and repositioning of OSB. Two factors dominated – the report of the Foreign Minister's Committee of Review, which gave the OSB leadership a mandate for change and growth, and the experience and perspective of the Bureau's new Director, Bill Armstrong. These two factors were strengthened by a determined Committee that unanimously supported renewal.

An established philosophy reinvigorated

Armstrong had helped Jim Webb manage the Australian Volunteers Abroad (AVA) program in its early years, so was steeped in the philosophy and practice of the program. He had travelled extensively for OSB, particularly in Papua and New Guinea, where he had built a network amongst partner organisations and volunteers. Some of the many volunteers he advised and mentored played important roles in OSB during his time as Director. Elizabeth Britten was primarily responsible for hiring him as Director; Mary Considine (Papua and New Guinea, 1966) became a key member of his senior management team, taking responsibility for overseas operations and helping think through what was needed to move OSB forward while keeping faith with the past.

AVA's foundational premises and Armstrong's personal philosophy were a natural fit. His philosophy had developed during his years of involvement with the Catholic Young Christian Workers (YCW) movement, with its strong emphasis on experiential learning and social responsibility, before he joined OSB in 1964. He worked at the YCW headquarters in Belgium in 1974 and the first half of 1975, after which he became the Australian National Coordinator for Action for World Development (AWD) from 1975 to 1981. He had been involved with AWD from its beginnings in 1971 when he served on the National Committee and then as its Victorian State Organiser. AWD was an interdenominational church-based development education campaign that exposed countless Australians to critical thinking about development issues and influenced the shape of debate about development in the Australian Council for Overseas Aid (ACFOA) and its member agencies.

AWD was very much part of the social and intellectual turmoil of Australia in the 1970s.[1] It took on board the theories of underdevelopment in the Third World, which inevitably pointed to overdevelopment in the West, and linked development with liberation. It did so in ways that challenged individuals to reflect and act, drawing on the work of Paulo Freire whose *Pedagogy of the Oppressed* (1972) promulgated his Action–Reflection– Conscientization model. Freire showed how structural analysis revealed who benefited and who did not from particular social actions or inactions, offering a sort of dialectical materialism for people more comfortable with Christianity than Marxism.

For AWD aid was never neutral, but always driven by political interest, as was particularly evident in aid from governments but also in NGOs channelling government funds. AWD was widely critical of the non-government development sector, condemning particularly the blatantly false advertising used in fundraising strategies for child sponsorship. AWD aimed to establish justice, not to hand out charity. In writing about the AWD approach, Armstrong pointed to the examples of the courageous stance taken by the Australian Council of Churches (ACC) in support of the people of Southern Africa, and the support that several agencies, including Community Aid Abroad (CAA) and Australian Catholic Relief (ACR), gave to East Timor and its people. Armstrong's clear vision of development was articulated in 1978 and published four years later around the time he began as Director of OSB. He insisted that "development is about people, the liberation of people, people taking command of their own lives, people participating in the decisions that shape their lives, people being free to love and build relationships, genuine relationships devoid of manipulation".[2]

Armstrong had also been on the Executive Committee of ACFOA since 1975, which meant that he was well known, particularly for his views on development education. Senior Australian Development Assistance Bureau (ADAB) officials respected him for his leadership in public discourse on issues of aid and development and the role of NGOs. For government officials a vocal NGO sector was an asset, because of its capacity and readiness to campaign on issues of development and, especially, on the size of aid budgets.

Armstrong's perspectives on aid and development brought an activist approach to OSB. Even though OSB seldom issued press releases, Armstrong was an extremely active lobbyist. He wrote to Ministers and other politicians on the social and foreign policy issues of the day, such as apartheid and Southern Africa, Cambodia, aid to Vietnam, among many others. Occasionally his letters were congratulatory, but more often they would advance arguments for Australia to adopt particular courses of action. His correspondence was sometimes robust, but never shrill, demeaning, or intended to embarrass. Armstrong ensured that every opportunity was taken to present submissions to and appear before parliamentary committees investigating myriad aspects of Australia's foreign and aid policies. In his submissions the history of OSB's work and relationships would be laid out, along with analysis of the issues at stake and the unique contribution Australian volunteers were making or could make.

In his first year or two as Director, Armstrong worked closely with the OSB Committee to arrive at a restatement of the organisation's aims and objectives and draw up an organisational structure that would carry it forward. Elizabeth Britten chaired the Committee, Hugh O'Neill was Deputy, and Philip Harris was Treasurer. Frank Engel, Chris Fogarty, Jeannine Paton and Bruce Thorpe continued as members. Four of the seven had been volunteers, and one (Engel) had been an initiator of VGS. OSB had a staff of 11, including the Director – nine in Melbourne and two in Sydney.

Early in his time as Director, Armstrong travelled interstate to meet returned volunteers to gauge and seek their support. They voiced their frustrations at having been unable to participate or have their views heard and were generally supportive of greater participation by returned volunteers, raising OSB's profile and taking a more open and collaborative approach to engagement with community and other organisations.[3] Interested returned volunteers moved quickly, forming groups in Sydney and Melbourne to establish returned volunteer associations, which were to be assisted by OSB but to remain independent of it. A greater role for returned volunteers had certainly been one of the recommendations of the Committee of Review's report, but it was a role that frustrated returned volunteers had actively pursued for some years before the review. Roger King, one of the most active returned volunteers, wrote to former volunteers in Victoria in December 1982, heralding the change in direction and inviting them to attend open meetings to discuss the support of Armstrong and the Committee for establishing organisations of ex-volunteers.[4] Their proponents envisaged several roles for these organisations, such as supporting volunteers, assisting OSB with publicity, recruiting and briefing volunteers, organising policy debates, lobbying, and providing an avenue for election to the Committee.

Although overwhelmingly positive, relations with returned volunteers were not without tension on issues of organisational governance. Some pushed vigorously for greater levels of returned volunteer representation on the Committee, with some even wanting it to be a Committee of Returned Volunteers – a model better suited to organisations that were entirely member-supported. It was difficult for them to sustain their campaign as most of the Committee were already returned volunteers, even though the Committee had no constituency or representative requirements for its membership.

The Committee of Review and a three-year plan

Of the 47 recommendations in the Committee of Review's 1981 Report, many related to particular countries or relatively minor administrative matters that would have been attended to by a well-run organisation. The Review also addressed some high-level strategic policies, the most important of which was a clear endorsement of the AVA program's high value and of its ongoing need for flexibility, responsiveness and community support, which meant that it should remain in the hands of an NGO. The Committee of Review also specified that, notwithstanding the changes it recommended to the organisational structure and practices of OSB, it was the organisation best suited to run the AVA program.

Leadership on the key questions of OSB's philosophical approach and identity was an early priority for Armstrong and an ongoing theme of his time as Director. In contemplating a vision for OSB, he knew it was essential to revisit its origins in VGS. He had spent time with volunteer graduates in Indonesia and experienced firsthand the fundamental value of relationship-building in their reasons for being there and in the way they lived. Inserting the spirit of the VGS program into the OSB of the 1980s also had the effect of rekindling an enthusiastic and emotional connection with former volunteer graduates who had lost touch with OSB in the 1970s. It brought people like Herb and Betty Feith, Don Anderson and Ken Thomas back in touch. Their support strengthened the efforts of O'Neill and Engel on the Committee to instil in volunteers and staff a sense of where the organisation had come from.

In October 1982, Britten wrote to all supporters to update them on the first ten months of OSB under Armstrong's leadership, informing them that the Committee, in several day-long sessions, had worked to clarify OSB's philosophy and policy and its response to the Committee of Review.[5] As Britten put it, the Committee saw OSB's role as a facilitator in "community building", bringing about an international "interchange of people who can bear witness to the fact that we are all part of a global village", and being more concerned with human development than large-scale projects or economics. This meant that OSB would continue its practice of selecting, briefing and sending groups of volunteers to work in developing countries for periods usually of two years at rates of pay similar to those received by local people. OSB would also act as a recruitment agency for specific positions overseas, with the costs being met by the employing agencies or governments and it would also undertake special projects in which personnel were the major component. At the time, OSB was investigating a possible project in Thailand to provide pre-embarkation orientation for refugees bound for Australia; it had also recruited an architect and two draftsmen to assist with reconstruction in Tonga after Cyclone Isaac in March 1982. Britten assured supporters that the Committee would work with associations of returned volunteers to ensure that they were represented in the Committee. She pointed out that, despite additional funding from government, the organisation still had to raise significant funds, and that it needed to look for new office premises.

Rather than seeking another office space to rent, the Committee decided it made better sense in the long term to buy, thus acquiring the certainty that property ownership brought to an organisation. Early in 1983 the Committee purchased a dilapidated engineering workshop in the inner Melbourne suburb of Fitzroy, at 71–75 Argyle St., for $155,000 and authorised expenditure up to $210,000 for renovations and repairs.[6] Following the decision to buy the Fitzroy property, OSB embarked on a more purposeful fundraising strategy. Letters were sent to supporters, and by supporters to people they thought might be interested. The request for funds covered the entire gamut of OSB's operations and plans: to improve the assessment of placements in-country; to enable multiple departures of volunteers; to provide language training and in-country briefings; to improve support for volunteers in the field and on their return; to make greater use of returned volunteers' experience in Australia; to extend operations to more countries; to increase the number of volunteers serving to 250; and to provide more suitable office accommodation by purchasing a building.

The appeal immediately raised $35,700, about a third of which came from former volunteers. The NGOs OSB approached were not so forthcoming; both ACR and ACC maintained their stance that, as OSB received significant government funding without restrictions, they preferred to use their funds for activities that the government would not fund.[7] (For example, ACR paid for the services of a bulldozer driver recruited by OSB for ACR's European counterpart, Coopération Internationale pour le Développement et la Solidarité (CIDSE), in Cambodia, well before OSB investigated the possibilities of a program there.)

Armstrong moved quickly to act on the most important of the operational recommendations made by the Committee of Review to improve and enrich the AVA program, reporting on these actions in August 1983.[8] They included the first mid-year departure of volunteers, the first in-country briefings in Port Moresby and Kuala Lumpur, the first language courses in Yogyakarta and Sabah, advertisements in the press, community service announcements on radio, upgrading the role of interstate representatives in promotion and selection of volunteers, and support for the Returned Australian Volunteers Abroad Association (RAVAA) who assisted with the June briefing in Sydney, and for Returned Overseas Volunteers of Australia (ROVA), who conducted a weekend workshop for returned volunteers in Melbourne. Returned volunteers Desmond Crowley and Alan Davis, nominated by RAVAA and ROVA, were appointed to the OSB Committee.

Meetings of serving volunteers had been conducted in Kuala Lumpur and Kota Kinabalu, Port Moresby, Mt Hagen and Rabaul, and it was planned to hold regular meetings in all countries. By June 1983, the number of staff had increased to 15, and it had become apparent that to strengthen OSB's ability to improve the quality of placements, staff in its overseas operations section would need to be relieved of first-round interviewing. These innovations were intended to improve the volunteer experience, but Armstrong pointed out that OSB continued to use the recruitment, selection and placement processes it had used for 20 years.[9] The significance of changes in practice lay in making better use of returned volunteers and of OSB's friends in promotion and recruitment. Changes were also made to the Development Worker Scheme (DWS); positions were publicly advertised and returned volunteers who registered their interest were sent information on the positions, but DWS was no longer reserved for them. AVA applicants could also be considered for DWS positions.[10]

Tony Street had attended the farewell function for departing volunteers as Minister for Foreign Affairs in January 1983, but by March Bill Hayden held the Foreign Affairs portfolio in a new government that was intent on squeezing the aid budget. Armstrong wrote to the new Minister and to the Chair of the Senate Committee on Foreign Affairs, Defence and Trade to argue that channelling an increased percentage of the government's aid budget through NGOs would improve the quality of aid. Throughout his tenure as OSB director, Armstrong actively lobbied politicians about the size of Australia's aid budget and how it should be allocated. He made repeated efforts to meet Hayden but did not succeed in doing so.

At the end of 1983 Armstrong met with ADAB to present the case for increased funding for OSB. His pitch was essentially that OSB had for two years followed the recommendations of the Committee of Review as closely as possible, which had led to increased numbers of volunteers, better placements, better briefing programs and language training. It had meant more involvement with government and with other NGOs. More adequate allowances had enabled experienced people to volunteer, thus prioritising the development cooperation agenda. The organisation was also pursuing new community development projects, made possible by relatively generous increases in funding. Armstrong argued that OSB was now at a point where an injection of funds would enable it to move forward rapidly.[11]

Early in 1984, Armstrong put together a three-year plan for July 1984 to June 1987. The plan reconfirmed AVA's dual objective of benefiting both people in developing countries and the Australians participating in the program. AVA provided personnel to work for local salaries under local conditions, so that they could establish links with local people. Having the volunteers live and work in a spirit of equality helped break down barriers; it was also substantially cheaper than any other method of making expertise available.

The three-year plan provided for OSB to have a presence in all Australian states by mid-1987. An overseas operations team had been established with responsibility for final selection and placement of volunteers, country briefings, language training and support. By increasing staff numbers, the team could spend more time in the countries where volunteers were placed to liaise with employers and assess potential placements. The plan also described a special projects section to focus on community development activities, in response to increased demand from community-based groups, especially in the Pacific Islands where, as well as the personnel requested, funds were needed to pay their salaries and for equipment. DWS personnel had been sent to Kiribati and the Solomon Islands, and also to Cambodia for ACR. A senior staff appointment was required to expand this work and ensure it was self-financing. The plan was to increase the number of volunteers in the field to 250 by 1986. To support the plan a budget of $1.655 million was requested for 1984/85, $2.14 million for 1985/86, and $2.675 million for 1986/87.[12]

Dilemmas

It was inevitable that the new momentum would pose new dilemmas for OSB – an inevitability that the organisation was aware of and even enthusiastic about. DWS, for example, showed potential for new ways of assisting developing countries, but also guaranteed that there would be conflict in realising this potential. There was clear demand in the Solomon Islands, Kiribati, Tuvalu, Vanuatu and Papua New Guinea for well-qualified and experienced Australians in a range of professions. It was also evident there was a supply of people prepared to serve for local salary and conditions with a supplementary payment to meet ongoing financial commitments in Australia. It was inevitable that this style of recruitment would conflict with the work of other recruiting agencies, but strong voices among OSB's leaders insisted that OSB should not waiver in its "commitment as a development and recruiting agency to continue to develop services which will benefit people in countries that we serve … if it results in commercial disadvantage for others, so be it".[13] Those voices thought it important that OSB expose as a myth the frequently stated idea that high salaries were necessary to attract qualified and experienced workers to developing countries. They also argued that schemes such as DWS would enable countries to spread the foreign aid they received further and move towards building expertise locally.

While the momentum and energy within OSB were evident, OSB's purpose, direction and limits were also critically examined. In a two-day meeting in July 1984, the Committee discussed many threshold and fundamental issues.[14] Was OSB a volunteer-sending organisation or a development agency? Was it too tied up in government departments and their hierarchies, instead of fostering development that involved the poor? There was a strong desire to spend more effort supporting community-based groups, but this would mean departing from the practice of requiring employers to pay local costs and would require OSB to fund volunteers and projects. It was also recognised that working in community development could entail political and even physical risk, as it often challenged the status quo.

Involvement in the issues of world development was bound to take OSB into politically controversial areas. The Committee's nuanced discussion of this inevitability asserted the need for the Bureau to inform volunteers and returned volunteers of such issues, while taking account of the situation of volunteers in the field. OSB staff and Committee members were free to express their opinions but were asked to also consider the impact their opinions might have on OSB operations. It was also recognised that OSB was under no obligation to be involved in every issue of world development and that it reserved the right to steer its own course on issues related to its operations. Apartheid in Southern Africa was the first issue to test these principles.[15]

The Committee discussed organisational independence in relation to fundraising. Independent sources of income were seen as desirable, but the value of fundraising was seen to arise more from its community education reach and was measured more in terms of the numbers of people reached than dollars contributed. Earning funds through providing services held strong appeal for the Committee, which was pleased to learn that ADAB had encouraged OSB to apply for a Bilateral NGO (BINGO) grant of $200,000 for the 1984/85 year to finance DWS recruitment for governments and community organisations in the Pacific.

Securing government funding

In June 1984 the report of an independent committee, set up by Bill Hayden in April 1983 to review Australia's overseas aid program and chaired by Sir Gordon Jackson, was tabled in Parliament. It recommended that Australian aid be rationalised so that Australia did what it was best at in fewer countries and that ADAB be transformed from an administrative agency into a professional development organisation. OSB was singled out for detailed commentary at the beginning of the report's section on technical assistance and the report was unambiguously supportive of OSB's role, its recent development and future growth: "An expanded volunteer program is desirable and requires a substantial forward commitment of financial resources within a 3–5 year rolling program. Without such a commitment the Australian volunteer program is unlikely to realise its potential in the Australian aid effort".[16]

This very positive finding, combined with the evidence of OSB's reforms since early 1982, gave OSB a much more secure platform for lobbying the government. It soon became clear, however, that the government was in no hurry to consider, let alone act upon, the Jackson Committee's recommendations. On getting verbal advice that the OSB's funding for 1984/85 would be the same as 1983/84, plus enough to cover inflation, Armstrong wrote to Dr Bob Dun, Director-General of ADAB, to explain that this would mean that OSB could not send as many volunteers and that a further $300,000 was required just to maintain its program on the current scale.[17] After several exchanges during July and August, Armstrong was largely successful in his lobbying; instead of the $1.5

million it had requested, OSB received $1.25 million, which included an additional $150,000 for a Pacific multi-country program.[18]

Armstrong realised he needed to tackle the government's apparent hesitation to implement the Jackson Committee's recommendations and did so in a letter to Foreign Minister Hayden. OSB's budget, as determined in the agreed three-year plan, was already in deficit. If the deficit was not made up in the 1985/86 budget, the plan could not be implemented.[19] He shared information about his lobbying with returned volunteers and supporters. The reply from Richard Manning, ADAB's First Assistant Secretary (Planning and Multilateral Division), placed OSB funding in a different context. He pointed out that the 27% increase over 1983/84 funding made the government's contribution of $1.1 million to OSB the largest single disbursement from the total funding allocation for all non-government organisations. He did not want to diminish OSB's achievements, but made it clear that no advance commitment to further increases would be made. The Jackson Committee's recommendations on NGOs, he added, were still to be considered and had been referred to the Joint Parliamentary Committee.[20]

Elizabeth Britten resigned as Chair of the OSB Committee in December 1984, having provided resolute and adroit leadership in bringing to an end the previous regime. She stepped down, confident in the Director she had appointed, and was succeeded by Hugh O'Neill, who in turn became a pillar of the organisation. O'Neill built on his experience as a volunteer graduate in Indonesia, his association with Jim Webb, and his leadership of the Australian Indonesian Association in Victoria to serve as an extremely involved and active Chairman for the next 15 years.

O'Neill chaired the meeting of the Committee March 1985, which Richard Manning had agreed to attend. Manning elaborated on his earlier correspondence and explained the depth of the gloom in Canberra. The government's aid budget was exhausted and this was affecting all programs and not just NGOs. He advised that, although it was unlikely that the Jackson Committee recommendations would be taken up in the 1985/86 budget, the government was committed to the volunteer program and OSB would not receive a smaller grant than in 1984/85. He suggested it would be worthwhile for OSB to explore options for ADAB funding beyond its Core Grant and to arrange an annual meeting of the OSB Committee with the Director-General of ADAB.[21]

The next step was to redraft the three-year plan. OSB was determined not to cut aspects of its operations that were bringing improvements and to retain the target of 250 volunteers in the field by 1986. The only savings to be found were in not pursuing innovation and not appointing new staff. Activity was to increase in project development, especially in the Solomon Islands, where there was an ongoing commitment of volunteers for the Solomon Islands Development Trust's Community Education/Rural Water Supply and Sanitation Project. The revised three-year plan for July 1985 to June 1988 requested an ADAB grant of $1.95 million of a total budget of $2.065 million for 1985/86; $2.25 million of $2.41 million in 1986/87; and $2.55 million of $2.9 million for 1987/88.[22] In June 1985, Armstrong and Hugh O'Neill met senior ADAB officers who could do nothing more than express sympathy and enthusiasm, directing them to see the Minister to put their case, but Hayden remained elusive. Further negotiation with ADAB about the funding necessary to maintain current levels of volunteer activity resulted in an ADAB Grant for 1985/86 of $1.8 million, still below what had been requested in the revised plan.

In November 1985, Senator Teague, who had chaired the Committee of Review into the AVA program four years earlier, informed OSB that the Foreign Minister had agreed to his request to publish the Committee's report and table it in Parliament.[23] Tony Street, Minister for Foreign Affairs at the time of that review, had been urged to publish it in August 1981, but a delay had been agreed to because it was thought that the recommendations would be better accepted and implemented without the attention that publishing the report would attract. With publication of the report imminent, Teague sought a formal response to his Committee's recommendations from OSB.[24] The OSB response stated that most of the 47 recommendations had been accepted and implemented and had been a valuable basis for restructuring OSB and its programs. It also pointed out that, although the recommended target of 250 volunteers in the field was accepted, it had only been possible to achieve 200.[25]

Action and reflection in OSB

The issue of government relations and the effort to turn the support for OSB frequently expressed by government officials into the forward commitment of funds were essential for the survival and expansion of OSB and its programs. The organisation's necessary preoccupation with its relationship with government also gave cause for deep reflection, discussion and debate on how the organisation was characterised. There was a tension between government funding and organisational independence. Where else would support come from? Was it necessary and/or appropriate to have fundraising campaigns? How should the organisation project itself? Should it have a public identity supported by a media strategy? The usual way for these issues to be canvassed was for the management team to produce papers that were workshopped with staff and presented to the OSB Committee for discussion. The debate proceeded through much of 1985, and the papers presented and discussed are evidence of intensely evaluative thinking.

Armstrong, looking back over the 30 years of VGS operation and 20 years of OSB, pointed to changes in individual Australians, in Australia as a nation and in the Third World.[26] He characterised DWS, begun in 1976, as a response to the need for highly experienced people in countries where OSB worked. The Scheme was an expression of the extent to which Third World governments valued personal motivations and development philosophies in their personnel, which were as important as technical competence in enabling successful partnerships. Unfortunately, in Australia and elsewhere, the term "volunteering" had connotations of amateurism and idealism. OSB had moved beyond pure volunteer programs into a range of project activity through which it was demonstrating its credibility as a professional development agency. Operationally, the DWS and the AVA programs were merged to meet the requirements for technical assistance and the social and political climate of the 1980s. Armstrong suggested that "volunteer" be replaced by "volunteer development worker" in any printed material, correspondence and discussion. The term duly entered the OSB lexicon and was widely used in written communications, although less in conversation, and was symbolic of a "grown-up" version of volunteering.

Fundraising

Armstrong had appointed Tam Lynden-Bell to be his Assistant Director for community engagement, fundraising and communications. They had served together in the ACFOA Executive Committee, Lynden-Bell's organisational base being the service club Apex. Lynden-Bell owned and operated successful pharmacy businesses and brought a unique real-world sharpness and energy to OSB, evident in his strong analysis in 1985 of past and potential sources of financial support, which shaped OSB's thinking on fundraising for years to come.[27] In its early years, OSB had been supported by contributions from private and community organisations, trusts and foundations and individuals. Even in 1967, half of the 80–90 new volunteers were sponsored by schools, colleges, churches, service clubs and the business community, including Forelanders Trust, Howard Norman Trust, Myer Foundation, Sidney Myer Charity Trust and high-profile Australian companies, such as Ansett Transport Industries, ACI, BHP, CUB, CSR, Comalco, CBA, CRA, IBM Australia, ICI, Johnson and Johnson, Kraft Foods, Nylex Corporation, Qantas Airways and Rheem Australia.

OSB had come about at a time of strong economic growth and Australian companies had been prepared to support OSB for the "identity and purpose" it provided to Australian nationalism, as well as being "a worthy means of adventure and service for our young people".[28] As circumstances changed, corporate support for OSB did not continue. As its reputation had grown, so too had the government grants it received and the organisation's dependence on those grants. Government grants in 1966 accounted for 66% of the total budget of $62,000; by 1984, they were 94.5% of the total budget of $915,000, although community support had grown in the intervening years by 50% to $33,000.

The OSB view had been that, however valuable government support was, the organisation's stability and continued independence relied on an adequate level of non-government funding or community-based support. Among the issues this raised was what should be considered an adequate proportion of non-government funding. Another was the importance of demonstrating independence through the attitudes, stances and actions of the Committee rather than through diverse funding sources. A further question was whether government grants were not in fact community-based (otherwise the government would need to be seen as a vested interest accountable to itself). Lynden-Bell's discussion paper suggested that having too much funding from one source was a risk only if that funding might cease. Governments of different persuasions had established a record of increasing funding to OSB over the preceding 20 years, which seemed to demonstrate bipartisan support for the Bureau's activities that should persist as long as OSB's management remained accountable and its programs continued to respond to community expectations.

The discussion paper's examination of non-government sources made it clear that service clubs would be less interested in contributing than in the past, although it was still worthwhile speaking to them, as a development education activity rather than with any expectation of raising substantial funds. The level of government funding eliminated any possibility of corporate donations or sponsorship and, when it came to public fundraising, OSB had a major image problem. "A public appeal depicting volunteers as 'angels of mercy' saving starving, pot-bellied children with big sorrowful eyes" would undoubtedly raise more than an appeal based on "furthering development education and devising long term solutions to third world problems," but would conflict with OSB's philosophy.[29] A limited appeal for funds directed at the organisation's own constituencies, who understood and/or experienced OSB's approach to development, was one thing, but the discussion paper made it clear that OSB should not pursue major public fundraising efforts and, furthermore, as it was not a fundraising charity, should not be seen to act like one.

It was considered wholly appropriate for Australia's international volunteer program to be government-funded, as it was in many other countries. Beyond the volunteer program, it was also considered appropriate and important for OSB to offer recruitment, training, project management and other services on a fee-for-service basis, thus earning untied funds, rather than receiving them as donations. In determining its fees OSB could strike a balance between the exorbitant rates of consultants and the cost-recovery approach of voluntary agencies. Overall, OSB should seek to ensure that its remuneration, whether in government grants or fees, was commensurate with the quality of the services provided. In the years to come, the question of fundraising was revisited from time to time, but the fundamental approach persisted – the organisation preferred to earn its income rather than seek donations.

Communications

Inevitably, consideration of fundraising led to the need for a communications policy, which was the subject of another discussion paper.[30] The organisation regularly produced newsletters, bulletins, press releases, pamphlets, advertising and public speaking materials, but no practice or policy brought these together. Jean Walsh, Press Secretary to the Premier of Victoria and later a member of the OSB Committee, applied her expertise to oversee a rebranding exercise. She advised that a policy was needed to ensure the organisation's image was consistent with its development philosophy.

In 1985 the organisation's identity was becoming diffuse. Australian Volunteers Abroad was well-known and the program's high profile was valuable in keeping the work of OSB in the public eye. Various terms in addition to "volunteer" were now being used in connection with OSB's work, such as volunteer development worker, development worker, and people in development. The name of the organisation, Overseas Service Bureau, was known, but only within a relatively narrow group of bureaucrats, academics and the NGO community. Staff and committee members discussed for the first time the need for clear objectives in the communication required for different purposes: in recruiting volunteers; in development education; and in lobbying politicians and bureaucrats. For the different audiences OSB needed to communicate with, the relative merits of television, radio and the press were analysed and assessed.

Structure and accountability

After three or four years of organisational reform, OSB found that changes in its operational environment called for new ways of working in some areas. The organisation had grown and new staff needed to be inducted into the OSB way, requiring deliberate effort to maintain the integrity of OSB's approach to development and to ensure that it was reflected throughout the organisation. Mary Considine took up this challenge, applying community development principles to enable staff to take stock of management challenges:

> All good development processes should start where people are at – and then go on to draw out of reflection on practice the new insights and understandings that can be put into practice. It is my belief that in looking at what we do and how we do it, we can see also what it is we believe about development for others and for us.[31]

In the preceding years the organisation had set sub-objectives, planned for them and implemented the actions on a range of fronts – greater numbers of volunteers in more countries; extended promotional work in Australia; improved support to volunteers; better briefing and training; higher levels of returned volunteer involvement – all of which had required more staff and more specialisation, as well as more structure and accountability in the workplace. A structure of functional teams had been put in place and increased efficiency. It was now recognised that certain activities, such as planning briefings and producing newsletters, extended beyond the scope of the functional team structure and required greater collaboration across the organisation.

OSB culture

After Armstrong took over as Director, the culture of OSB was completely refashioned, arising in part from the philosophy of development Armstrong promoted. Within the context of the development sector, OSB was distinguished by the simple, profound and accessible vision his philosophy had engendered. In essence the vision held that development is not something anyone can do to anyone else; development is a process in which all participate, but which can be thwarted by poverty, injustice, racism and any violation of human rights. The appeal of this vision drew people to the organisation; a press advertisement in 1984 for a field officer position attracted 150 applicants.

The backgrounds of the staff were many and varied. A small number knew Armstrong's outlook and style from their experience of him at AWD; others had come across him at ACFOA, but the majority had been exposed to and internalised his approach during their time as volunteers. They were from a very diverse range of professions and occupations, including pharmacy, local government, agriculture, building trades, and academia, and all of them had accepted lower salaries to work at OSB.

OSB staff lived the philosophy the organisation was imbued with. The Bureau operated with only as much hierarchy as good governance and accountability demanded. Beyond that it operated with an openness and an egalitarian style that were evident in robust debate of ethics or political economy and in weekend working-bees providing labour to the builders refurbishing the newly purchased property; even the builders shared in the ethos.

The approach to information management could not have been more different under Armstrong from what it had been when Martin was Director. In 1983 it was established that all documents provided to the Committee would also be provided to all Assistant Directors unless directed otherwise by the Committee.[32] Meetings were arranged to ensure regular contact between staff and Committee. The Staff Manual described the process for handling incoming mail; all mail, unless marked confidential or private, was opened at a morning meeting and seen by the Executive Director and Assistant Directors, or their representatives, before distribution to the appropriate sections.[33]

Collaborating with government and the NGO community

Training programs

At the annual consultation between ADAB and the NGO community in September 1982, OSB was encouraged to explore using its accumulated experience to assist other agencies with training their personnel before they went overseas. Early in 1983 Armstrong convened a meeting of interested agencies, including Australian Red Cross and the Australian Organisation for Disaster Relief Operations (AODRO), as well as some smaller agencies. A proposal was drafted for an "institute" to undertake this work, although the "institute" was never imagined as a physical entity but as an extension of OSB's work and located within it. Planning began early in 1984 for a residential course to be piloted in September–October that year. As there was not sufficient capacity in OSB's staff to design and implement the program, Armstrong invited his former colleagues at AWD to take on the task, confident that they shared OSB's approach to development and adult education. The five- to six-day courses, called People in Development, ran for several years thereafter, providing pre-departure briefings for development workers and staff from OSB and other agencies.

Abraham Baeanisea (SIDT) with Bill Armstrong at OSB's Melbourne office, September 1985. Courtesy AVI

At OSB's Melbourne office, 1985. L to r: Bill Armstrong, Mary Considine, Diane McDonald, Courtesy AVI

Staff of OSB's Overseas Section in 1985. L to r: Roger Holt, Graeme Bruce, Mary Considine, Peter Britton, Lyn Creek, Glen McIntyre, Frank Mannix, Helen Sinclair, Trish Farrelly. Courtesy AVI

Geoff Black, community development worker with Lekutu Community Centre, Fiji, 1985–86, with his son Hamish. Courtesy AVI

L to r: Bill Armstrong, Executive Director, OSB; Dr Bob Dun, Director-General AIDAB; Chris Fogarty, Deputy Chairperson OSB Committee, Canberra, 1987. Courtesy AVI

Hugh O'Neill calls OSB Annual Meeting to order, September 1987.
Courtesy AVI

OSB Committee members, October 1987. L to r, back row: Desmond Crowley, Robin Gray, Chris Fogarty, Alan Davis; front row: Judith King, Frank Engel, Margaret Christie. Courtesy AVI

OSB's new premises from 1984 at 71–75 Argyle St, Fitzroy, Melbourne. Courtesy AVI

Chris Fogarty introduces Governor-General Sir Ninian Stephen at a Canberra function, 1989. Courtesy AVI

Joint Agency Working Group

As funding for the government's overseas aid tightened under the new Labor government in 1983, Neville Ross, Head of ADAB's NGO Section, saw an opportunity to increase the proportion of the aid budget channelled through his NGO section. One of the strategies Ross used to achieve this was to encourage Australian NGOs to establish a super-agency that could operate large-scale programs and, therefore, attract substantial funding.[34] He envisaged a consortium of identifiably Australian agencies with compatible approaches to development. Discussions in early 1984 involved Australian Freedom from Hunger Campaign (AFFHC), CAA, Women and Development Network of Australia (WADNA) and OSB, but CAA was the only organisation enthusiastic about the prospect of a super-agency, with the others preferring a looser arrangement, with collaborative measures determined project by project.[35]

The Joint Agency Working Group (JAWG) put a proposal to ADAB requesting funding for joint project planning missions to Southern Africa, the Pacific and Indochina, and in mid-1984, JAWG undertook investigations in Mozambique, Zambia and Zimbabwe. Mozambique was assessed as the country most in need of assistance, both because of its acute humanitarian needs and because the expertise of a very experienced Australian doctor, Julie Cliff, working with the Ministry of Health, was available there. The project was designed as an integrated program in health, agriculture, fisheries and water, located in Inhambane Province in the south of Mozambique. An initial 12-month rehabilitation and reconstruction phase was to be followed by a three-year development phase. It was agreed that CAA would manage the project, working with OSB on recruitment and selection of the project team; AFFHC would be responsible for financial administration. Initially it was thought that WADNA would monitor the project to ensure that women's rights were considered and that women directly benefited, but WADNA withdrew before the proposal was finalised. The project was funded in March 1985 for an initial 18 months.[36]

As no funds were available for JAWG to conduct a planning mission to Indochina, ACFOA separately coordinated a visit to Vietnam, Laos and Cambodia by a delegation from several of its member agencies, including AFFHC and OSB.[37] In the Pacific, WADNA had conducted a major mission in 1982 and subsequently agreed to employ two women to work on strengthening links in the region. WADNA agreed that their work would support JAWG objectives and produced a report that was the basis for further work carried out in the Pacific. In October 1985, JAWG concluded that its original project was now complete and that the exercise had demonstrated the usefulness of a collaborative approach to project identification.[38]

Government relations: towards an agreement

In July 1986, ACFOA alerted its member agencies to the fact that Hayden had offered aid cuts to the government's Expenditure Review Committee and stated that the government would not adhere to the commitment it had made in November 1985 to increase foreign aid.[39] OSB was not spared, learning in August that it would receive $1.8 million for 1986/87, the same amount as in 1985/86, and $15,000 for the Multi-Country DWS.[40] By this time OSB had built a structure to support 250 volunteers in the field, but could not afford to send that number. In June 1987 there were 200 volunteers in the field. It was working in more countries, often placing very experienced volunteers with families and commitments that required additional financial support.[41]

Without adequate core funding from government and with little will to engage in public fundraising, the only alternative for OSB was to supplement the core funding by engaging in more contracted programs, projects and consultancies with different sections of ADAB, and directly with partner countries such as the Botswana teachers' program. The success of this strategy, however, rested on securing and protecting the core funding, and the political reality of the time was such that the core funding could no longer be assumed. OSB was just one of the 130 NGOs receiving funds from the government, but it received 20% of the total funding for NGOs. Some at OSB argued that if it were seen as the government's volunteer-sending agency, perhaps as a quango, it might access more funds. Others argued that an organisation receiving more than 90% of its funds from government could not really claim to be an NGO.[42] In a sense, the OSB's volunteer program was now suffering the consequences of the decision made by government in 1965 and again in 1981 not to establish a government volunteer program but to support the organisation that had already created one. These were sensitive issues for OSB, which had forged an identity larger and more complex than that of a volunteer-sending agency and saw itself as a development organisation with its own stances and distinctive styles of operation.

Armstrong was determined to clarify the status of OSB and its relationship with government, but was fully aware of the risks implicit in doing so. OSB could assert its status as an NGO and receive government funds through the same mechanisms as all other NGOs. The amount of government funding would fall and OSB would have to invest heavily in fundraising, with no certainty of success and with considerable diminution of its integrity, so it was never an option. Armstrong argued it was important to recognise the special relationship through which OSB held responsibility for operating Australia's volunteer program and its special identity as a private community organisation receiving substantial government funding to enable it to uphold this responsibility. The obligations on both sides of the relationship – the provision of adequate funding and the operation of an agreed level of programming – needed to be recognised and documented.[43]

In March 1987, Armstrong, sometimes with Chris Fogarty, conferred with ADAB's Director-General and his senior staff in four meetings over two days. All were positive about OSB, its operations and relationship with government. Armstrong came away confident that the 1987/88 budget would at least support 200 volunteers in the field, that there would be opportunities to sell projects to other parts of ADAB and the opportunity to seek funding through Committee for Development Cooperation

(CDC), a joint ADAB–NGO mechanism for subsidising NGO projects.[44] By mid-1987 ADAB had declared its intention to draw up a Record of Understanding in relation to OSB's core funding which would include the extent of the forward commitment to OSB, the range of services the government was prepared to pay for and a review of the relationship between government and OSB. It was acknowledged that core funding for the volunteer program should include full program costs including in-country costs as well as resettlement costs and some funds for raising community awareness.

The 1985 agreement on the Multi-Country Program (Pacific) DWS was extended in June 1987 to June 1988 to cover an additional 20 people, making a total of 41 supported through this program in 1987/88.[45] It remained unclear whether the proposed Record of Understanding would provide for DWS in core funding. It was mooted that a new arrangement might deny OSB access to project funding through the CDC. ADAB's intention was to work on the agreement and review the relationship at the same time, consulting with OSB about questions the review should address to clarify the relationship and the range of services the government was to pay for.[46]

In November, this process took on a new significance when AIDAB[47] warned Armstrong that other organisations, including AFS Australia, Australian People for Health, Education and Development Abroad (APHEDA), CAA, Palms (Paulian Lay Missionary Society), and Interserve (a Protestant missionary organisation), were looking to enter the volunteer arena and seeking government support. AIDAB needed a clear rationale for government support for OSB and wanted the Record of Understanding process to provide that.[48] The Terms of Reference, agreed in May 1988, clearly stated that the objective of the review was to strengthen the basis of cooperation between AIDAB and OSB and establish in contractual form their long-standing financial relationship.[49]

AIDAB Director-General Bob Dun confirmed that he regarded it inappropriate for OSB to remain part of the CDC Project Subsidy Scheme. He reiterated that AVA was highly regarded and that AIDAB would prioritise government support for OSB within the NGO sector. He added that the budget climate was unpredictable and speculated that funding for the OSB might be more secure if it came from Country Programs (the largest part of AIDAB's budget) rather than the NGO allocation which was contained within the smaller Global Programs.[50]

When AIDAB had assembled the questions it sought answers to for its review in July 1988, OSB undertook to canvass the ideas and views of returned volunteers, its staff and supporters and other NGOs.[51] OSB's response to AIDAB's questions was a comprehensive statement of the state of the organisation, with a restatement of its objectives.[52] The few non-AIDAB sources of support were listed – Victorian State Government ($30,000); Botswana Government ($98,164 over 3 years); individual and community donors ($10,695); Arthur Andersen ($6,500) – but these amounts were dwarfed by the estimates of salary and benefits that volunteers had foregone ($5 million in 1987/88), free advertising ($3.8 million) and a host of discounted professional services.

By 1988, the AVA program was operating in 25 countries with OSB associates also working in the Philippines, Mexico, Mozambique and El Salvador. In Southern Africa the program had grown from three volunteer placements in 1984 to 62 in 1988, and from one to 11 in Indochina.[53] The AVA program was scaled down in Malaysia and Kiribati after Japan and USA increased the numbers of volunteers they made available for free. Small Pacific Island states had found it difficult to fund salaries for volunteers and security concerns in Papua New Guinea had led to a reduction in the number of volunteers there. In its response to the AIDAB questionnaire, OSB put the case that increased funds would enable it to do more in the increasing number of countries where the local salary component of the AVA program model could not be met. OSB wanted to continue sending older, more experienced volunteers, as well as opening opportunities for young people early in their careers. The response noted that, while OSB, whose staffing complement had risen to 57, 50 of whom were in the national office in Melbourne, had productive ad-hoc meetings with AIDAB at all levels, there was no regular formal consultative mechanism with senior staff.[54]

AIDAB and NGOs

Dun continued to be concerned about finding the best way to secure funding for OSB. He knew the Department of Finance never liked AIDAB locking in multi-year commitments and that the aid budget was likely to be reduced in favour of trade and commercial activity. With OSB already the largest recipient of NGO funds, it would be difficult to achieve an increase. He suggested that OSB's funding come more from Country Programs, arguing that this would look better and involve greater interaction between OSB and AIDAB. Australian Executive Service Overseas Program (AESOP), Palms and Interserve would also move into regional and country programs, thus separating volunteer agencies and their programs from the NGO section of AIDAB.[55]

As part of its review of its relationships with NGOs, AIDAB's Policy Branch produced an internal policy paper on the AIDAB–NGO relationship, which noted its value in enabling the Australian government to provide effective grass-roots aid and acknowledged and encouraged community concern.[56] The policy paper differentiated agencies that managed voluntary technical assistance activities but did not raise substantial funds from the general public as other NGOs did. Their public contribution lay in the services they provided at less than market cost and their activities did not fit easily with the project model that was central to AIDAB's funding mechanism for NGOs, the Project Subsidy Scheme or the proposed Program Subsidy Scheme.

AIDAB had used two organising principles – one put diverse activities together because they were implemented by NGOs, and the other considered program objectives (emergency aid, refugees, relief, etc.) rather than who was delivering the services. In the proposed reform of its relationships with NGOs, only the second principle would be followed. NGO professional development activities would move to the academic and research area within AIDAB's Global Programs area; NGO development education work would move to the public information and development area; and voluntary technical assistance, including volunteer programs, would move to Country Programs.

AIDAB outlined its position at a meeting in May 1989.[57] AIDAB would introduce a Record of Understanding for the volunteer program (including one with AESOP). This agreement would provide for core funding and the right to seek additional funding from other parts of AIDAB. It envisaged a three-year forward commitment. AIDAB would have a seat on OSB's "Board of Directors" and a regular process of review and reporting would be set up. A newly created Development Centres and Volunteer Programs Section in AIDAB would administer the relationship and would also look after the Australian Centre for International Agricultural Research (ACIAR), the International Development Program (IDP) and the National Centre for Development Studies (NCDS).

OSB was taken aback and responded that core funding it received was only for the AVA program and that OSB remained an NGO. For AIDAB to sit on the "Board" would raise several issues, including a perceived loss of NGO status and increased government control. The "Board" (Committee as then defined) did not represent particular constituencies and, furthermore, an AIDAB representative on the "Board" would have to be involved in decisions beyond the AVA program. AIDAB argued that it provided nearly 100% of AVA's funding and that an AIDAB representative on the "Board" would formalise the existing informal relationship and would not be able to veto any decisions made by the "Board", pointing out that it already had representatives on the Boards of IDP, ACIAR and AESOP. A meeting with the OSB Committee was scheduled for 2 June to take the matter further.[58]

While the Committee remained pleased with the prospect of formalising relations with AIDAB and could see advantages in having an AIDAB representative, they saw disadvantages in the possibility of conflicts of interest and confidentiality breaches. There was also the legal question of whether a Committee position could be reserved for AIDAB, so the Committee raised the possibility of an AIDAB representative having observer status at its meetings.[59] Armstrong wrote to John Holloway, AIDAB's Deputy Director-General to convey both the Committee's pleasure with the AIDAB proposal and its concerns about confidentiality and potential conflict of interest; he raised the question of whether they would consider the suggestion that an AIDAB representative have observer status on the OSB Committee.[60]

John Holloway and Louise Morauta of the AIDAB Policy Branch attended the June meeting with the OSB Committee members, together with six senior OSB staff. Holloway pointed out that the amount of money the government gave OSB to support its program had become large enough to warrant formalising OSB's relationship with government in a manageable and accountable way. The arrangements AIDAB proposed were designed to protect OSB's funding and protect the volunteer program; they were to be seen as a partnership with AIDAB rather than a take-over by AIDAB. AIDAB representation on the Committee was intended to show responsible management, as it had with IDP and ACIAR without undermining their independence.[61]

The Committee endorsed in principle the proposal that a senior member of AIDAB participate as a member of the Committee.[62] In consideration of the forthcoming Record of Understanding, the Committee resolved to use one of two vacancies for this purpose and invited John Holloway, whose personal commitment had impressed them, to join the Committee in a private capacity. AIDAB would be asked to consider the fact of his appointment when they considered their representation on Committee.[63] By inviting him directly they had preserved their right to choose Committee members and circumvented the legal question of reserving a seat for an AIDAB representative.

The subtleties of these negotiations did not impress the broader NGO community, which was concerned by the precedent having an AIDAB representative on OSB's Committee set. Armstrong explained to Dun that, while the Committee had willingly agreed to AIDAB's representative being a full member, they would prefer the representative to have observer status and asked if the matter of full membership could be reconsidered.[64] Armstrong assured Holloway that his invitation to join the Committee stood and Holloway confirmed that his personal interest in OSB had been long-standing.[65] Bob Dun agreed that it would be appropriate for the AIDAB representative at OSB Committee meetings to have observer status and that the representative would be at Director level, normally the Director responsible for OSB funding.[66]

Agreement

Foreign Minister Gareth Evans signed the agreement between the Commonwealth of Australia and OSB relating to government support for OSB's Voluntary Technical Assistance Program in July 1990.[67] It provided for continuing grants, determined annually and paid quarterly. Prior to every annual budget consultation, OSB was to present a three-year plan comprising an operational plan for one year and indicative costings for the two years following.

The operational plan for 1990/91 for Australian Voluntary Technical Assistance Program (AVTAP) was sent to AIDAB at the end of August. Despite the agreement, OSB's funding issues had not been resolved. Armstrong, in a letter accompanying the operational plan, explained that the target of 250 volunteers in the field had been reached in January 1988. With its experienced staff, the number of requests on hand and volunteers available, OSB was in a position to maintain 300 or more volunteers in the field. Armstrong pointed out that the newy signed agreement did not specify the level of continuing government support. Secure funding and expanded opportunities for OSB had been discussed for more than two years but had still not eventuated. AIDAB had indicated the Core Grant would be $3.549 million, which was less than the grant for 1989/90 and $1 million less than planned. Without additional funds through regional and multi-country allocations there would be no new volunteers in January 1991 and the number of volunteers on assignment would reduce from 286 to 185 in January and to 160 by July 1991. It was feared that a sudden change of this magnitude would have an ongoing operational impact.[68]

Armstrong sent outlines of three programs of voluntary technical assistance to be considered for Country Program funding in 1990/91 (Indochina $640,000, Papua New Guinea/Pacific $540,000, Southern Africa $150,000) to support discussion of OSB funding at the first High-Level Meeting under the new agreement early in September. OSB had to accept that, in the budgetary circumstances of the current government, its core funding would be reduced and that other sources of AIDAB funding would be required to provide for 250 volunteers in the future.[69]

In September 1990 OSB announced that it had cancelled its AVA mid-year departure group for 1991. OSB's agitation was at least partially successful, in that AIDAB agreed to an additional $400,000, which increased the Core Grant to $3.95 million. It still fell short of the $4.55 million requested for 1990/91, but was thought to be enough for 60–70 volunteers to be placed in January 1991. OSB staff discussions with AIDAB's Country Programs area gave no indication of any paths to additional funds.[70] Holloway attended the November OSB Committee as a member and an AIDAB observer was in attendance as well. Armstrong informed the Committee that, although the Minister had agreed to the further $400,000, OSB had been told to expect decreases in future and had been encouraged to seek other sources of funding.

In June 1991, at the Second Annual High-Level Meeting under the agreement, AIDAB announced they would conduct yet another review of the effectiveness of the AVA program as quickly as possible and would reveal the Terms of Reference and what was expected of OSB.[71] The terms of the agreement provided for a joint evaluation of AVA and it was this that AIDAB was acting on. The review was triggered by yet more change within AIDAB, as a result of which the International Organisations Section, which managed the agreement with OSB, was to be dismantled and responsibility for OSB's funding was reverting to the NGO Section. The circle was now complete.

The decade had been characterised by the intensification of OSB's relationship with government, resulting in a more formal relationship that reflected broader changes in the way government saw its role and the responsibilities of NGOs. While these changes were an irresistible trend, the remarkable features in the relationship were the respect and enthusiasm amongst senior AIDAB officials for OSB and its programs. They too were confronted with challenging policy and budget environments and found creative ways of trying to increase or at least protect OSB's funds. Variations on this theme continued in the 1990s, but the emergence of a less supportive attitude from parts of AIDAB highlighted the issue of OSB's dependence and a need for greater diversity in its business model.

CHAPTER 5

Diversification and Dependence (1991–2002)

In August 1990, just a month after OSB and Foreign Minister Evans had signed the agreement on government support for OSB's Voluntary Technical Assistance Program (AVTAP), AIDAB informed OSB that its grant would be substantially less than planned, not even matching the previous year. The organisation lobbied hard and got $400,000 restored to its grant, but it was now clear that the limits of government support for the volunteer program had been reached. As there had been a steady decline in government spending on overseas aid in the preceding six years,[1] this came as no surprise. The OSB would need to identify other sources of funds, so the OSB Committee asked the Executive Director to prepare a strategic plan by July 1991.

After 12 months of consultation and analysis in the most thorough examination of the organisation's purpose and objectives in 30 years, the plan, *Future Directions*, was published. It enunciated a mission statement entirely in line with the organisation's founding principles, and deliberately avoided the concepts and terminology of international aid:

> The Overseas Service Bureau provides opportunities for Australians to live alongside people in developing communities and work in partnership with them in order to:
>
> - foster cross-cultural relationships and international understanding;

- assist in the development of their own and other communities; and
- contribute to a peaceful and just world.[2]

The organisation's principal concern was human development, explicitly understood to include development in Australian communities. Experiential learning, also described as a process of action and reflection, was highlighted as a key element in how people grow and change.

The plan committed the organisation to four key objectives: to conduct volunteer programs such as Australian Volunteers Abroad; provide recruitment, briefing and training services for others engaged in technical assistance; implement people-centred projects and programs; and, increase public awareness of aid, development and cross-cultural issues. A further five enabling objectives made it clear that the organisation knew that, to achieve its key objectives, it would have to change the way it managed people, maintained its culture, and networked and positioned itself. The need for improvements in processes and in policy development was singled out in one particular objective that committed OSB to an ongoing practice of evaluation.

The discourse that gave rise to *Future Directions* was not a winner-take-all debate. It was recognised that unresolved dilemmas were fundamental to the organisation and, contrary to standard practice, should be named and explored in the plan. While the starting point was the need to diversify sources of income, maintaining the organisation's independent, non-profit nature and its ethos was considered vital. Another central tension was the value placed on cost-effective technical assistance as against the learning experience of living and working in communities. Rather than attempt to resolve this issue, it was determined that its two dimensions be held in creative tension.

Future Directions contained no financial descriptions or projections, no numeric targets or timetables. It was not a business plan but a prescient and determining consideration of strategic options for the future. It reflected an era when OSB did not see itself as a business or use the language and tools of business, but knew it would have to move in that direction and was expressing its ambivalence and reservations. It was realistic about the limits to government support for volunteering, was energetic in looking for opportunities to make the most of its specialised skills in managing people, and was keen to market project management to expand its portfolio. It remained committed to development education. The dilemmas, issues and tensions identified in the plan dominated the next decade as OSB worked through and lived out these contradictions.

Future Directions' plan implied expansion, so the organisation moved quickly to increase staff numbers and strengthen its management structure. New management units were established for recruitment, program development and training, public information and education, in addition to the country-based operational areas.[3] Changing the organisational structure to manage the changing portfolio of work became a recurring theme of the next decade. By May 1992, changes had enabled program-based reporting to the Committee and separate coordination of work on AVA and projects.[4] Monitoring and evaluation of programs were agreed to and budgeted for in new activities. Some progress was made in providing recruitment services and staff of Westpac and ANZ taking up international appointments in the Pacific Islands and Asia benefited from OSB's cross-cultural training and country-specific briefings. The growth anticipated in *Future Directions* had begun and emerged in project-based work and fee-for-service activities, rather than in the AVA program.

Budget support

Concern about the uncertain fate of the government's 1992 aid budget drove OSB to participate in ACFOA's 1991–92 campaign to lobby for its expansion. It distributed kits to returned volunteers to encourage them to lobby their Members of Parliament in the lead up to the 1993 election. The kits addressed both the quantity and quality of aid and included analysis of Labor and Coalition policy papers.[5] Armstrong wrote letters to the Treasurer (John Dawkins), Minister for Foreign Affairs (Gareth Evans) and Minister for Trade and Overseas Development (John Kerin).[6] The lobbying achieved a one per cent increase in the aid budget and, significantly, greater recognition of the role of NGOs, particularly in programs concerned with women, environment, HIV/AIDS, and reconstruction in Cambodia. The budget papers mentioned the AVA program's effectiveness specifically in justifying an increase in its funding, later confirmed to be 60.6% for 1992/93 (from $4.14 million to $6.46 million).[7]

This unexpected expression of confidence in OSB made it a fortuitous time for Chris Fogarty to replace Hugh O'Neill as Chairman of the OSB Committee. OSB had not sought an increase of this size and had planned to maintain a program of approximately 250 volunteers in the field at any one time, but now it had to plan for a program of 450 volunteers.[8] Such a substantial increase could not be achieved in one step; the Operational Plan presented to AIDAB for 1992/93 increased the number to be placed from 161 to 247, bringing the number in the field at 1 July 1993 to 354.[9] One avenue to boosting the number of volunteers was to increase the participation of younger people, which was controversial because it highlighted policy tensions and differences in how some staff and Committee members saw the organisation and its programs. The percentage of young people serving as volunteers had been declining since the AVA program began in 1964. In the mid-1980s this was not seen as problematic, as OSB had become proud of its record in recruiting well qualified and experienced professionals to provide technical expertise. Younger, less experienced applicants were generally encouraged to re-apply once they had more experience. Those on the OSB Committee and management team who supported the objective of providing opportunities for experiential learning had wanted to redress the imbalance, so the Committee agreed in 1989 to increase the number of volunteers under 25 in the January 1990 program. Eight young volunteers went to Africa and Asia, most of them as teachers, but the initiative lapsed until late 1992 when the Committee supported a proposal for a Volunteer Graduate Program within AVA for 30–40 additional volunteers under 25 for 12-month assignments, but only 17 were placed in January 1993, largely because of continued resistance to engaging younger volunteers by some staff who thought it undermined OSB's professional image as a provider of technical assistance.[10]

Managing projects

Developing and managing projects introduced new complexities to the organisation and required a change in management style. Managing in the AVA context was necessarily fluid and flexible, as variables tended to balance each other. Difficulties in identifying appropriate assignments in one region would often be offset by additional opportunities in others; the overall impact of volunteers not completing assignments would usually be negated by those who extended their time. As in the AVA program, OSB's projects still involved putting carefully selected and prepared people into appropriate positions, and monitoring and supporting them, but, unlike AVA, project contracts specified locations, numbers, duration of assignments and often the skill level required. Funds for projects mostly came from AIDAB's Country Programs, so the projects had to demonstrate a contribution to Country Program's objectives. Securing and administering project funds was much more time-consuming and costly and required different approaches and skills. Processes for appraisal and design, implementation, monitoring and evaluation had to be embedded in the project management cycle.[11]

Projects had become an essential component in OSB's business arrangement with AIDAB, but their funding was complex. OSB, like other NGOs, found that AIDAB was not prepared to cover the full cost of overheads and administration. AIDAB assumed that OSB's organisational costs were covered by AVTAP and that projects should therefore be costed at a marginal rate. Beneath this assumption lay AIDAB's misunderstanding about NGOs and their not-for-profit status; they did not realise that NGOs had to make a modest surplus at least, so that they did not run at a loss.

At its annual policy and evaluation weekend in August 1993, the OSB Committee was presented with a stocktake of project activity; ten projects had been completed in 1992/93 and a further 12, all funded by AIDAB, were underway, including eight in Cambodia and Vietnam. In addition, the groundwork had been completed for new projects to commence with funding from the Australian Centre for International Agricultural Research (ACIAR) whereby Australians would support ACIAR's research partners in Zimbabwe (veterinary science) and Kiribati (aquaculture). An AIDAB project in Western Samoa responding to the widespread destruction wrought by Cyclone Val at the end of 1991 was designed to strengthen building and building inspection practices to cyclone-proof standards and involved specifying and procuring a substantial amount of building material. All other projects were small groups of volunteers working on defined activities for pre-determined periods of time in countries where there was little or no local financial contribution and the entire cost was paid from aid funds.

OSB staff became skilled at meeting AIDAB requirements to get project funding, which rose in 1991/92 from 6.6% of total income to 17%. It doubled in 1992/93 to $1,860,000, but was dwarfed by the increased grant for AVTAP, so as a proportion of total income it rose from 17% to 21%. It fell again to 16% ($1,332,000) in 1993/94, rising again to 18.3% ($2,133,560) in 1994/95.[12] AIDAB-funded project activity declined as work in Vietnam and Cambodia was increasingly absorbed into the core volunteer program. Innovation continued outside the AIDAB relationship, and in 1994 the Commonwealth Department of Employment, Education and Training (DEET) wrote to all state education departments inviting participation in a new Australian Teachers in Asia Program. Designed jointly by OSB and DEET, this two-year program was to increase teachers' capacity for work in international environments and to strengthen educational links. It targeted teachers who were unemployed or facing redundancy and prepared to teach for a year in schools in Indonesia, Vietnam, Malaysia, China and Thailand.[13]

Training and recruitment services

Of the program areas designated in *Future Directions,* the slowest to take off was providing services in recruitment and training (or briefing) for other not-for-profits and for private sector companies. Although businesses with international interests recognised the value of cross-cultural training and country briefings and were prepared to pay for these services, OSB was never wholly supportive of working with the business community. While many thought it inappropriate to work with the corporate world, others could see that it was building relationships with people in the developing world on a scale that dwarfed NGOs and even government agencies and that, if OSB's know-how and professionalism could improve the way the corporate world conducted those relationships, OSB's input could only be beneficial. Furthermore, any profit OSB made from selling these services could be used to subsidise unfunded activities.

Recruitment services undertaken for Save the Children Fund Australia (SCFA) came about as a result of a close association between OSB and SCFA's Executive Director who appreciated that recruiting a team to work in Cambodia needed the professional services of recruiters who understood that country. Other NGOs in the international development sector were intensely competitive and chose not to use OSB's offerings, but recruitment services were of interest to some Aboriginal communities in rural and remote Australia, as they appeared to help address difficulties they faced in employing appropriate people. Early adopters of the services were a community bakery (Mi-Patha Association) in Wadeye and Marra Worra Worra Aboriginal Corporation in Fitzroy Crossing.

Engaging with Aboriginal Australia

In 1992, the OSB Committee made clear their intention to move ahead with Aboriginal issues that had been an unfocused interest of the organisation for many years.[14] Pre-departure briefings had always included sessions on racism in Australia and the history of Aboriginal dispossession and the struggle. The urban-based activists who presented and sometimes hosted these briefings tended to convey a sense that black issues were for black people and well-intentioned white people were neither necessary nor welcome to engage with them. People familiar with and experienced in the circumstances of the Aboriginal organisations central to Aboriginal communities in remote areas held a different view. These organisations relied on people they employed as administrators, organisers, trainers, storekeepers, and health professionals, and if these people were incompetent or abused their power the organisations were held back. Albany-based accountant Ron Richards, who had many years' experience with Aboriginal community organisations and enterprises in the Kimberley region, put it to OSB that it was morally obliged to apply the community development skills it had acquired in Third World countries to Aboriginal communities in Australia. For nearly a decade he had persisted with this message,[15] and had introduced OSB to other experienced consultants who combined a community development perspective with first-hand knowledge of particular areas. They appreciated OSB's success in finding people to live and work successfully in Third World countries and argued that people like these would be able to adapt to life in remote communities and work in the interests of those communities. They identified with OSB's philosophy and its approach to community development and appreciated its diffidence about entering the field uninvited and that its intentions were limited to providing paid services in recruitment and allied areas. They agreed to introduce OSB to key people in particular regions and organisations.[16]

In July 1993 the writer travelled with consultant Geoff Langford to Alice Springs to meet with members of the Aboriginal and Torres Strait Islander Commission (ATSIC), Office of Local Government, Pitjantjatjara Council, Tangentyere Council, Central Land Council and other aboriginal organisations, before travelling to Ernabella, Fregon, Amata and Umuwa, the administrative centre of the Aṉangu Pitjantjatjara Yankunytjatjara (APY) lands. A visit to the West Kimberley region followed a month later, where Ron Richards had briefed Aboriginal organisations and encouraged them to engage with OSB about their staffing needs. The level of demand for OSB's services in the organisations was unexpectedly high. By the end of 1995, community organisations had made 26 appointments on advice from OSB, following a process of advertising, shortlisting, interviewing and checking references. Eleven appointments (of accountants, architects, administrators, executive officers and nurses) were in the West and East Kimberley; six (marketing and office managers, a women's centre coordinator, a mechanic and a council clerk) were in Central Australia; nine (doctors, an accountant, an education coordinator, an essential services officer and a town clerk) were in the Barkly region and the Top End.

Consistent with *Future Directions,* two major development education programs were conducted in 1993/94. The Beyond Borders Youth Tour (BBYT)[17] brought together 22 young people from Africa, Asia, the Pacific Islands and Aboriginal Australia in a five-week tour of regional and remote areas of Australia, following an orientation week of training in public speaking, leading discussion groups and talking to media. They met with service clubs, welfare services, environmental organisations, women's groups, unions, schools and universities.[18] Later in 1994 the Melanesian Women's Tour brought seven women from Papua New Guinea, the Solomon Islands, Vanuatu, Irian Jaya, New Caledonia and Fiji to Australia for a month-long tour of five states.[19] Both tours drew substantially on the voluntary contribution of time and effort of returned volunteers and benefited substantially from sponsorship and support from travel and hospitality companies.

Some development education activities were for Aboriginal people exclusively. Late in 1992, UNESCO asked OSB to facilitate Australian involvement in a program linking indigenous Sami people from Sweden and Norway with San (Bushmen) people in Namibia. The three groups, co-ordinated by the Nyae Nyae Development Foundation of Namibia and financed principally by Sweden, Norway and Finland aid agencies, were to travel together as they compared their experiences of land rights issues. OSB secured AIDAB funds for four Aboriginal Australians recommended by the Kimberley and Cape York Land Councils to participate in the 19-day exchange in November 1993.[20]

OSB's emphasis on community education, especially the importance it attached to working with returned volunteers, set it apart from other agencies internationally. OSB was unusual in maintaining offices in Australia's state capitals which had important functions in promoting OSB programs and recruitment but whose major function was community education through assisting returned volunteers in their transition back into Australian society and providing opportunities for them to share their experiences. By providing practical advice and supportive environments and networks, OSB's state offices encouraged returned volunteers to stay involved in the community on issues of international development and to assist volunteer recruits to prepare for the volunteer experience. Returned volunteers were active participants in public forums held around Australia on issues related to social justice and aid and development, such as trafficking and child prostitution in Asia, the realities of NGOs in India, and violence against women in El Salvador. Some involved collaboration with other organisations such as ECPAT (End Child Prostitution in Asian Tourism) and International Women's Development Agency.

Two years after *Future Directions* had been published, it was evident that, although there had been growth in all four of OSB's program areas – AVA, projects, services, and community education – the AVA program continued to dominate. OSB's Operational Plan for 1993/94 budgeted a total expenditure of $10.49 million, of which $6.95 million was for AVTAP, $3.26 million for projects and $280,000 for the general account. The AVA plan was to place 300 new volunteers in the year, which would more than double the number of volunteers in three years and take the number in the field to 490 in June 1994, requiring two recruitment campaigns and four briefings per year, and a continuous process of placement.[21] Considerable progress had also been made in achieving the enabling objectives of *Future Directions*. The number of staff had grown to 85 by the end of May 1993, almost double what it had been at the beginning of 1992, bringing complexity to the organisation that called for further adjustment to its structure.

Volunteers and the government's aid program

Each year the OSB Committee held an extended meeting, usually over a weekend involving roughly equal numbers of senior staff and Committee members, to allow for more thorough discussion of policy and direction. At the August 1993 meeting, the key issue that arose was increasing discomfort that OSB had become part of Australia's aid program. It was argued that OSB had run a very successful volunteer program based on certain abiding principles – partnership, living and learning together, and building bridges of understanding based on equality and justice – but these were not the principles of the Australian government's aid program. Within the concept of aid was a notion of superiority; those who have give to those who don't. Eventually aid would be outmoded, but there would always be a need to foster and develop relationships, so OSB needed to maintain its awareness of the fundamental distinction between its principles and the concept of aid.[22] These concerns were exacerbated when OSB examined the trend in AIDAB to downplay humanitarian concerns and emphasise the commercial benefits of the aid program, in which the Development Import Finance Facility (DIFF) scheme – essentially a subsidy to Australian companies managing infrastructure projects – was the fastest growing component. Philip Flood, Director-General of AIDAB, insisted that Australia's commercial interests should be reflected in all AIDAB programs and strategies.[23]

By the end of 1993 the growth of project work in OSB's portfolio had also raised philosophical questions, as it was recognised that projects required different relationships with "employers" in the countries benefiting from such work. Armstrong, in particular, was keen that staff were aware of the potential threat to OSB's philosophy, methodology and ethos that lay in the structures and systems for delivering projects, at one point exclaiming to his managers, "A lot of people here think they are working for an aid agency".[24] In a reprise of the earlier Committee discussion, he made sure that managers and staff were aware of his concerns and that technical assistance did not necessarily work towards justice, development and the recognition of human rights.

Foreign Affairs Minister Gareth Evans, with Chris Fogarty and Bill Armstrong, signs OSB's agreement with AusAID for the OVTA program, Canberra, 1995. Courtesy AVI

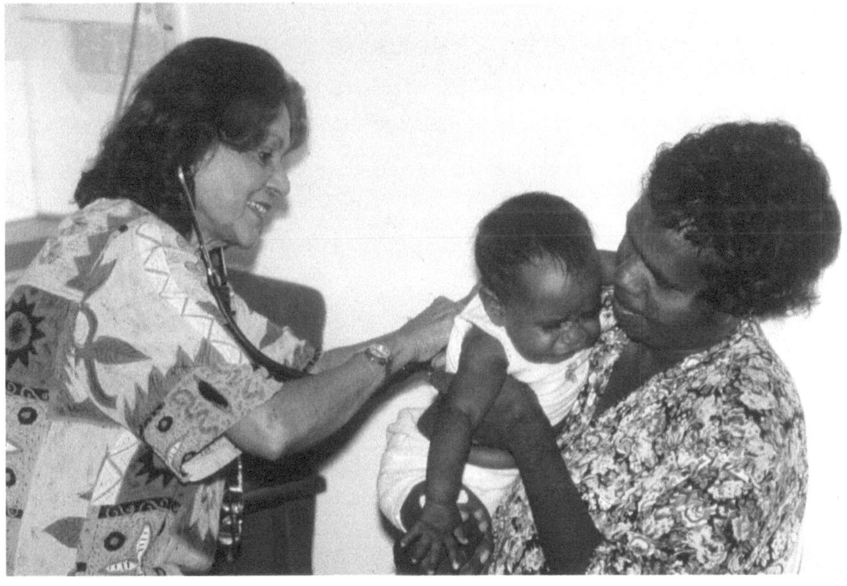

Dr Ulita Nair, recruited for Anyinginyi Congress Aboriginal Corporation, Tennant Creek, 1997. Photo Dennis Schulz. Courtesy AVI

TAYAP launch at Australia–Thailand Ministerial Economic Commission meeting, Canberra, February 1997. Thai delegation members with Minister for Foreign Affairs Alexander Downer, TAYAP participants James Nichols and Kate Lockart, and Minister for Trade Tim Fischer. Photo AUSPIC. Courtesy AVI

TAYAP horticulturalist Kate Lockart at the Buriram rural development project. Photo TV Asia 1998. Courtesy AVI

Georgia Noy, marine scientist holds her audience in the Philippines, 1999–2000. Photo Ken Lawson. Courtesy AVI

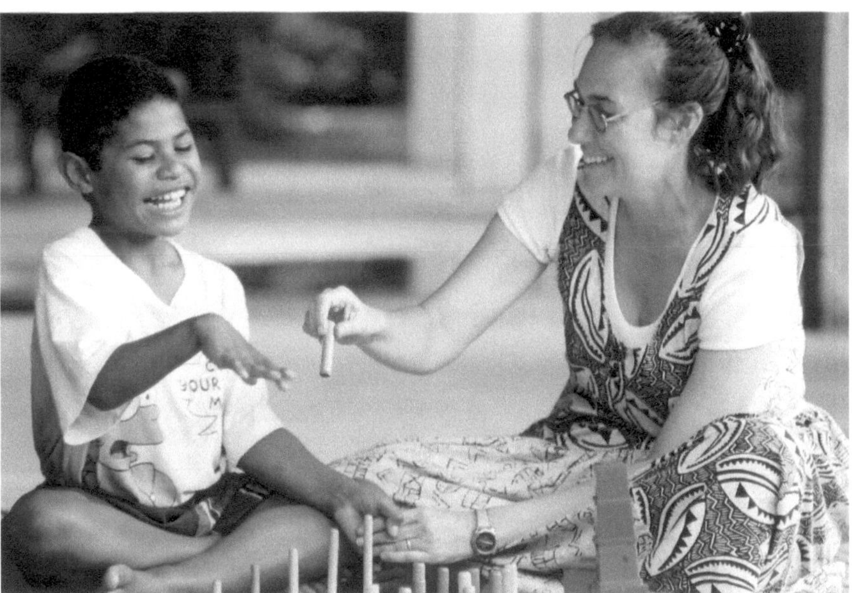

Leigh Dix, occupational therapist in Fiji, 1999–2001. Photo Will Salter. Courtesy AVI

Bob Meyenn, AVI Board Chairperson, 2000. Photo Viv Mehes. Courtesy AVI

OSB had now become less vulnerable to the impact of a reduction in the AVTAP grant, which dropped from 95% of total income in 1992/93 to 65% in 1993/94, but if project funding was included, AIDAB still contributed more than 90% of OSB's total income. As the 1994 budget was awaited, there was little optimism. OSB had proposed a plan for 240–250 new volunteers costing $8.8 million and in March 1994 encouraged returned volunteers and supporters to lobby members of the Expenditure Review Committee (ERC). Although funding cuts had been expected, much to everyone's surprise, funding for volunteer programs was increased for 1994/95.[25] OSB's AVTAP grant was increased by 33.5% to $8.95 million, bringing the proposed target of 500 volunteers in the field in 1995 into clear view.[26]

Relations with government

Although OSB was keen to develop relationships with NGOs and businesses in initiatives consistent with its philosophy, its strongest relationship continued to be with the Australian government. It was at times important for OSB to explain that it was not an arm of government, and AIDAB continued to show that it appreciated OSB's non-government status and its capacity to establish contacts in communities where government agencies could not. AIDAB also appreciated OSB's capacity to source and manage high-quality technical assistance personnel, increasingly engaging OSB to recruit for specific positions outside its existing programs from January 1995. These positions were all in government departments or agencies in the Pacific Islands and are further discussed in Chapter 9.

While management restructuring, staff training programs and the recruitment of additional staff had increased levels of professionalism in OSB, they had also increased its cost base. Operational costs had also increased, as volunteers in most countries required financial support beyond what local agencies could contribute to their costs.[27] Without additional support from AIDAB, OSB would have to cut the AVA program. A positive ministerial reaction to OSB's request for more funds encouraged AIDAB to ask it to present a three-year plan and budget by the end of 1994,[28] thus ensuring that funding was a key issue at the February 1995 OSB Committee meeting. AIDAB observers had attended OSB Committee meetings since early 1990, with little impact on proceedings, but the observer at this meeting, Gerard Guthrie, actively gave and received messages, letting the Committee know that Flood and the Minister for Development Cooperation and Pacific Island Affairs supported an increase in funding. He also told them of AIDAB's intention to conduct a review of the effectiveness of volunteer sending organisations including AESOP, Palms and Interserve.[29]

In a series of meetings with Flood early in 1995, Armstrong pointed out that the AVA program's operational expenses had increased because of expanded programs in very poor countries (Vietnam, Laos, Eritrea, Mozambique and Kiribati), because there had been budget cuts in health, education and social services in some countries, and because of inherent underfunding of certain focus areas, such as refugees, women, HIV/AIDS and environment. He put the case that, as the volunteer program grew, so too did the Australian community's voluntary contribution. OSB saw the financial support from the government as underwriting that community support. Four hundred volunteers in the field had foregone an average Australian salary of $20,000, totalling $8 million for the preceding year which matched the funds contributed by the government.[30] Flood conveyed his wish for AusAID[31] to have a representative on the OSB Committee, pointing out that recent funding boosts increased AusAID 's interest in OSB's policy and management decisions and proposing that OSB's Articles of Association be altered to accommodate the appointment of an AusAID representative as a full member of the Committee.[32] In negotiations, AusAID made it clear that a $10 million budget contribution was available in 1995 if it had a seat on the Committee and $8.9 million (no increase) if it did not. Armstrong's response was that $10 million was not enough to maintain 500 volunteers in the field with appropriate support and that $11.5 million would be required.[33]

A meeting was convened between AusAID (Philip Flood and colleagues) and OSB (Committee Chairman Chris Fogarty, Committee member Sally-Anne Watts and Armstrong), at which Flood talked of his commitment to a strong volunteer program, but admitted that the strength of OSB's management had been raised as a concern. Flood insisted that $10 million was the maximum possible budget contribution and that it was contingent on OSB's agreeing to have an AusAID nominee on the OSB Committee,[34] which they did after further discussion with the Committee.[35] In subsequent correspondence with Minister Bilney, Fogarty was assured that he had no concerns about OSB's management and that he was well informed of OSB activities.[36]

New brands

Despite OSB's ongoing efforts to achieve greater recognition as an organisation, the AVA program remained better known. Early in 1995 a consultant was engaged to help develop a communications strategy to promote OSB as a vital organisation worthy of continued government and community support. The strategy explored ways to cultivate supporters and raise the organisation's profile through its publication program and media exposure.[37] It highlighted the fundamental relationship between OSB and its programs and recommended consistent branding and packaging of the programs, while ensuring that product and service names were subsumed within OSB's identity. Alongside Australian Volunteers Abroad, Beyond Borders was introduced to encompass tours, exchanges and other community education activities, and Project Partners for all project management activities. People Prepared came into use as the umbrella term for recruitment, training and briefing services.

Once the four names proposed by the communications strategy for grouping OSB's activities had been agreed and articulated, operational units were encouraged to generate stories for the Public Affairs Unit to push to the media. Coverage increased dramatically, with 36 radio interviews in six months, ten stories in print media and one TV program.[38]

New challenges

In August 1995 the OSB Committee and staff countenanced, for the first time, the possibility that AusAID would call for tenders to manage Australia's international volunteer program.[39] OSB had no significant competitors, but recognised that it could not assume its protected status would be maintained into the future and that competition could develop amongst technical assistance providers, such as universities, state government agencies and other NGOs. The Committee decided to commission John Baker to conduct a financial, management and efficiency review of its own by the end of the year. Baker, a former senior public servant and diplomat, had developed many management and leadership development programs, especially for senior executives in the Australian public service. He had advised OSB in the past and the Committee thought his insights into the best management style and structure for OSB would be useful, and that having Baker conduct the review would send a strong message to AusAID. OSB was facing new challenges. Whereas government scrutiny had previously focused on program management and field performance, the focus had shifted to accountability, where funding came from and how funds were used. There was a stronger appetite for testing an organisation's efficiency and for questioning to whom it was accountable; where did it get its support, other than from government, and to whom did it report? Another challenge to emerge at this time was that OSB staff who were members of the Australian Services Union began negotiations for an industrial agreement.

Strategic directions

The opening pages of the three-year plan for 1995/96–98/99, *Strategic Directions*, adopted in December 1995, summarised the organisation's growth.[40] In 1982/83, 186 Australians worked in OSB placements, most of them through the AVA program. By 1994/95, 770 people were participating, including 670 AVAs in 44 countries, 90 project personnel in 20 projects, and 12 in Aboriginal communities. Other people had participated in community education tours and exchanges. OSB saw itself as one of Australia's leading agencies in international development, but struggled with the reality that AVA was better known than OSB. One major strategy for the coming three years was to raise the public profile through a comprehensive communications and marketing agenda. A second major strategy, related to accountability, effectiveness and efficiency, proposed ongoing review of the Committee's role and composition and the management structure, and continuing to develop evaluation schedules and accounting and reporting systems. It was envisaged that programs in the Asia and the Pacific would be the principal focus, the largest being Indonesia and Papua New Guinea, although OSB was keen to maintain its presence and activities in Latin America and Africa.

AusAID's *Review of the Efficiency and Effectiveness of Australian Volunteer Programs*, released in June 1996, concluded that the volunteer programs were efficient and effective. It reaffirmed the principle of recognising the value of the voluntary contribution made by volunteers in analyses of cost-sharing between the agencies and the Australian government, and suggested that in-kind support from academics, consultants and other sources should also be noted. Compared to international volunteer organisations in other countries, OSB was assessed as efficient. The Review found no evidence that OSB was overstaffed, as some within AusAID had alleged, and cited John Baker's conclusion that OSB's management systems, morale and performance compared favourably with public sector organisations of similar size. It recommended that AusAID develop a policy specifying the principles and objectives of its support of volunteer agencies and that agencies reassess the structure and membership of their governing bodies. It also recommended that OSB stop government-funded activity in Latin America and withdraw from Thailand over five years.

These recommendations had to be put on hold as a change of government in March 1996 raised the prospect of budget cuts across all portfolios, and the new Minister for Foreign Affairs, Alexander Downer, commissioned a wider review of Australia's aid program.[41] OSB took comfort in the fact that Downer, having made it clear he would only support NGOs that could demonstrate community support, had accepted that OSB had demonstrated community support in volunteers' wages foregone. He also declared he was comfortable with OSB's assessment of the value of the AVA program at $30 million, of which the government contributed $10 million.[42] Downer indicated he had "long been convinced of the worth of volunteer programs", and referred to the benefits they brought to developing countries, the volunteers and Australia. He then noted his recent announcement in Bangkok of a 50:50 Youth Ambassadors Program to assist in language training, environmental projects and vocational training in Thailand, substantially supported by private sector funding from Thailand and Australia.[43]

50:50 Youth Ambassadors Program

The idea for the 50:50 Youth Ambassadors Program emerged from a discussion between Downer and his friend Mechai Viravaidya, a prominent politician, activist and social entrepreneur, renowned for promoting condom use in Thailand to control birth rates and, later, HIV infection. Downer announced the program in Bangkok on 22 April 1996, before Department of Foreign Affairs and Trade (DFAT) or AusAID staff knew what it was. They were briefed some days later by Greg Hunt, Senior Adviser in the Minister's office, who explained that Mechai expected substantial support from the Thai business community, as the concept was to be developed in association with 50th anniversary celebrations of the King's ascension to the throne. Funds would be raised from Australian businesses with Thai interests, and the Australian government would also contribute. The program would offer 12-month assignments to young Australians who had just completed their training; they would be in rural areas assisting with English language teaching, environmental projects and vocational training. AusAID was to prepare a submission for the Minister on how the program would operate. If it was approved, AusAID would ask its officer in Bangkok to discuss the program further with Mechai, especially its association with the King's anniversary.[44] OSB agreed to prepare a project design and was then informed of the discussion between AusAID's Bangkok staff and Mechai, who had attempted to clarify the program's title. Mechai asked if 50 referred to 50 volunteers in the King's 50th anniversary year. AusAID put its view that the title signified a partnership in which program costs would be shared equally between Australia and Thailand. Although the program was intended as an opportunity for private sector involvement in development cooperation, the Australian government would commit seed funding for the first year. Mechai requested a longer term commitment from the Australian government. He had not secured any funding from the Thai government and, doubting the ability of Thai private sources to fund half the program's costs, proposed a more modest program.[45]

The 1996 review of volunteer programs had recommended that programs cease in Thailand within five years, consistent with AusAID's view that as a middle-income country Thailand could "graduate" from the aid program. It therefore suited OSB to have the opportunity to proceed with this initiative given its non-aid terms of reference. With a November deadline for its project design proposal, OSB began to liaise with the Australia Thailand Business Council (ATBC) and the Australia Thailand Chamber of Commerce (ATCC), both of which agreed to promote the scheme to their member companies. OSB already knew Mechai, having previously cooperated with the NGO he led, Population and Community Development Association (PDA). OSB's project design specified up to 50 placements over five years to 2001, with the first group of six to be placed by April 1997. These initial placements would cost $104,000 and a further $127,000 would support the fundraising strategy.[46] Now known as the Thailand Australia Youth Ambassadors Program (TAYAP), the scheme was launched by Downer at the meeting of the Australia–Thailand Ministerial Economic Commission in Canberra in February 1997, where it was promoted as an innovation to promote personal linkages between the countries' future cultural, business and community leaders. The initial six placements were to be followed by 12 in the next financial year, with further placements dependent on the strength of business sector support for the program. The Minister believed that the investment yield from a trust fund of $10 million would maintain a program of 50 volunteers each year, but accepted that it would be sustainable at a smaller scale with $4 million.[47]

Given the uncertainty as to how much could be raised from the private sector for the program, OSB recommended that the Australian government commitment be maintained at the same level or reduce over three to five years. A promotional video featuring Hugh Morgan AO and brochures pitched at the business community were developed; launches and meetings were planned for Sydney, Brisbane and Bangkok hosted by companies active in the ATBC. Business leaders with experience of Thailand needed no persuasion of the value of cultural literacy and language acquisition for doing business in Thailand. They applauded the program, but said that it was precisely the kind of program that should be funded by government rather than by business. The Sydney launch of TAYAP for the private sector was hosted by National Australia Bank on 22 October 1997 and promoted to all ATBC members. Addressing the launch, Downer encouraged "the private sector to see involvement in aid activities as a way of bringing tangible benefits to itself", adding that "association with an NGO like OSB can enhance a company's reputation".[48] Thirty people attended the event, half of them from AusAID, DFAT, the Thai Embassy, Thai media representatives and OSB. Of the 16 business people in attendance, six were from NAB. The business community had shunned the Minister's invitation to contribute and Downer neither attended another TAYAP function nor spoke of it to OSB again.

As the vision of a trust fund was unlikely to succeed, OSB negotiated for the TAYAP contract to be amended to a sponsorship model of fundraising. By May 1998, 17 TAYAP volunteers were on assignment. Sponsorships were set at $30,000, and the first to be taken up was by engineering firm Sinclair Knight Merz on the basis that one of its young talent would benefit from the program and in turn benefit the company. He was placed in an environmental program in a rural area where his profound learning experiences encompassed cross-cultural issues and sustainability and development. Such was his personal transformation that he never returned to the company or to engineering, which highlighted a fundamental flaw in the sponsorship model.

At the Committee's Policy Weekend meeting in August 1996, Scott Dawson was welcomed as AusAID's appointee. He informed the Committee that the Government's grant to OSB's volunteer program in 1996/97 was $9.498 million, $500,000 less than the previous year, forcing a cut to the program size and other savings. The Committee noted that on 30 June 1996 there were 510 people in the field (427 AVAs, 69 project personnel and 15 in Aboriginal organisations). It also discussed the importance of a management restructure with clearer lines of responsibility for program management, serviced by a number of task-based areas. Also discussed was a proposal to establish an Ambassadorial Group of up to 50 people who would champion OSB for two or three years, informing the organisation of community trends and opportunities and providing access to important people and places.[49]

Audit issues

The OSB Committee also confronted issues raised by AusAID's auditors,[50] particularly OSB's use of accrual accounting and the rent OSB charged to AVTAP for the use of its buildings. OSB's assets were held in a separately managed General Account and each OSB program was charged rent at commercial rates determined by an annual valuation. The AusAID auditor maintained that OSB was making a profit from program funds, even though OSB used any surpluses to underwrite unfunded development activities. From discussions in ACFOA circles, Armstrong concluded that a pattern of critical issues had been raised by one particular auditor in the audits of NGOs and stressed that a clear strategy was needed to deal with this.[51] The fundamental issue facing the Committee was that, as a company, OSB was obliged to follow accrual accounting procedures, whereas the government worked on a cash accounting basis. It presented Scott Dawson with a potential conflict of interest, leading him to clarify his understanding that, although nominated to the Committee by AusAID, he was not its representative but an independent member of the Committee with a duty not to disclose Committee proceedings to AusAID. In spite of this, he excused himself from Committee meetings when the auditor's draft report was under discussion. Noting that the audit issue had to be resolved before progress could be made, Armstrong stressed the importance of not letting AusAID set OSB's policy framework.[52]

Eventually, in early 1997, AusAID accepted OSB's evidence that AusAID had received and accepted its reports and financial statements as far back as the first quarter of 1990, which dealt with most of the auditor's recommendations, leaving unresolved only the issues of rent paid by the AVTAP program and of whether OSB should report to AusAID on a cash or accrual accounting basis. The audit report was finalised at the end of April and included the recommendations that:

- "Recurrent costs" within the core agreement should be defined to exclude provisions. Acquittals were to be purely on a cash basis including the costs of bringing volunteers home, and employees' Long Service Leave and Annual Leave.
- The internal rental charge, by one profit centre (General Account) to the detriment of another (AVTAP), should be limited to actual costs associated with the maintenance and ownership of the building. It was also recommended that AusAID consider whether to recover the past surpluses of rent paid over actual property expenditure.[53]

As expected, there were cuts to the government's aid budget in the Commonwealth Budget for 1997/98. Armstrong, as ACFOA President, led a press conference with 12 other NGO leaders to express concern at the cuts, pointing out that

> the Government squandered a significant and timely opportunity to rebuild Australia's badly tarnished international reputation. Cuts to aid simply compound a self-defeating image of Australia as a country that is isolationist, doesn't care and is behaving like an ostrich … Coming on top of last year's 10% cut, this further 3% reduction is simply a miserable measure.[54]

The press conference, held in Parliament House and broadcast throughout the building on its internal television network, provoked a frenzied response from Downer who berated Armstrong. Armstrong's relations with the government plummeted. A meeting scheduled that week for OSB Committee members and senior staff to meet the Minister for Foreign Affairs' Parliamentary Secretary, Andrew Thomson, was cancelled without explanation or any plan to reschedule. OSB also learnt that the AusAID Executive had discussed yet another draft audit report on OSB's dealings with AusAID. Armstrong wrote to Thomson, pointing out that, on the basis of the earlier draft audit report, both AusAID and OSB had a problem; because OSB was required under the Companies Act to present financial reports on an accrual basis, its accounting system had been configured to meet this requirement. He reiterated that AusAID had never questioned the validity of OSB's reports.[55] He enclosed a position paper dated May 1997 describing the AVA program as a three-way partnership between the Australian government, the Australian community and the international community. The strength of community support was attested by the 18,000 people who inquired about volunteering in 1996 and by the 68% recognition factor in polling conducted by Quadrant research in May 1997. With bipartisan support, Commonwealth funding for the program had increased, but Australia was lagging behind other countries. The paper requested that the AVA program be recognised as an important national program in which the Australian people were key stakeholders, that the government make a financial commitment to the future of the AVA program, that the program receive triennial funding with annual review, and that discussions be held to determine the most appropriate funding channel.[56]

Armstrong documented the history of OSB's financial management arrangements. He pointed out that lack of any certainty about ongoing government funding had underpinned OSB's decision to purchase property as an asset base. The building had been purchased with a loan in 1984 and was made useable by the volunteer labour of returned volunteers, staff, Committee members and supporters. Until the 1990 agreement, there had been no requirement in government grants that surpluses (or interest) had to be returned to AusAID or used only for the particular project or program that AusAID had funded. It was common practice in the international development community to use surplus monies for organisational development and other programs. With no guarantees and many risks, having an asset made it possible for OSB to raise funds to meet its obligations in the event of emergencies overseas, having to wind down its activities, or possible litigation. As well as satisfying the Companies Act requirements, accrual accounting was necessary to provide for liabilities that came with legal and moral responsibilities for staff and volunteers.[57]

Armstrong provided AusAID with his confidential background paper when they met to resolve the audit issues. He noted that AIDAB observers at OSB Committee meetings since January 1990 had been privy to all discussions and had access to all Committee papers, and that AusAID had a nominated officer as a full member of the Committee since October 1995. The negotiations resulted in Points of Agreement that addressed among other matters, capping provisions at their June 1996 level, the basis of rents charged, the repayment of accumulated unexpended grant funds, and the assessment of OSB's assets and current and future obligations and liabilities.[58]

Twelve months after the initial audit report a basis from which to proceed had been agreed, but this basis had to take account of the way AusAID had reshaped its working relationship with NGOs. AusAID's review of the effectiveness of NGO programs in 1994/95 had recommended greater clarity in the relationship between AusAID and NGOs, with streamlined administration and stronger accountability. In 1996, AusAID's funding of NGOs had been audited by Australian National Audit Office, which had recommended more monitoring. In response to these two reviews, AusAID had developed an umbrella contract for use by all NGOs, with features and requirements specific to each activity to be set out in an exchange of letters (EOL).[59] The umbrella contract required organisations to acknowledge AusAID support in their public information and to obtain written consent from AusAID before issuing any formal media statements critical of AusAID; it assigned all intellectual property to the organisations.[60]

Interim arrangement

AusAID decided on an interim one-year arrangement for AVTAP in 1997/98 and issued OSB with an EOL specifying the same budget figure as 1996/97 ($9.498 million), which was a decrease in real terms of 2% (10% over two years), and specifically excluding Latin America. AusAID agreed to hold further discussions on longer term options for the volunteer program, including the possibility of a commercial arrangement.[61] Despite changes in the contractual arrangement and the nature of AusAID's presence on the OSB Committee, the first EOL under the umbrella contract continued to describe the Commonwealth's ongoing support to OSB for its AVA program.[62] Since April 1997, in consideration of the importance of the AVA program to OSB and the increased intensity of liaison required with AusAID, the AVA program had its own executive director, David Penman, a director at OSB since October 1994.

Project work continued to be a significant component of OSB's activities. Between June 1995 and June 1997, OSB sent 30 submissions and one tender to AusAID, 13 of which were successful. Whereas AVTAP was funded through AusAID's relatively small global fund, projects gave OSB access to the much larger bilateral aid funds disbursed through AusAID

Country Programs. This enabled OSB to operate in countries that did not fund the in-country costs of volunteers and to design and implement technical assistance programs with different premises and cost structures. Of the total OSB staff of 104 full-time equivalents, including 15 in state offices, 12 were dedicated to project development and management. People Prepared was also growing, particularly in training and briefing services for corporate clients; an agreement with a leading relocation company, AustraliaWide Relocations, whereby OSB provided cross-cultural training and country- and city-specific briefings in the suite of services the company offered its clients, substantially increased demand for these services.

Expanded services to Aboriginal communities

Demand for recruitment services from Aboriginal communities continued to grow, as OSB's reputation in this area grew, but operating on a fee-for-service basis alone was not viable. Many Aboriginal organisations did not see staff recruitment as a business cost that should be budgeted; others made poor recruitment decisions before turning to OSB for help. It was clear that an effective recruitment service in remote communities could only succeed with government support, which would need to include a subsidy. From early in its work with Aboriginal communities, OSB had been encouraged and supported by the Julalikari Council Aboriginal Corporation (JCAC), led by David Curtis and Elliot McAdam. Early in 1997, OSB renewed discussions with Curtis, elected ATSIC Commissioner for the Northern Territory Central Zone in 1996, and McAdam, JCAC General Manager, about the possibility of working in partnership to further develop the recruitment service and to consider joint ventures. Curtis undertook to raise recruitment at a national level in ATSIC. JCAC had become a major training and employment organisation in its own right, providing a range of services, including housing construction and maintenance, Community Development Employment Program, Night Patrol, Skillshare, Landcare and outstation infrastructure development.

JCAC was fully aware of the financial losses, wasted opportunities and anguish in Aboriginal communities caused by inappropriate recruitment practices and low staff retention rates, and signed an agreement with OSB in August 1997 to explore working together to promote an expanded recruitment service.[63] Specifically, JCAC helped OSB prepare a case for financial support for the service and lobbied the Northern Territory and Commonwealth governments. Yapakurlangu Regional Council of ATSIC, based in Tennant Creek, endorsed OSB's work and urged all ATSIC Regional Councils in the Northern Territory to use OSB's services; an arrangement was made for OSB to speak at a meeting of all the Northern Territory Regional Councils.[64]

The expanded service, known as Remote Recruiting, was made possible through the involvement of ATSIC, Local Government Association of Northern Territory (LGANT) and JCAC. ATSIC allocated $125,000 initially, and again in 1998/99, to support Remote Recruiting, granting it to JCAC to engage OSB to manage the service. LGANT offered furnished office accommodation in Darwin for two years and $25,000 for start-up costs, which it received from the Northern Territory Department of Housing and Local Government. Projections indicated that OSB's unfunded expenditure could be progressively reduced with a small surplus in 2000.[65]

The Committee's 1997 Policy Weekend began with updates on the year's activities, including viewing a new media announcement for the AVA program and a new promotional video.[66] Other achievements included securing a project to develop disaster preparedness in the Pacific Islands and the production of a video for Ansett Australia to be screened on flights to Bali, which raised issues of cultural sensitivity with a light touch. There was a presentation on the recommendations of the Simons Review of Australian aid, followed by discussion of the role of boards and their relationship to management. The Committee also discussed threats to community organisations from government agencies, which increasingly disregarded organisations' values and saw them purely as service deliverers and contractors. OSB had noticed a new orthodoxy in its dealings with government bureaucracy, whereby discussion tended to focus on unit costs, numbers and countries. In discussing the draft strategic plan for 1997–2002, the Committee identified three key challenges: the relationship with government; maintaining the central role of the AVA program; and organisational governance.[67] The plan placed the long-term viability of OSB in expanding the development of people-to-people links with the private, public and community sector. The Committee remained determined to avoid using the language of the aid industry.

Before entering discussions with AusAID on a future agreement, Armstrong met with the new Parliamentary Secretary for the Minister for Foreign Affairs, Kathy Sullivan. She had met volunteers in the field and was enthusiastic about the AVA program. OSB presented to her the case for multi-year funding, requesting:

- a commitment from the Australian government to the continuation of the AVA program
- guaranteed three-year rolling funding with annual negotiation of the third year's funds
- a separate budget line and an exemption from compulsory competitive tendering arrangements based on the special relationship which had endured for more than 30 years and the 1996 review finding that the program was managed effectively and efficiently
- increased funding to support higher numbers of volunteers in the field (1,000 in 2000–1)
- recognition that the geographical spread of AVA should be wider than Australia's official development cooperation agenda.[68]

The Committee decided to develop a business plan against which managers could report, proposing to bring together the *Strategic Directions* document, the business plan and the budget at the May 1998 Committee meeting.[69] They focused on the respective roles of Committee, CEO and senior staff, clarifying that the Committee's responsibilities were governance and legal liability and included employing the CEO, determining strategic directions, values and vision, and representing the organisation. The staff were responsible for strategic planning, developing and managing programs, implementing new ideas, promotion and marketing, and reporting to stakeholders. OSB staff and the Committee shared responsibility for "defending the faith" and opening doors. It was agreed that Committee meetings needed to focus more on goals and that the Committee would attend to its composition.[70]

Two significant events had an impact on OSB's relationship with government in the first half of 1998. In May the Prime Minister announced a $10 million initiative to place 500 young Australians over two years in the Asia-Pacific region. The Australian Youth Ambassadors for Development (AYAD) was to be managed by a team within AusAID, with delivery of program components to be put out to open tender, thus ignoring OSB's experience with TAYAP and effectively creating a competitive environment where previously OSB had enjoyed a strategic monopoly. In late April OSB received the first draft of a new contract that indicated that OSB was to be a service provider to government, and that the government-funded volunteer program would be tied to the objectives of the government's bilateral aid program, requiring OSB to report against these objectives for every placement. OSB resisted where it could, proposing many changes to the draft.[71]

New agreement

A revised agreement for the Overseas Voluntary Technical Assistance (OVTA) program was signed on 7 August 1998 to provide for the next five years. The Commonwealth's aim remained to provide funding for a "voluntary technical assistance program" through the AVA program and, as OSB had the relevant expertise, AusAID agreed to accept OSB's offer to provide services for the AVA program.[72] The contract obliged OSB to provide an annual work plan, deposit the funds in a separate bank account, and to obtain all approvals and authorisations required from the developing countries. AusAID required a medium-term strategy by the end of 1998, setting out AVA program objectives and strategies in accordance with the priorities of the Commonwealth's aid program, which included contributing to poverty reduction and improving sustainable development. The contract specified cash accounting be used, but allowed for rent for OSB buildings and facilities to be applied. As in the umbrella agreement, OSB was required to acknowledge Commonwealth funding in all public communications and seek AusAID comment on any communication critical of the Commonwealth's role in the project. OSB owned the intellectual property it created and gave AusAID licence to use it. Countries eligible to benefit included 13 in Africa and Palestine, but excluded Latin America where OSB could operate using its own funds if it chose to. The first EOL, also signed on 7 August, further acknowledged that OSB had run the AVA program, Australia's largest voluntary technical assistance program, for over 30 years, on a partnership principle that brought benefits for volunteers and for host communities. The OVTA program budget to be managed by OSB was set at $9.783 million for 1998/99.

OSB continued with its broad focus. Project Partners had submitted eight bids/proposals in the first quarter, but was operating in deficit and recognised that to would take three years to remedy this. A major expansion was planned for People Prepared to increase its income by 71% to $853,000. The Committee was revising and updating the company's articles, whereby OSB would remain a company limited by guarantee and introduce a Council of up to 50, including all current Committee Members and patrons, which would elect a President and Deputy President, meet annually and receive reports from a Board elected by Council, but would have no policy or administrative function.[73]

Work had continued on the strategic framework for 1998–2002, *Putting People First*, which included re-examining and reframing OSB's purpose: "OSB aims to contribute to a peaceful and just world by fostering cross-cultural relationships and international understanding between people; and by participating in the social and economic development of communities".

OSB remained caught in its existential dilemma; it railed against the prevailing economic orthodoxy, but was committed to becoming a significant player in the paradigm it opposed. It envisaged developing more people-to-people links involving government, business and the wider community. It reiterated some of the key messages of *Future Directions*, declaring human development to be OSB's principal concern, and upholding experiential learning as the key to people's growth and action for change.

The Public Affairs Unit had generated significant media coverage about volunteers and their experiences, particularly on metropolitan and national radio and in the press, including feature articles in news magazines. These colourful stories were easy to place, but achieving traction for recognition of the organisation was difficult because of its rather dated name. Despite concerted efforts to promote the name over four years, its recognition actually declined.[74] An investigation of the organisation's name recommended that Australian Volunteers International (AVI) be adopted as its new name,[75] which happened when a new constitution was adopted in April 1999. Professor Bob Meyenn, who had been a volunteer in the Solomon Islands and was Dean of Education at Charles Sturt University was elected Chair of the newly constituted Board, and jurist and former governor-general, Sir Ninian Stephen, became the first President of the AVI Council.

People Prepared had developed a plan for recruitment services through 1998/99–2000/01. Recruitments for overseas positions (for OSB/AVI-managed projects and external clients) were set to increase from 90 to 146. Remote Recruiting planned to increase its recruitments from 40 to 80 over the three years. One thousand interested and qualified people registered for consideration. People Prepared's training services were also finding new markets. In the last quarter of 1998, 12 briefings were conducted for corporate clients, and training services were provided to BHP's Global

Leadership Program. For Qantas and Ford Motor Company, OSB was the preferred provider, and Crown Worldwide Relocations, with whom AustraliaWide had an agreement, identified OSB as their preferred cross-cultural trainer and briefing provider.[76]

Eight months after introducing the OVTA agreement, AusAID announced its intention to negotiate a replacement. As the new contract arrangements were to include a statement of aims and strategies, the medium-term strategy was no longer required. The annual work plan was also no longer relevant, as new arrangements would include changes in price, reporting and payments.[77] The new agreement set an agreed price per volunteer per year, which included management fees, risk factors and inflation. Based on an assumed distribution of placements (46% to Asia, 36% to the Pacific Islands and Papua New Guinea and 18% to Africa), the agreed price was $25,300. In line with changes across all Commonwealth agencies, budgeting and reporting was now accrual-based. AusAID had developed a performance information framework that required all activities and programs to have "meaningful and measurable performance indicators" from July 1999, which were to be achieved by compiling a table of volunteers who had returned for each key result area (sector), specifying their name, country, placement objective and achievement rating.[78] Variation in the price could be proposed if there had been a variation in the regional split of more than 5% over six months. The OVTA budget for 1999/2000 was $9.959 million.[79]

It was inevitable that the assumptions underlying the price mechanism would prove unsustainable. In March 2001, AVI sought an increase in the agreed price to $28,600. African placements remained on target at 18%, despite the withdrawal from Zimbabwe in May 2000 because of intractable civil and political unrest. Placements in the Pacific Islands and Papua New Guinea were down to 28.1% compared to the target of 36%, volunteers had to be withdrawn because of civil and political unrest in the Solomon Islands, and continuing political uncertainty in Fiji had reduced program opportunities. Asian placements had expanded, largely because of an increase in volunteers in East Timor, where volunteer assignments were twice as expensive because living conditions necessitated short-term assignments. Furthermore, the value of the Australian dollar had dropped by 25% since the commencement of the revised contract.[80]

Conscious that the OVTA contract was to expire in June 2003, Armstrong (whose contract as CEO had been extended to June 2002)[81] was anxious that discussions of its extension should begin and sent a proposal to AusAID Director-General, Bruce Davis, in August 2001.[82] He pointed out that, in addition to the $10.8 million funding AVI would receive for OVTA in 2001/02, an estimated $8.2 million was expected to implement other AusAID-funded projects involving volunteers. Altogether this involved more than 1,000 postings in the financial year. Armstrong proposed a memorandum of understanding to confirm the relationship between the Australian government and the Australian community regarding the Australian volunteer program and to recognise the expanded possibilities. He argued for an overarching contract as a framework for specific programs and services, including OVTA, specialist voluntary technical assistance, such as the Pacific Technical Assistance Facility (PACTAF) and Staffing Assistance Program for East Timor (SAPET),[83] volunteer roles in bilateral projects managed by Australian Managing Contractors, and volunteers in multi-lateral projects and programs. He argued for an outputs style contract, such as the PACTAF/SAPET contracts, where management fees were agreed upfront and actual operational costs were reimbursed, adding that, since 1967, AVI had managed 40 projects funded by AusAID.

Davis supported the idea of a strategic alliance with a broad new contractual arrangement and sent his Deputy, Charles Tapp, who had joined AusAID from CARE early in 2000, to meet with AVI in Melbourne late in 2001.[84] Tapp acknowledged the need to revise the current contract but explained that the AusAID Executive would not be able to focus on a broad agreement until the end of March 2002. He proposed that the OVTA contract be amended to address increases in recruitment costs and the need to increase the number of volunteers to achieve the months required. His aim was to have the amendment ready by February 2002 and for it to carry through to the original contract's end in June 2003.[85]

These changes were not made and the increased cost of volunteers forced AVI to suspend volunteer placement in 2002. By this stage the percentage of AVI's income derived from sources other than OVTA funding had risen to 44%, compared to 28% in 1998/99.[86] Meetings were held and negotiations continued between senior AVI staff and AusAID through the first half of 2002, but it was clear that AusAID had no intention of agreeing to any new arrangements until a new CEO was in place at AVI, after Armstrong's extended contract had ended. AusAID's concern that AVI's costs were excessive became apparent through the protracted negotiations, prompting David Penman to encourage AusAID to review AVI's operations at the earliest opportunity and end unfounded speculation.[87]

Between 1991 and 2002, AVI devised and implemented successive strategic plans to keep pace with changing circumstances, while preserving and defending its original principles and core activities. As it did so, AVI was transformed into a much larger organisation with a broad range of activities and with considerable influence and widespread credibility. Its expenditure grew from $4.8 million in 1990/91, when there were 365 volunteers, to over $20 million in 2001/02, when the number of volunteers exceeded 1,000. It had a new name, a new constitution, a Board of Directors and a Council, and it had more than 100 committed and experienced staff. It had negotiated formal memoranda of understanding with the governments of the expanded list of countries where it worked on diverse programs and services, and had concluded an industrial agreement with the Australian Services Union.

Bill Armstrong's leadership through these 12 years had been a crucial factor in AVI's success. He lived and breathed the organisation's ethos, while enjoying the respect of the NGO sector, as President of ACFOA from 1994 to 1997, and of AusAID staff and executives. The mood and environment in AusAID steadily changed through the 1990s, especially under the influence of Foreign Affairs Minister, Alexander Downer. Neo-liberal thinking had taken root in government circles in the late 1980s, but it was in the 1990s that it overwhelmed government thinking. A fundamental suspicion of NGOs and a determination to keep them out of policy debates crept in, leaving no room for the old-style government–NGO partnership; the procurement of services had to be competitive and value-free. Gone were the days when AusAID officers, faced with awkward circumstances, would shepherd OSB to areas where funding was more plentiful or secure. Furthermore, in the new environment of AusAID a line of thought had emerged that considered AVI too strong and too privileged – as a protected species that needed to toughen up and face competition. Bringing AVI to heel was never going to be easy while the esteemed Armstrong was CEO, a fact that AusAID acknowledged by using delaying tactics to render him ineffective in his last year of office.

PART III

Development in Practice: Selected Programs (1980s–90s)

CHAPTER 6

Indochina: Working in Times of Transition

The destruction and genocide wrought by the Khmer Rouge in Cambodia was not fully revealed to the world until after the regime had been overthrown early in 1979 by the Vietnamese military. Although there was no disputing the scale of the killing and the intensity of human rights abuse perpetrated by Pol Pot and his Khmer Rouge colleagues, the Australian government's political response to the genocide was not equally clear. Against the advice of Foreign Minister Andrew Peacock and his department, Prime Minister Malcolm Fraser insisted that the Australian government continue to recognise Pol Pot's regime, condemned the Vietnamese invasion and occupation of Cambodia, and suspended Australian aid to Vietnam. The Australian government's overriding concern at this time was not to cause offence to the United States or to the Association of Southeast Asian Nations (ASEAN).

The Australian government's position on Cambodia did not change when a Labor government was elected in 1983. What was different, however, was that Foreign Minister Bill Hayden participated very actively in diplomatic efforts to resolve the diplomatic imbroglio. He travelled in the region, meeting formally and informally with the various parties and bringing them all, except the Khmer Rouge, together at seminars and even floating the idea of an international war crimes tribunal.[1] ACFOA proposed to Hayden that NGO channels be used for official aid to Vietnam and Cambodia using BINGO (Bilateral NGO) grants.[2] The Australian government took up this option and used NGO funding as a way of maintaining contact with the Cambodian regime through the difficult conflict resolution process until the United Nations Transitional Authority in Cambodia (UNTAC) was put in place in February 1992, following the Paris peace accord in October 1991.[3]

In this political context, OSB sought opportunities to engage with Indochina in the early 1980s. OSB's staff and Committee had been opposed, with varying levels of intensity, to Australia's military involvement in the Vietnam war and was keen to be involved in post-war development in Vietnam, Laos and Cambodia, all of which had been deeply affected by the conflict. The organisation's combined objectives of providing assistance, building relationships, knowledge, and understanding seemed particularly appropriate, but doors needed to be opened. The opportunity came when ACFOA sent a month-long goodwill mission to the three countries of Indochina in June 1985. As well as conveying goodwill, the delegation was to identify NGO projects and collect information for community education purposes in Australia. The delegation was led by Graham Alliband, National Director of Australian Freedom From Hunger Campaign (AFFHC) and formerly a Foreign Affairs official at the Australian Embassy in Hanoi when Australia suspended its aid to Vietnam. He was accompanied by staff from ACFOA, Save the Children Fund Australia (SCFA), World Vision Australia, and the author, representing OSB.

Laos

The first country visited was the Lao People's Democratic Republic where the Australian Embassy had helped arrange meetings with ministries, multilateral organisations and the extremely small international NGO community. The delegation was received at the Ministries of Health, Agriculture and Education, mainly by their Vice-Ministers, who were very forthcoming, in some cases even arranging additional meetings for delegation members to follow up their lines of inquiry. United Nations agencies were well represented in Vientiane and presented detailed briefs on the extent of the need and opportunities for development assistance. They also emphasised the frustrations of working in a country with poorly developed infrastructure and communication systems, where political formation and correctness took precedence over economic and social progress. The staff of United Nations specialised agencies and international NGOs cited these factors as reasons why the Lao were unlikely to be interested in foreign volunteers.

We found, to the contrary, that some Lao officials were very interested in the prospect of assistance from foreign volunteers. Many of them had extensive exposure to technical assistance and training programs from Eastern bloc countries. The training offered in these programs had often missed the mark; for example, Lao had qualified as railway engineers in East Germany after years of study, knowing that Laos had no railway system. Soviet advisers had often displayed the same discourtesy, ignorance or arrogance as the worst Western advisers in other countries. The Lao had also had positive encounters with United Nations Volunteers (UNV) in a range of specialisations, although there had been very few of them. Drawing from these experiences, the Lao officials commented that volunteers were better to work with than advisers because they didn't mind working and staying with the people. Australia was invited to be part of an expanded UNV program and was also asked to consider providing specialist teachers of English as a foreign language to the teachers college and other Institutes. The officials also showed an early interest in nurse educators.

OSB pursued these ideas immediately and by January 1986 had recruited an Australian civil servant with experience in international development programs to work within the United Nations Development Program (UNDP) to oversee the expansion of the UNV program in Laos. By 1990 nine AVA volunteers had been placed in Laos, mostly in government institutions.

Vietnam

In Vietnam, the delegation was hosted by AIDRECEP, an agency of the Communist Party of Vietnam formed in 1977 to coordinate all aid from countries other than Eastern bloc countries, whether multilateral, bilateral, or NGO. The delegation's visit to Vietnam preceded the Doi Moi economic reforms initiated in 1986, which shifted the country towards a market economy and eventually brought about some relaxation in social regulation and interaction. The visit was highly organised and tightly structured and the delegation was fully escorted to every meeting. It was clear that the drivers assigned to the delegation were people of prestige and authority, presumably from being trusted as drivers during the war. Very little English was spoken and French was used reluctantly, so the delegation was totally dependent on the AIDRECEP interpreters. Because of the language issue, it was immediately apparent that if Australian volunteers were assigned to Vietnam their interaction with Vietnamese colleagues would be stilted at best, and given the social and political milieu, any fraternisation would be an awkward prospect.

Fraternisation was, however, a compulsory and highly organised component of the ACFOA delegation's schedule in Vietnam. AIDRECEP determinedly demonstrated Vietnamese hospitality, of which alcohol consumption was a very large part. After a day in Thanh Tri District, not far from Hanoi, visiting clinics, livestock production and women's union activities, dinner was a formal occasion with toasts repeatedly proposed and celebrated. At one point the Vice-Chairman of the People's Committee demanded to know why one of the Australian delegation was not drinking the toasts. The delegate explained that drinking alcohol was against his religion – an unsatisfactory explanation as far as the Vice-Chairman was concerned and he immediately retorted: "A man who doesn't drink is like a flag that doesn't fly!" On other occasions, the after-hours discussions were less formal and often turned to where people had been during the war. Two interesting things arose in these discussions. One was the number of women who had been military commanders and now had significant positions in the Party; the other was the respect they expressed for Australian soldiers, as if good fighters were worthy enemies.

It quickly became evident that the skill in high demand that Australian volunteers could bring to Vietnam was the teaching of English as a foreign language (TEFL). The first highly experienced TEFL teacher was placed later that year, commencing a major theme in OSB's work in Vietnam. Once the Doi Moi reforms were in place and Vietnam wanted to open its economy up to the world, the training of English-language teachers who could teach effectively in schools became a priority for OSB project work, with financial support from AIDAB.

Cambodia

With no scheduled passenger flights between Ho Chi Minh City and Phnom Penh, the delegation flew in a Hercules chartered by the Red Cross and configured for transporting supplies. In Cambodia there was no Australian Embassy and no officials in the Cambodian government to coordinate our visit. The Vietnamese presence was evident, but as a political and military strength that did not extend to technical aspects of service delivery. Government departments only functioned with assistance from international NGOs. The delegation put together a schedule of meetings and visits by requesting transport and other logistical assistance from these NGOs. Because the Khmer Rouge were still attacking roads and railways, the distance we could travel from Phnom Penh was severely limited, and a strict night-time curfew in Phnom Penh was policed by military checkpoints.

The delegation met many Cambodian leaders and aid workers who were in Phnom Penh at high-level diplomatic receptions. The key meeting was undoubtedly with Hun Sen, Prime Minister and Foreign Minister of the People's Republic of Kampuchea. In a long and broad-ranging discussion he referred to his recent three-hour meeting with Australian Foreign Minister Bill Hayden, clarifying that it had been an "accidental meeting" which they had initially intended keeping secret until Hayden insisted on making it public. Hun Sen was quick to support the idea of having Australian volunteers in Cambodia, even suggesting that Australian technicians bring their own equipment so they would not have to grapple with confusing Soviet equipment. He suggested that it would be very useful for Australian NGOs to have an office in Phnom Penh, adding that he understood from his meeting with Hayden that Australian NGOs were the Australian government's "back door" through which it would provide assistance; he expressed confidence that Australian volunteers could come through that back door too.[4]

Cambodia's particular challenges

The ACFOA delegation's visit to Vietnam, Laos and Cambodia significantly boosted our knowledge and awareness of conditions in all three countries and stimulated agency programming in each of them. Cambodia was the most problematic, as conflict persisted, traumatising the population and inhibiting the functioning of any infrastructure or communication system. It was diplomatically isolated and Australia had no representative there. Aid agencies wanting to commence operations needed logistical and communication assistance within the country to operate, which accentuated difference amongst agencies. Agencies from Australia that were part of an international organisational framework or alliance had access to the resources of their international colleagues. World Vision was already established with an international staff that included Australians; Australian Catholic Relief (ACR) worked through their European counterpart Coopération Internationale pour le Développement et la Solidarité (CIDSE); Community Aid Abroad (CAA) was able to work through Oxfam; and the Australian Quakers through the American Friends Service Committee. Other agencies, mostly secular home-grown Australian organisations such as AFFHC, OSB, Australian People for Health, Education and Development Abroad (APHEDA, the Australian Council of Trade Unions' aid organisation) and

SCFA, were left to make their own arrangements and began talking with each other about working together. AFFHC, APHEDA and SCFA raised in ACFOA's Indo-China Sub-Committee the notion of jointly engaging a project administrator who could also act as a representative in Phnom Penh. By October 1985 it was clear the Australian government would support the idea, but APHEDA and AFFHC could do nothing further until January 1986, when they planned to request government funding for it as part of their Cambodia program costs.

OSB's unique style of collaboration meant it was quite accustomed to operating without in-country offices, relying instead on staff travelling from Melbourne to negotiate arrangements and to support volunteers. In the countries where it operated, OSB relied on relationships it had established with partner organisations, which were the volunteers' employers and, as such, were expected to exercise the rights and responsibilities of employers. However, it was clear that OSB would not be able to operate in its usual way in Cambodia. It could not expect to identify local employers with the necessary level of professional confidence and management experience. Furthermore, domestic, regional and international communications and logistics were extremely difficult. Consequently, in November 1985 OSB indicated its interest in being part of the Joint Australian NGO Office (JANGOO) arrangement, joining its management committee and taking on the financial commitment involved.[5] The Australian government saw the advantages of having unofficial Australian representation in Phnom Penh as a symbol of Australia's interest in Cambodia, a source of information, and a way of conveying messages, and made the JANGOO possible by supporting the agencies involved.

Joint Australian NGO Office in Cambodia

Jennifer Ashton was JANGOO's first administrator and as the only staff member she had a particularly complex role to play. As intended, the office represented the four Australian agencies in Cambodia, liaising with both the Cambodian Government and an increasing number of international NGOs in Phnom Penh. To give an example of how this worked for OSB, in late 1987 Ashton passed on to OSB a request she had received from the Ministry of Foreign Affairs' Department of Asia and Australia. It was a fairly detailed request for veterinary assistance at chicken and pig farms belonging to the Municipality of Phnom Penh, which needed advice and training on breeding stock, animal production and vaccines. She visited the municipal farms to meet the request's initiators and was able to verify from other sources that the municipality and its farms were viable entities to work with. An Australian veterinarian with relevant experience was recruited in January 1988, who before long had acquired new poultry in Thailand as breeding stock, flying back to Phnom Penh with the birds in the seats next to him.

Also in November, Ashton sent to OSB an account of her meeting with the Minister of Culture to discuss the nomination of a very experienced ethnomusicologist to meet a request that a visiting Cambodian delegation had initially discussed with OSB in Melbourne. Many in the NGO community were disparaging of this idea as they saw no relationship between culture and development, and dismissed it as irrelevant in Cambodia's straitened circumstances. The Minister, however, was very clear about the importance of rebuilding the artistic and spiritual dimensions of life as well as the material. The Khmer Rouge had destroyed cultural artefacts and knowledge along with physical infrastructure and crops. As life after Khmer Rouge domination became more tolerable, there was a spontaneous explosion of dance troupes in some parts of Cambodia, which set for the Ministry the huge task of researching, documenting and training in Khmer cultural forms. The Minister was insistent that the ethnomusicologist under discussion would be very valuable, but strongly advised that the role be described as documenting and writing, warning that any mention of teaching would raise suspicions in the Ministry of the Interior who would have to approve the submission.[6] The permissions were successfully navigated and the ethnomusicologist went to Cambodia at the same time as the veterinarian.

JANGOO as unofficial embassy

With its establishment in July 1986, JANGOO was the first ongoing Australian presence in Cambodia since the Khmer Rouge had seized power in 1975. It therefore made perfect sense for JANGOO to act as an unofficial embassy, or at least to discharge some of the functions normally associated with diplomatic missions. The consular role of looking out for Australians was one such function; another was analysis and reporting. As early as March 1987, Hayden had indicated his interest in receiving reports from JANGOO on the situation in Cambodia. The management committee decided that the first report would be on the food situation in Cambodia and the second would be on the political situation.[7] Ashton was providing services to an increasing range of stakeholders. When she visited Australia in September–October 1987 she had meetings with each of the four agencies collaborating in JANGOO, two in Sydney and two in Melbourne. She attended the annual ACFOA Council meeting and the ACTU's Annual Congress, and separately briefed AIDAB and the Department of Foreign Affairs and Trade in Canberra.

The AIDAB/NGO Co-operation Program had a rolling program of project review visits to countries where AIDAB was funding the work of Australian NGOs. In October 1987, Vietnam was to be reviewed, but this review had a wider regional remit. For this review Bill Armstrong was the NGO representative and Geoff Leach was the AIDAB officer. As official Australian government aid to Vietnam was still suspended, Australian government funds were channelled through multilateral organisations and the NGOs. They commented that, although the NGOs were making a significant contribution, there was a need for large-scale investment in infrastructure that was beyond the scope of NGOs in terms of the scale and expertise required.

The review team's greatest concern, however, related to the uncertainty of political reconciliation in Cambodia. Looking forward, they envisaged two scenarios, both of them problematic, which they outlined in their report:

> In 1990 without a political settlement there is no doubt that either the present government will require to equip itself far better in order to fight the Khmer Rouge or the Vietnamese will need to remain and continue to protect the Kampuchean people, thus risking the refusal of the rest of the world to recognize Kampuchea. On the other hand, if a political and military solution is found which enables Kampuchea to confidently move ahead, it is likely there will be such a massive response and injection of international aid both multilateral and bilateral so as to swamp the country and possibly cause incredible dislocation to the people.[8]

They were right in their forecast about the impact of overwhelming aid, although it probably took longer to reach that point than they had anticipated. By the end of 1989, JANGOO was channelling the largest bilateral aid program in the country, both in terms of the range of activities and expenditure.[9]

In the circumstances of Cambodia's political and diplomatic isolation and with Australia taking on a more pro-active role, JANGOO had become indispensable. To discharge this central concern effectively required particularly skilled and flexible diplomatic talent. Furthermore, the increasing volume of work in identifying projects, building relationships and managing communication lines with ministries, departments and other organisations called for more resources than JANGOO had at hand. JANGOO's management committee agreed that Alliband would assess the staffing needs of the office, and each of the four agencies provided him with their requirements.[10] The Administrator's role was advertised in August 1988 in time for a handover in Phnom Penh from November ahead of a 1 January 1989 start. It was significant and symbolic that the new Administrator, Lyndall McLean, took leave from Australia's Department of Foreign Affairs to take up the appointment. She was known to many of the JANGOO committee from her time as Chargé d'Affaires in the Australian Embassy in Hanoi at the time of the ACFOA delegation's visit in 1985.

Motor vehicles were scarce in Phnom Penh in 1985. Morning scene at Central Market. Photo Peter Britton

Veterinarian Peter Frecklington with the Deputy Manager of Tokthla Chicken Farm, Phnom Penh, c.1988. Courtesy AVI

Left

Ethnomusicologist Bill Lobban in the workshop of the Fine Arts School in Phnom Penh, c.1989. Courtesy AVI

Below

Bill Armstrong visits OSB's Forestry Project in Vietnam with Australian Ambassador, Graham Alliband, 1990. Courtesy AVI

Left

Joan Healy, community development worker at Krom Akphiwat Krom, Battambang, 1995. Photo Bill Armstrong

Below

Archivist Peter Arfanis with a colleague at Cambodia's Council of Ministers, August 1999. Photo Andy Eames. Courtesy AVI

Penny Everingham, agroforester, with a colleague at Cambodia's Forestry Department, August 1999. Photo Andy Eames. Courtesy AVI

Michelle Hart demonstrates digital map-making at Hanoi's Research Training Centre for Community Development, July 2002. Photo Will Salter. Courtesy AVI

Optimism, concern and advocacy

In ACFOA's Indo-China Sub-Committee in 1989 there was a growing consensus that a settlement of Cambodia's military and political turmoil might be possible and, therefore, greater optimism about the possibility that bilateral aid from Western governments could commence. In this context Australian NGOs had begun to air three major concerns. As Armstrong and Leach had indicated in the report of their visit to Vietnam in 1987, there were doubts about the ability of Cambodian Ministries and Departments to absorb a sudden influx of aid, as they lacked experience in determining their own priorities and the skills in dealing with bilateral aid managers. The Australian NGOs thought they had a responsibility to lay the foundations for a future bilateral aid program and believed they should continue to play a role in that bilateral program once it began.[11]

The momentum was certainly growing and was visible enough to attract comment from the *Far Eastern Economic Review* in its report on Australia's move to soften its line on not dealing with the Vietnamese-backed government in Phnom Penh. The report used as evidence two visits by a Hanoi-based Australian diplomat and a visit by AIDAB, and Australian NGO contacts with Australian firms investigating opportunities to conduct business in Cambodia.[12]

Armstrong had long been a strong voice for peace and a persistent critic of the Australian government's apparent tolerance of the Khmer Rouge's presence in the internationally recognised Coalition Government of Democratic Kampuchea. In mid-1989 he renewed his attack, railing against the failure of Western governments to act against China's arming of the Khmer Rouge, thus enabling the survival of the force responsible for two million deaths between 1975 and 1979. Now that Vietnam had undertaken to withdraw its troops by September 1989, he argued, it was all the more important to deny the Khmer Rouge any diplomatic or military support.[13] A few days later he argued that Australia's support for including the Khmer Rouge, still a well-organised force along the Thai–Cambodian border, in an interim coalition was too dangerous, even if Pol

Pot and his cronies were excluded. He pointed out that the Australian aid community was fully aware of the need to integrate the 40,000–50,000 Khmer Rouge fighters and their families back into Cambodian society, but this depended on disarming Khmer Rouge soldiers and removing them from the control of the commanders who had been responsible for the killing fields.[14]

McLean's report in November 1989 was not reassuring, but it was also not alarmist: "Curfews have been reintroduced. Pailin has definitely fallen. Prices of food items are skyrocketing. A draft evacuation plan exists. Things are tense but there is a confidence that the Hun Sen Government will be able to resist the Khmer Rouge".[15]

JANGOO was a remarkable example of four agencies collaborating successfully at both operational and management levels. Those outside the non-government development sector have often expressed surprise at the ferocity of competition between agencies, especially when fundraising was involved. Among them is renowned journalist and film-maker John Pilger, who returned to Cambodia in 1989 to make a new documentary *Cambodia: Year Ten*, as a sequel to his 1979 documentary, *Year Zero: The Silent Death of Cambodia.* It was shown on Australian commercial television in November 1989, and Pilger had asked that it be followed with an appeal for funds to be directed to the four agencies involved in JANGOO. In a masterpiece of unprincipled marketing World Vision used the screening to broadcast their fund-raising advertisements. After negotiations with World Vision, the JANGOO management committee settled on dividing the funds raised among all five agencies.[16]

In mid-1990, communications from McLean to JANGOO's constituent agencies covered a range of issues. One was a constant theme – the importance of lobbying the Australian government to challenge the Coalition Government of Democratic Kampuchea seat at the United Nations and to recognise the Hun Sen government. A new issue had also emerged relating to the need for a mechanism to coordinate international NGOs in Cambodia, as there were now 34 agencies. A Cooperation Committee for Cambodia (CCC) had been proposed which presented the dilemma of whether to register with the proposed committee as JANGOO or as four separate agencies.[17]

OSB's response to fellow JANGOO members was that the CCC as proposed was configured purely to meet the needs of the foreign agencies and made no reference to linking with the Cambodian government. There was no evidence the proposal had even been discussed with the government, let alone any recognition that the Cambodian government had a legitimate interest and right to coordinate the activities of foreign NGOs.[18] This was symptomatic of an attitude in the NGO community in Cambodia that persisted for at least another decade and probably derived from the early NGO experiences in Cambodia, when NGO resources and budgets far exceeded those of the Cambodian government and its agencies. It also seemed to reflect an attitude that as non-state actors they had more moral authority than the state.

Australian government aid and the role of NGOs

There were real fears that, after years of building their experience in Cambodia and delivering assistance that was appropriate and appreciated, NGOs would be pushed aside as bilateral programs were planned and implemented. OSB's fears were realised at the end of 1990 when AIDAB informed OSB that funding for its English Language Training (ELT) programs in Cambodia and Vietnam would cease. AIDAB did not want to commit to a three-year program when it was likely that it would need to include an English language focus as its bilateral program developed.[19] Graham Alliband, who had returned to diplomatic service in 1988 when he was appointed Australia's Ambassador to Vietnam, confirmed that he had recommended new funding for OSB's existing programs, but had not been told that it would cease.[20] AIDAB agreed to reconsider its decision on the Vietnam ELT program, but only after telephone calls and representation from the Vietnamese Ministry of Education in Hanoi. They recognised that it was unlikely a new bilateral English language capacity could be put in place before the end of 1991 and that it was better to avoid a lull by proceeding with the workshops OSB had planned for 1991.[21]

By April 1991, funding had been approved for a program for ELT specialists to work in Vietnam for two years. They would conduct two six-week summer vacation workshops in Hanoi for senior secondary school teachers and pre-workshop orientation courses for volunteer tutors and counterparts who were to assist in the program. Four experienced TEFL teachers joined OSB's ELT consultant, Barbara Mullock, to conduct the workshop series from July to September. AIDAB also reinstated the Cambodian English language project, which was not to build teachers' capacity to teach English but was a niche project to teach English to senior Cambodian officials so that they could communicate more effectively with international representatives. Beginning in September 1991, it drew on OSB's experience in teaching English to high-ranking Communist Party members in Vietnam.[22]

Hopes for any improvement in Cambodia's situation were very much pinned on the push for a United Nations intervention, initiated and advocated for by Australian Foreign Minister, Gareth Evans. Negotiations to bring this about were intense and those involved benefited considerably from the experience and know-how of Lyndall McLean, the well-regarded diplomat who had taken leave to run the JANGOO office.[23] McLean was also directly engaged in planning to re-establish an official Australian presence in Cambodia, where she subsequently resumed official diplomatic service. She also assisted with arrangements for the Australian contingent in United Nations Advance Mission in Cambodia (UNAMIC) in October 1991.[24]

John Holloway, Deputy Director-General of AIDAB and OSB Committee member, became Australia's Ambassador to Cambodia, arriving in Phnom Penh in November 1991. He was preceded in October by OSB senior staff member, David Penman, who was to establish an official presence for OSB, initially sharing an office with the British and New Zealand volunteer organisations, VSO and VSA. In recognition of Armstrong's leadership on the Cambodia issue, ACFOA nominated him as the NGO Adviser to Minister Evans in the Australian Delegation to the Ministerial Planning Conference on the Rehabilitation and Reconstruction of Cambodia in Tokyo in June 1992.

Laos and Vietnam: ongoing programs

OSB's programs in Indochina largely followed the path set during its first visit as part of the ACFOA delegation in 1985. In Laos, a reasonably diverse volunteer program was developed. Between 1986 and 1995, 43 volunteers took up their assignments. The teaching of English dominated, but other placements required volunteers with experience in knowledge management, income generation, and even agricultural production. Almost all were located in or close to Vientiane and all were in ministries, other state institutions or organisations affiliated with the Lao People's Revolutionary Party.

In Vietnam, the volunteer program was much more substantial, with 107 volunteers between 1986 and 1995. Apart from two small projects in agroforestry and midwifery training, all assignments related to English language teaching. Some placements were designed to upgrade the English language skills of officials in government departments or institutes, who needed English for specific purposes in a variety of professional or technical areas. The vast majority of OSB's activity was concentrated in teacher training programs, both pre-service and in-service. OSB engaged some highly experienced ELT professionals, former volunteers who had gone on to become experts in applied linguistics. They worked with the Ministry of Education to determine how to bring maximum benefit to schoolchildren, without withdrawing teachers from classroom service and taking into account teachers' already substantial out-of-hours commitments and transport difficulties.

A training package was developed for delivery in full-time intensive workshops during the summer vacation. It focused on upgrading both the English language proficiency and the pedagogical skills of

Vietnamese teachers of English throughout Vietnam. All sessions modelled communicative, student-centred learning and teaching strategies. The 1990 Summer School workshop program, which AIDAB was initially reluctant to fund, was enthusiastically received and generated additional demand from the Vietnamese Ministry of Education for more and progressively larger programs over the next four years.

Cambodia in transition

The process of transition in Cambodia presented new opportunities for OSB and the volunteer program. OSB was the point of entry for Australians into the UNV program and was therefore well placed to respond when in 1992 UNV called for volunteers to work with UNTAC. Some of the UNV roles were as electoral officers in district centres helping to prepare for and administer the election planned for May 1993; one of the volunteers, a retired Australian judge, ended up working with UNTAC as their Human Rights Assistant.

As part of the 1991 comprehensive settlement process, approximately 370,000 Cambodian refugees were to be repatriated from camps along the Thai–Cambodia border and resettled. In an environment where the Khmer Rouge had been neither effectively contained nor disarmed, the repatriation and resettlement exposed those involved to extreme risk. Even logistically it was a complex exercise, and there were no Khmer speakers in the United Nations force. The United Nations High Commissioner for Refugees (UNHCR), which had carriage of this operation, contracted OSB to recruit Khmer-speaking Australians and 11 Cambodian Australians were found to work for UNHCR as interpreters, radio operators and in other positions. The first five recruited from the Australian Khmer community in 1991 were so successful that the project was extended into 1992 and again in 1993. The 11 volunteers were also a conduit for assistance from the Khmer community in Australia. Some of them chose to stay on in Cambodia, newly married to Cambodian women.

In this setting of the movement of peoples in 1992, OSB began its involvement in a remarkable community development project based on the activities of Joan Healy, a Josephite nun who had been working in a Cambodian refugee camp known as Site 2. In the badlands along the Thai–Cambodia border, the various camps were under the control of different political military groups. Only Khao-I-Dang was controlled by UNHCR; it was never attacked, was relatively safe, and refugees there could be eligible for third country resettlement. None of these characteristics applied to the Khmer Rouge-controlled Site 8 or to Site 2, which was controlled by the Khmer People's National Liberation Front led by anti-Communist Son Sann.

In Site 2, Healy forged an effective relationship with health worker Meas Nee which they continued to develop in Battambang.[25] Healy's travel to and work in Cambodia with repatriated Cambodians was supported by OSB, whom Healy, as she crisscrossed the country, kept apprised of what was happening, suggesting ways that volunteers could assist. More returnees settled in Battambang than in any other province and it was a logical centre for international NGOs to establish themselves. Meas Nee spoke English and had had responsibilities in Site 2, giving him skills that he could draw on to find work in Battambang and support his family. Healy and Meas Nee assembled a team that was supplemented by two OSB volunteers, Mal Simmons and Moira O'Leary, community development workers with deep experience as volunteers in Africa and Pacific Island countries.

The OSB project, Rebuilding Local Communities in Battambang Province, enabled the establishment and operation of a local community development organisation over two years from 1993. Given its small budget any purchases for the project had to be decided cooperatively. The first priority was motorbikes so that the team could visit villages in the province, but with no insurance available they deliberately chose underpowered bikes that bandits would despise. They linked a radio transmitter to the UNTAC network for security reasons, with each team member given hand-held two-way radios.[26] The villages selected by the project to work with were very poor and had no other NGO working with them. The villagers had to be willing to work together, regardless of whether they were repatriated returnees or locals or of different political factions. In the run-up to the May 1993 election Khmer Rouge attacks became so frequent that the project team had to suspend their village visits for a while.

The team reached agreement with monks to build a centre in the grounds of a *wat*, registering their organisation as Krom Akphiwat Phum in 1995. After a few years, the organisation had taken root and became renowned for its use of community development approaches in a conflict and post-conflict situation. Meas Nee completed a PhD at Latrobe University in 2000 that analysed social reconstruction in post-conflict situations and continues to be much in demand as an inspirational community development worker, teacher, consultant, manager and leader.

The unusual circumstances presented by the conflict and reconstruction in Cambodia demanded an unusual volunteer program. In summary, OSB initially supported the agencies of a government Australia did not recognise, then played an invaluable role in support of the United Nations administration, before backing an innovative community development project which directly addressed the social trauma of the conflict. It was not until 1996 that OSB's program in Cambodia started to take on the scale and shape of a regular capacity-building program with 16 volunteers from diverse professional backgrounds placed in government departments and state institutions, as well as in foreign and local NGOs.

OSB's non-government status and independent leadership enabled it to play a particularly interesting and valuable role, especially in Vietnam and Cambodia. It went beyond being the Australian government's "back door", as Hayden had described it. Certainly OSB as an Australian organisation and its volunteers who were Australian citizens (or at least residents) were able to participate in activities not supported by Australian policy; it succeeded because of OSB's prowess in establishing relationships and building trust. Teaching English to high-ranking party officials in pre-Doi Moi Hanoi was an exercise that rested principally on high levels of trust and discretion; it was negotiated entirely in non-government channels and was not a project that could be handed to government or private agencies. The same was true of teaching English to senior officials in the Phnom Penh government prior to the international agreement. Even recruiting Khmer-speaking Australians to work in UNHCR required adroit navigation of the deeply divided and politicised Cambodian community in Australia. In Indochina in this era, OSB was able to achieve exceptional results, with the support of the Australian government.

CHAPTER 7

Africa: Working in the Frontline States

From its beginnings the AVA program provided Australians with opportunities to locate themselves in and identify with a decolonising world. In the 1960s many African countries were confident in their newly won independence. They were also aware that colonialism had left them with an inadequate skills base and invited international volunteers to participate in developing their new nations.

In the first three years of the AVA program (1964–66) volunteers went to Tanzania, Nigeria and Zambia. Nigeria had become independent in 1960 and Zambia in 1964, the same year that Tanganyika and Zanzibar came together as Tanzania. Over several decades the AVA program placed dozens of Australian teachers in schools in Tanzania. The programs in Nigeria and Kenya had briefer histories, ceasing in 1971. There was a short flurry of activity in Lesotho in the mid-1970s when four Australian agriculturalists worked with the United Nations Food and Agricultural Organization (FAO). The biggest program was in Botswana where ten volunteers served from January 1970 to December 1979, all but two as teachers or teacher trainers. Throughout the 1970s OSB's programs in Africa were small, and by the end of June 1983 there were six volunteers on assignment in Africa, all of them teachers in Tanzania.[1] By December 1984 the number had fallen to two, but this number was soon to increase dramatically as the organisation's interest and investment in Africa grew.

The optimism expressed in contributing to nation-building in independent countries in Africa was increasingly overshadowed by the realities of South Africa's apartheid regime and its occupation of South West Africa (later Namibia), which had a political and psychological impact on the whole of sub-Saharan Africa, especially in the countries closest to South Africa where apartheid brought violence and immediate physical threat.

Anti-apartheid campaigns

In the 1970s Australians from all walks of life were galvanised by two issues – Australia's participation in the Vietnam War and apartheid. Australians were angry about apartheid. When South Africa's Springbok Rugby Union team toured Australia in 1971, there were widespread protests around the country during which 700 people were arrested and many more injured in clashes with police. In Melbourne, 5,000 protesters faced lines of police with their batons drawn and charging police horses.[2] In Queensland the state government declared a state of emergency.

Churches and unions were deeply involved in the protests, as were NGOs in the aid and development community. The first public campaign that ACFOA launched was about apartheid, following on from the Springbok tour protests of 1971.[3] The immediate target of the anti-apartheid movement's campaigning was the Australian cricket team's tour to South Africa planned for 1972. Churches, unions and others put so much pressure on members of the Australian Cricket Board that its Chairman, Sir Donald Bradman, cancelled the tour, stating that Australia would not play cricket with South Africa while apartheid was in force.[4]

In January 1973 ACFOA organised a development education conference in Canberra. One of a series of conferences funded by the Government, it was designed to examine questions such as the nature of development, how development could be built into country studies and what educational methods would best insert social justice into formal education. That was before a formidable Zimbabwean activist took the podium and turned the conference into an opportunity to confront conference participants with their "complacent racism". Sekai Holland berated her audience for continuing to participate in an exploitative system and denounced their aid as neo-colonial in a remarkable performance that caused those present to speak freely about how deeply and personally it had affected them.[5]

A second ACFOA campaign in 1974 gave rise to the Campaign Against Racial Exploitation (CARE), formally launched by Australian Council of Trade Union leader Bob Hawke in December 1974, which became the dominant anti-apartheid group in Australia thereafter. CARE coordinated the campaigns and lobbied successive Australian governments. Despite Allen Martin's involvement in ACFOA and OSB's origins in asserting and demonstrating racial equality, OSB did not engage in the issue of apartheid. Although individual staff members may have been involved, there was no commentary on the issue in any of the bulletins and newsletters OSB sent to volunteers in the 1970s.

In the 1980s OSB, under Bill Armstrong's directorship, did engage with the issue and it had a substantial impact on the organisation. In 1983 OSB supported CARE, paying an affiliation fee that gave OSB staff access to up-to-date information in CARE's newsletters and bulletins. CARE was instrumental in bringing representatives of both the African National Congress (ANC) and South West African People's Organisation (SWAPO) to Australia and helping them establish offices.[6] The presence of these liberation movements in Australia and OSB's interaction with them changed the way OSB responded to apartheid, which had a direct impact on its programming decisions.

African liberation movements in Australia

In South Africa ANC had gone underground after it was banned in 1960. Outside South Africa it was broadly recognised as representing the otherwise voiceless people of South Africa and some governments accorded it official recognition. ANC sent Sonwabo Edwin (Eddie) Funde to Australia as its representative in Australasia and the Pacific in late 1983.[7] Despite formal requests and considerable lobbying by supporters, the Australian government would not provide any kind of diplomatic privilege, funding or in-kind support to ANC, or to SWAPO when it followed 18 months later. ANC was provided with space in the Sydney Trades Hall and established its mission to Australasia and the Pacific there. The South African Embassy launched an intensive disinformation campaign in the Australian mainstream media, branding ANC as terrorists and forcing Funde into a media offensive.[8]

SWAPO's Head of Women's Affairs in Lusaka and Women's Council Central Committee member, Susan Nghidinwa, visited Australia in 1984.[9] OSB made a donation towards the cost of her visit and hosted her in its offices, where she spoke to all staff on the situation in Namibia and SWAPO's struggle. Following her reports back to SWAPO's headquarters on the state of anti-apartheid activism in Australia, Hadino Hishongwa, a founding member of SWAPO in 1960, arrived in March 1985 as SWAPO's representative in Australia.[10] In September 1985 CARE organised a national conference on Namibia, which OSB attended and supported as a sponsor.

SWAPO received no assistance from the Australian government but, like ANC, depended on crucial support from unions and churches, including the Uniting Church which provided office space in Melbourne. The Uniting Church's strong support for ANC and SWAPO extended to explicit support for armed struggle – a stance that caused many to leave the church.[11] Both the ANC and the SWAPO representatives faced acute financial difficulties and suffered racist attacks, break-ins and robberies. Funde and his family were nearly killed when his home was shot at in 1989 in an attack organised by Jim Saleam, currently the Chairman of the Australia First Party in New South Wales.

Before coming to Australia, both Funde and Hishongwa had been assigned to Sweden where they had enjoyed both official recognition and generous funding and facilities. In Australia, the government allowed the ANC representative to consult with the Department of Foreign Affairs, but not as an official representative of the South African people. SWAPO's standing was slightly higher, but still not official, because Australia had a seat on the United Nations Council for Namibia. Both needed to prioritise fundraising and make good use of in-kind support. Funde received valuable administrative support from APHEDA (the Australian Council of Trade Unions' international development organisation), which was also located in the Sydney Trades Hall. His most remarkable fundraising venture was the establishment of the Mandela Foundation of Australia, launched in May 1988, which through its dinners and concerts successfully projected a respectability such as that associated with Sydney's North Shore. Sponsors came from both sides of politics and included the then Prime Minister Bob Hawke, former Prime Ministers Gough Whitlam and Malcolm Fraser, Ian McPhee, Alexander Downer and Don Dunstan.

On several occasions, OSB received requests for funding from ANC for such things as assistance with administrative support or school kits on South Africa, Namibia and the frontline states. OSB did not provide financial support but put Funde in touch with returned volunteers who assisted in both Sydney and Melbourne. OSB did, however, cover Funde's costs when he travelled to Melbourne to address outgoing volunteers at their pre-departure briefing, as OSB considered it essential for all volunteers to be aware of the realities of apartheid and the struggle against it. When Funde was not able to attend the briefings he arranged for his Melbourne-based assistant, Terry February, to attend and speak. Before OSB knew of February's ANC connection, OSB staff knew him as the photocopier mechanic who regularly came to the office to repair or maintain its machines. February was also the main speaker at an OSB staff development seminar in August 1985;[12] the fact that his brother was a fighter in the ANC's armed wing added to his authenticity as a speaker.

Although there were opportunities in other parts of the African continent, OSB determined that its Africa program would focus on providing assistance to the countries known as the frontline states – the countries bordering or close to South Africa which were most affected by the conflict that characterised the long struggle for freedom in South

Africa. After 1960, the anti-apartheid forces operated mainly from their bases in exile. Although these forces obtained support and funding from many international sources, the support of neighbouring states was militarily and politically crucial. The term "frontline states" was not just a geographic designation; it was an alliance established in 1975 between Zambia, Botswana, Tanzania, Angola and Mozambique. It provided material, diplomatic, logistical and political support to the nationalist movements fighting for independence in Rhodesia, South West Africa and South Africa. Once Zimbabwe gained independence, it became the sixth frontline state in 1980, completing the circle of anti-colonial and Marxist inspired countries around South Africa and forcing it to rely more heavily on military means to destabilize its neighbours with raids and bombings, and by fomenting dissidence and funding surrogate armies to fight civil wars in the frontline states. The economic solidarity of frontline states was given form in 1980 in the Southern African Development Co-ordination Conference (SADCC), later the Southern African Development Community (SADC).

Teachers for Botswana

The Ministry of Education in Botswana re-established contact with OSB in 1983, making a general request for teachers in April 1984. Botswana had decided to expand their education system to provide a minimum of nine years education to all children by the mid-1990s. They had 505 Botswanan teachers, but to accomplish their goal they needed to recruit 250 teachers from abroad to teach in schools while they invested in teacher training.[13]

OSB was aware that Botswana was relatively prosperous compared to other countries in Southern Africa, but the Botswanan request provided an opportunity to work in the frontline states, to demonstrate solidarity, build links and learn more about what was involved in working in this part of the world. In May 1984 OSB appointed a staff member, Graeme Bruce, to work specifically on the Africa program. He had been one of several volunteers at Botswana's Francistown Teachers College in 1974–75 and was therefore familiar with conditions in Botswana and knew people in the Ministry of Education. He visited Botswana and Zimbabwe in September 1984, and it was agreed that OSB would recruit an initial six volunteers to go to Botswana in January 1985 before committing to larger numbers. Four secondary teachers were also assigned to Zimbabwe in January 1985.

In May 1985 the Botswanan Ministry of Education requested 20 teachers each year for three years, offering to pay return airfares as well as local salaries, with other costs to be negotiated. OSB saw this as an opportunity that could be managed as a separate activity. For the first time OSB could plan to recover full costs, outlined to the Ministry in June. In August the Ministry confirmed their request for 20 teachers to start in January 1986 and their willingness to pay $200,000 over two years.[14] OSB agreed to an initial year, with further recruitment subject to a review in April 1986. The Bureau also got Botswana to agree that OSB staff would be included in discussions about which schools would receive the volunteers, that placements would also be sought in teacher training colleges, and that primary school teachers with three years training would be acceptable in junior secondary schools. The Ministry was completely satisfied with the teachers who arrived in 1985 and conveyed their appreciation to OSB Assistant Director Tam Lynden-Bell, who travelled with the volunteers and joined their orientation in Gaborone, also meeting with senior Botswanan officials in Gaborone and representing ACFOA at the sixth SADCC Summit in Harare.

The Australian High Commissioner in Harare was very keen for OSB to expand its placement of teachers in Zimbabwe as well. Given the burgeoning demand for teachers in Africa and elsewhere, OSB appointed a recruiter to specialise in teacher recruitment. Fees paid by Botswana made funding this additional position possible.[15] In August 1986 OSB informed Botswana they would continue with the special program, appointing a second staff member in September to help develop and manage its growing programs in Africa.

From January 1985 to December 1988, when the teachers' program funded by the Botswanan government came to an end, 32 Australian teachers were assigned to work with the Ministry of Education. Each of the principal stakeholder groups had benefited. Botswana appreciated the professionalism of the Australian teaching staff and would have happily continued with the arrangement had they not secured large numbers of teachers from India at cheaper rates. For the Australian teachers, as for volunteers in other countries, there were challenges in working with rigid curricula, old-fashioned teaching methods and corporal punishment. Their physical conditions varied widely, with some living in suburban-style housing in established towns with large expatriate populations, but most living in quite humble circumstances in small concrete-block houses or even traditional *rondavels* some of which had neither electricity nor running water. A few were housed in school compounds a considerable distance from a main road.

For OSB the Botswana Teachers Program provided the experience of managing a separately funded multi-year project which extended the scope of its work beyond the routine of core-funded activity. Not only was the program funded from non-core sources, it was funded by the host country and was a powerful example of delivering larger-scale service for a fee. At more than $250,000 over three years, the program was by far the biggest of OSB's projects in the 1980s.

OSB was able to leverage the teacher program with a range of other assignments to support Botswanan organisations involved in conservation and non-formal education. Volunteers with trades backgrounds worked with the Brigades Movement, providing sustained support over several years. Established by Patrick van Rensburg, a South African educationalist and anti-apartheid activist who settled in Botswana and established the Foundation for Education with Production, the Brigades operated as semi-autonomous schools in rural centres that generated income by applying the skills that students learned. AVAs later worked with schools in Zimbabwe run by part of the same network, the Zimbabwean Foundation for Education with Production (ZIMFEP).

Living amidst violence

The Botswana project provided the practical experience of living and working in frontline states where a defining feature was the ever-present threat of violence, a reality that was thoroughly discussed by OSB staff and volunteers at a meeting in April 1986. In the first half of 1985 several houses in Gaborone had been bombed and their occupants killed. It was clear that these houses and people had been specifically targeted, which helped the volunteers put the events into perspective, although they remained concerned. In June 1985 a convoy of South African Defence Force soldiers drove into Gaborone and targeted ten houses and villages. Twelve South African exiles were killed and some bystanders were seriously injured, amongst them British and Dutch citizens. In May 1986, South African forces launched simultaneous air and ground strikes against Botswana, Zambia and Zimbabwe. Occasional car bombs and letter bombs continued to target particular members or supporters of the liberation movements and served to remind volunteers of the need to be alert. Without any volunteer management capacity in Botswana, the security and safety of volunteers had to be addressed by correspondence, occasional phone calls and regular meetings. Volunteers advised and coached each other about how to behave at roadblocks, and a cell system was set up comprising groups of five or six volunteers, each with a leader and a central point of contact.[16]

A response to the violence in the region was the establishment in 1987 of the Dukwi refugee camp by the Lutheran World Federation (LWF) for UNHCR about two hours' drive from Francistown in Botswana. The camp provided sanctuary to refugees from many African countries, but especially from Zimbabwe. Although many of the Zimbabwean refugees were able to go home in 1980 after Zimbabwe won its independence, deepening hostilities between Mugabe's Zimbabwe African National Union (ZANU) and Nkomo's Zimbabwe African People's Union (ZAPU) caused many more refugees to flee. AVA volunteers worked for LWF at the camp from January 1986 to April 1989. It was difficult at the time to get an accurate picture of what was occurring in Matabeleland in western and south-western Zimbabwe, where the refugees came from, but it was clear that the security situation was not good, as 12 people were shot dead on the Bulawayo–Victoria Falls road within one month. This violence was variously attributed to local banditry or to continuing South African support for the radical arm of Nkomo's ZAPU. What was certainly not known at the time was that systematic genocide of Ndebele, the Bantu-speaking people of western Zimbabwe, was being perpetrated by Mugabe's Fifth Brigade, who had been specially trained for the purpose by North Koreans.[17]

The violence in the region to which the program was exposed and the determination of Southern African colleagues to bring an end to apartheid and the occupation of Namibia had a profound impact on OSB staff working closely on this program. They lobbied management and put pressure on the OSB Committee to take a public stance in support of the anti-apartheid movement in South Africa and the struggle for independence in Namibia. Other NGOs had done so and publicised their stance, but they were not working in the frontline states. The OSB Committee was prepared to go only as far as stating the organisation's view on development and the values it espoused and its opposition to "violations of human rights and structured racism".[18] The Committee later added the important principle that whenever individual Committee members or staff were considering making statements about issues on which they (rightly) had strong feelings, their first consideration should be the safety and well-being of volunteers and their colleagues in the field.

OSB's decision to concentrate its Africa activity in the frontline states was in itself a very strong statement. OSB held this position until 1994 when the first AVA went to South Africa to work in Amanzimtoti near Durban in a community education program under the auspices of the YMCA. In the same year OSB took its first steps beyond Southern and Eastern Africa to the Horn of Africa and began working in Eritrea.

Mozambique

An ADAB-funded collaboration with Community Aid Abroad (CAA) and the Australian Freedom from Hunger Campaign (AFFHC) in a coalition known as the Joint Agency Working Group (JAWG) introduced OSB to Mozambique. The JAWG project conducted a design exercise in 1984 to outline an integrated development program encompassing health, water supply and agriculture in Morrumbene, a coastal district in Inhambane province. The first development workers for the project were briefed in January 1985 and departed soon after.

Mozambique's geography gave it singular importance in Southern Africa. Its three deepwater ports had for many years of Portuguese rule handled all trade in and out of Zimbabwe, Zambia, Malawi, Botswana, Swaziland, Transvaal and Natal. Mozambique therefore played a significant role in the fight for independence across Southern Africa. In the late 1970s at the height of the Rhodesian independence war, Mozambique's support was crucial for those opposing white-minority rule in Rhodesia. Mozambique's liberation front FRELIMO, which had come to power after the Portuguese left in 1975, provided logistical support and camps for training. Mozambique cut Rhodesia's access to the sea and in return had their supply lines disrupted by Rhodesian commandos operating in Mozambique. After Zimbabwean independence in 1980, the two countries were closely linked. Mozambique's role in the region's economy was recognised within SADCC as predominantly in transport and ports. South Africa formed from the remnants of Rhodesia's commandos the Mozambique National Resistance movement, RENAMO. This classic surrogate army, often referred to as bandits, maintained the offensive by sabotaging infrastructure and conducting terrorist raids. In March 1984, South Africa and Mozambique signed the Nkomati Accord, a non-aggression pact under which Mozambique undertook to neither shelter nor support the ANC and South Africa agreed to stop supplying RENAMO.

The Nkomati Accord seemed a propitious indicator when JAWG put their proposal to ADAB and prepared to begin its project. The first to arrive in Mozambique were the project's field director and agriculturalist, who encountered logistical difficulties that were far greater than imagined. Acquiring equipment was difficult and transporting it risky, as years of sabotage had crippled the country's infrastructure. Direct communication between Maputo and Morrumbene was impossible until a radio link was established in 1986. Because road travel was unsafe, the only way to get from to Morrumbene was to fly to Inhambane and cross the bay by boat. Contrary to expectations, the Nkomati Accord was never implemented; Mozambique did not expel any ANC operatives and South Africa continued its support of RENAMO. Fighting actually intensified, leading to rapid increases in the numbers of internal refugees, congestion and insecurity. The project acquired its own motorboat, which was the only one in the district and the only means of getting the Australians out if Morrumbene came under attack.[19]

Mozambique's security situation continued to deteriorate throughout 1986, prompting JAWG to write to each member of the project team and make it clear that they had total freedom to leave the project for security reasons at any time. Team members were encouraged to discuss their decision to leave with others but their right to make a decision independently was upheld. As well as making it clear that individuals had the right to make their own decisions, JAWG also made it clear that the four stakeholder groups (the project team as a whole, JAWG, the Mozambique authorities and the Australian government) also had the right to ask the team to leave Morrumbene at any time, with four stages in the withdrawal – to Inhambane, to Maputo, to somewhere outside Mozambique (probably Harare), and to Australia.[20]

The project in Inhambane was a powerful demonstration that inter-agency collaboration had its limits and many inherent difficulties. With hindsight it could be argued that the security assessment was naïve in its hope that the Nkomati Accord would bring peace. There was also confusion about the development philosophy underpinning the implementation of the project. Disputes arose because of the team structure and management practices in the field. Communication flows and the relationship between the team and JAWG back in Melbourne were never clear enough.[21] Tangled lines of loyalty complicated relationships between team members and with the Mozambican departments they were attached to. Some of the team had a close and previous association with CAA; others felt more loyalty to OSB which had recruited and supported them.

As a consequence of cuts to the government's aid budget, the project budget needed to be adjusted. The proposed changes cemented the antagonism within the team, which fell into two irreconcilable camps. In early 1987, AFFHC National Director Graham Alliband visited the project to see if he could make recommendations for its future. He concluded that "the origins of these staffing differences, which were also reflected at the JAWG level, have been structural. They have stemmed from the cumbersome and incoherent management structure inherent in the JAWG management arrangements". He referred to differences from the outset between CAA and OSB on the suitability of key project personnel. He also commented on the "real limitations to the spirit of cooperation on the CAA side". While commending the project as meeting genuine needs and deserving of further support, he could not salvage inter-agency cooperation in Mozambique.[22]

OSB and AFFHC both withdrew from the Mozambique project, thus ending Australia's first experiment in forming and operating an NGO consortium. Although OSB withdrew from this project, it continued in Mozambique, welcomed by the government of Mozambique in the signing of a memorandum of understanding with OSB. This agreement governed the placement of more than 60 volunteers up to 2007, most of whom were placed with the Ministry of Health and as lecturers in Mozambican universities, with some engaged in agriculture or veterinary services. The security situation remained a concern but was successfully managed by stationing volunteers in provincial capitals, from which they travelled on a daily basis to conduct any work needed in villages and rural areas.

Aid to Africa

Quite apart from the contest between apartheid and the liberation movements in Southern Africa, Africa was very much in the news in the mid-1980s. The widespread famines of 1984–85 attracted the attention of musicians and sportspeople. Band Aid recorded music for release to the Christmas market in 1984; the Live Aid concerts in 1985 were followed by Sports Aid in 1986. The publicity for these campaigns was so far-reaching that it tended to dominate the way people thought about Africa and drew sharp responses from people involved in development education, including Bill Armstrong. In OSB's October 1985 *Newsletter* he noted that "the world has sufficient food to feed its population; the problem is not inadequate production but inequality of distribution", and commented further "in no way do I wish to belittle the effort of Bob Geldof and the millions of people who gave in good faith, [but] it is absolutely vital that we face up to the reality of the situation and understand the real causes of the African crisis".

Live Aid may not have solved Africa's crisis, but it drew popular attention to it as never before. In a different way the attention was accentuated with the Australian release in March 1986 of the romantic drama *Out of Africa*, starring Robert Redford and Meryl Streep. Interest in volunteering in Africa surged in 1986, driven by a mixture of humanitarian and romantic sentiments.

In 1986 ACFOA established for the first time a committee to improve coordination among member agencies and with the Australian government on aid to Africa. In its 1986 budget the government announced that it would fund a Special Assistance Program for South Africa and Namibia (SAPSAN) to the tune of $5 million over five years. The Australian government had smartly found a way out of its dilemma. Politically there was no way it could support the ANC or SWAPO without being accused of supporting armed struggle. On the other hand, it was entirely defensible to financially support Australian NGOs such as APHEDA or OSB in their humanitarian assistance to refugees. Funding this program was a signal to ANC and SWAPO to approach OSB with requests for assistance in specific skill areas to which OSB was able to respond, thus creating volunteer projects funded by the government's SAPSAN.

Working with SWAPO in Congo

Hishongwa was interested in securing volunteers for the Nyango refugee settlement for Namibian refugees in Zambia. He identified needs for teachers, mechanics, occupational therapists, water engineers, agriculturalists and community development workers and suggested that the settlement could take four Australian volunteers. Early in 1987 his priority had changed and he requested teachers with English as their first language for a SWAPO school at Loudima in the People's Republic of the Congo. By the end of February 1987, Hishongwa had discussed this with ADAB, the Australian Teachers Federation (ATF) and with OSB staff member Graeme Bruce, and immediately conveyed the request in a letter to Armstrong that included news of SWAPO headquarters' willingness to accept Bruce as one of the teachers (physical education).[23] Within a week, CARE's National Convener had contacted OSB offering assistance, the ATF had confirmed their support, SWAPO headquarters had confirmed the request, and ADAB's Africa desk had encouraged OSB to apply for funding through SAPSAN. Funding was approved to recruit and support two teachers, the first of which served from August 1987 to July 1989 and the second, a science teacher, from January 1988 to December 1989.

The settlement at Loudima had been built in 1981 with funds contributed by UNHCR, Norway and Sweden, the unspent portion of which were used to build the school in 1987.[24] The school was extremely well resourced with new classrooms and housing. Approximately half its 40 teachers were Namibians and most of the others were from Scandinavian countries. The facilities and standard of living in Loudima were much higher than the Namibians could enjoy on their return home. The allowance paid to the students was more than the average income of a fulltime worker in Congo, but sustained and repeated interruptions to their schooling in Namibia meant that educational standards were very low. Some third-form students were 28 years old. Namibians were able to return to Namibia in November 1989 for the parliamentary election facilitated by the United Nations, and funding was set aside to bring students and teachers who were continuing at the school back to Loudima after the election.[25] OSB had intended, and had AIDAB funds for, a third teacher at Loudima, but ended the project in December 1990, as the school board had decided to leave Congo in December 1991.

With the prospect of independence, which was officially declared in March 1990, OSB's attention shifted to assessing the possibility of volunteers working in Namibia, liaising with volunteer organisations in Europe who were preparing to recruit and send volunteers to Namibia. As early as January 1990 it had become clear that teachers and nurses would be in high demand. The first Australian volunteers to Namibia in January 1991 were two secondary school teachers assigned through UNV, also separately funded by AIDAB. They were joined later that year by a volunteer stationed in UNDP as the UNV Program Officer to build and coordinate the UNV Program. AVAs worked in Namibia in increasing numbers and diverse roles for the next 25 years.

Working with the ANC in Tanzania

ANC's request for volunteers also focused on education, which became a high priority for ANC after the Soweto uprising of 1976. They began to establish educational facilities for exiles and their children, initially at Mazimbu in central Tanzania on land made available by President Nyerere. When the first college became too small, an additional facility was built at Dakawa, about 50 kilometres away. The Dakawa Development Centre served as an orientation and rehabilitation centre for exiles returning from Mozambique and Swaziland, offering not only formal education but also training in a variety of skilled trades. The OSB volunteer selected to work in this vocational training centre taught and developed the curriculum over three years from January 1991 to December 1993.

January 1985 was a pivotal moment for OSB's programs in Africa with the mobilisation of 12 volunteers to Botswana, Zimbabwe and Mozambique to join the two remaining volunteers in Tanzania. In the ten years before the end of 1984 there had been 78 AVAs in Africa, with the majority (52) in Tanzania. In the ten years after January 1985, 306 OSB volunteers worked in Africa. Botswana and Zimbabwe hosted large programs with about 100 volunteers in each. New programs were begun in Swaziland, Mozambique, Namibia, Malawi, and, in 1994, in Eritrea. Most of this activity was funded through the core volunteer program, but there were other significant projects that were separately funded. Some were generic in nature, such as a technical assistance program in Swaziland working with government departments and agencies. Most projects, however, appropriately focused on the most significant development issue of the era in Southern Africa, HIV/AIDS. Beginning in South Africa (KwaZulu-Natal) working with local NGOs in youth-focused community education programs, OSB developed considerable experience managing peer education programs. It continued to do so through the 1990s in Zimbabwe, including with factory workers, until intractable civil unrest and uncontrolled inflation made it impossible to continue there after May 2000. The experience of working in Southern Africa from the mid-1980s provided OSB with valuable learnings in risk management which served it well, not only in the rest of Africa but worldwide.

Suzanne Lau Gooey, pharmacist at Zimbabwe's Ministry of Health, 1990–92. Courtesy AVI

Veterinarian Jenny Turton assisted with research into tick fever in cattle at Zimbabwe's Central Veterinary Laboratory, 1993–96. Photo Debra Plueckhahn. Courtesy AVI

Dot Kingston advised and worked on women's literacy programs for Eritrea's Ministry of Education, 1995. Photo Debra Plueckhahn. Courtesy AVI

Paul Mellenhorst, curator/administrator at Nhabe Museum, Maun, Botswana, is interviewed for an AVA video, June 1997. Courtesy AVI

CHAPTER 8

Indonesia: Working with Civil Society

The first twenty years of Australian volunteering in Indonesia, outlined in the story of the Volunteer Graduate Scheme in Chapter 1, established a firm basis for the AVA program to build on throughout the 1970s. Almost all volunteers worked in universities and other educational institutions where they taught English. The demand for volunteers to teach English in Indonesia, in workplaces as well as in the classroom, was insatiable and remains so today, despite the emergence of innumerable private English-language teaching providers.

One notable exception to the preponderance of language teachers amongst volunteers in the 1970s was Mary Johnston whose significance was referred to in Chapter 1. After her return to Indonesia Johnston worked in a public health NGO, establishing in 1974 with colleagues a new organisation, Yayasan Indonesia Sejahtera (YIS), which is today one of Indonesia's largest and most respected NGOs. They wanted to make a philosophy of community participation more central to their work and to present a secular identity, although the broader NGO community always linked YIS with its Christian origins. Johnston continued as a volunteer until 1988, making a contribution that stands out as legendary.

New wave of Indonesian NGOs

Indonesian NGOs had existed since the early twentieth century, but in the 1970s they mushroomed at all administrative levels, from village to national. Many of the new organisations to emerge were linked through informal networks. The expansion in civil society can, to a certain extent, be attributed to the lack of opportunities for civic participation and political expression. Indonesia's New Order government in the 1970s was quite effective in depoliticising the community. Political parties were banned below regency level and the military-dominated regime acted as if it had achieved a post-political ideology-free era of stability. Indonesia's lower classes were designated a "floating mass", free of political concerns and devoted to economic development, leaving the armed forces to rule the people and protect them with the assistance of graduates and technocrats.[1]

The rapid emergence of so many NGOs provided many avenues for socially engaged intellectuals, students and local leaders to become involved. With the support of foreign funders, Indonesian NGOs developed into essential providers of services and built a capacity for social and economic research. They identified social and intellectual spaces the centralised government had not completely shut down and cleverly exploited these opportunities. It was a complex world they inhabited. They combatted poverty and promoted welfare by pursuing modes of development that were different to the officially sanctioned ones. Any open criticism of government put their existence at risk, and they relied on informal support and advice from sympathetic officials to continue their activities. NGO work in social and economic development had to be "non-political"; nevertheless, the organisations that comprised the NGO movement were at the same time conscious catalysts in the promotion of democratic values and processes.[2]

Feith's new Indonesian friends

Johnston's experience had paved the way for volunteers to work with Indonesian civil society, but Herb Feith gave further encouragement. He had resigned from the OSB Committee in 1972, but welcomed Armstrong's leadership of the organisation and re-established contact with him in the early 1980s, having also renewed his connections with Indonesia. The Indonesian tragedy of 1965–66 which resulted in the death of 500,000 or more alleged Communists, followed by ongoing human rights abuse and the single-minded pursuit of developmentalism that characterised Suharto's New Order made Feith's relationship with Indonesia and Indonesians so problematic that he did not visit the country for seven years. In the late 1970s his involvement in peace studies took him back to Indonesia where he engaged with a new group of friends and colleagues, who were socially engaged intellectuals and leaders in the NGO movement. In particular he gravitated towards a circle of critical intellectuals associated with Lembaga Penelitian, Pendidikan dan Penerangan Ekonomi dan Sosial (LP3ES, Institute for Social and Economic Research, Education and Information) and its prestigious journal *Prisma*.[3]

They were searching for alternative ideas for Indonesia's development and experimenting with community development programs. They also managed a publishing program to bring to Indonesian readers translations of the best and most recent Western academic writing on social, economic and political development. Among the circle were Dawam Rahardjo, head of LP3ES, Daniel Dhakidae, editor of *Prisma*, Aswab Mahasin, another leader at LP3ES, and Adi Sasono, whose organisational base was Lembaga Studi Pembangunan (LSP, Development Studies Institute). Abdurrahman Wahid had also come into this circle on his return to Indonesia from study in Egypt, Iraq and Europe. He was to rise in 1984 to the leadership of Nahdlatul Ulama (NU), the largest organisation of traditional Islam in Indonesia, and, in 1999, to become the first President elected after the fall of Suharto. In the late 1970s and early 1980s Wahid was a cultural activist, journalist, commentator and teacher. As a consultant to LP3ES, he was invaluable in introducing the organisation to the world of *pesantren,* the traditional Islamic boarding schools led by religious teachers who were the backbone of NU.[4]

Civil society's challenges

Feith saw the potential for developing productive links with Australia and introduced OSB staff to his new Indonesian friends, thus enabling a shift in OSB's programming. From 1982 on, working with Indonesian civil society became an important theme in OSB's work in Indonesia. Suharto's military-dominated New Order was at the peak of its powers and regime officials were inclined to perceive the term "non-government organisation" as actually signifying "anti-government organisation". NGOs felt this perception to be a threat to their existence and a terminology evolved to avoid any reference to their organisations' relationships to state or government; they were instead referred to as "institutions for developing community self-reliance".[5] The NGOs' default approach was to seek to collaborate with each other and to avoid open conflict with the authorities.

Indonesia was at the same time experiencing a wave of killings known as "mysterious shootings". A global economic recession and lower oil prices had caused an economic downturn in Indonesia. Cuts to food and fuel subsidies and a substantial devaluation of the rupiah had immediate consequences, especially for the poor, which led to a crime wave, particularly of robbery. In response, thousands of Indonesians were killed in a program of extrajudicial killings between 1982 and 1985, carefully planned and involving the military and police. The shooters were mainly undercover military officers and the bodies of those they shot were more often than not left in plain view. The program was piloted in Yogyakarta and then spread by military commanders to other cities once its effectiveness had been demonstrated. Military and police units worked their way through blacklists of known or suspected criminals.

In January 1983 a group of eight new volunteers arrived in Yogyakarta for language training before taking up their assignments, only to be confronted immediately by news of the killings. Their Indonesian colleagues countered their concerns by reassuring them that only criminals were at risk and that the shootings were a good solution that brought comfort and a sense of security to the lives of ordinary people. Only the most outspoken human rights activists were publicly critical of the killings.

Volunteers in Jakarta-based NGOs

Three of the volunteers had accepted assignments in Indonesian NGOs based in Jakarta, joining another who had begun working with Adi Sasono at LSP in 1982. One joined an organisation concentrating on small-scale agricultural development and the others, including me, joined LP3ES. My assignment had been at the instigation of Feith who had supervised my research in Indonesia in 1970–71 on the Indonesian army's self-image[6] and had been a supportive colleague ever since. He was aware of my interest in returning to Indonesia to experience the country in ways that would contrast with my previous experience which mainly involved the military.[7] He suggested I contact the OSB as he thought there could be an opportunity through its AVA program to work with LP3ES.

The role at LP3ES was initially configured to assist its community development team, but the LP3ES leaders wanted to take advantage of my experience in research and writing and fashioned a role to suit. It proved to be an unparalleled opportunity to get to know and work with a group of engaged intellectuals who were serious critics of the regime's approach and saw it their business to have their concerns discussed. In a highly censored environment they knew just how far their publications could push sensitive issues without receiving the phone-call no-one wanted. *Prisma* was an Indonesian language monthly with an exceptional reputation for serious scholarship and for being a relatively free space. I worked principally as editor of an English-language quarterly *Prisma,* usually translating a particularly interesting article from a recent issue of the Indonesian monthly and building on that theme by commissioning further articles by practitioners and academics. The networks of NGO intellectuals, development practitioners and critical academics overlapped substantially.

Apart from its publishing program and its team of contract researchers, LP3ES also managed a community development program in Central Java, eventually setting up a branch office in Klaten. Another of its operations was a *pesantren* development program funded by the Friedrich-Naumann-Stiftung (FNS), a German foundation with a mission to promote liberalism. This far-sighted and significant program pioneered community development in the *pesantren* context, working with religious teachers and the communities directly and supported by the invaluable advice and involvement of Abdurrahman Wahid.

The program's success was well leveraged, leading to the formation of specialist organisations and influencing others. The *pesantren* development program and its FNS funding were moved into an organisation established for the purpose, Perhimpunan Pengembangan Pesantren dan Masyarakat (P3M, Centre for Pesantren and Community Development). One of its programs aimed to strengthen awareness of women's reproductive rights using Quranic and broader Islamic idiom. It gave rise to an Islamic women's organisation, Rahima, which moved beyond women's reproductive rights into broader agendas of women's rights.

NGO space more constrained

The arrangements under which Indonesian NGOs had to work were further tightened in the mid-1980s. The New Order continued its efforts to depoliticise civil society as a whole and to discourage adherence to any ideologies other than the official Pancasila (the Five Principles of the State). In effect, no organisation could conduct any activity without the government's consent, especially foreign NGOs. The authorities were particularly concerned about foreign NGOs operating or funding activities in Indonesia for two reasons – they were NGOs and they were foreign. In 1985, Indonesia's Cabinet Secretariat took on the responsibility of overseeing all government and non-government projects financed in any way by overseas agencies.

Foreign NGOs had to meet two conditions to be allowed to work in Indonesia: one was a positive report from BAKIN (State Intelligence Coordinating Board); the other was a Memorandum of Understanding (MoU) with a suitably aligned technical ministry. While the activities of OSB were always scrutinised by BAKIN and other intelligence agencies, it never had a MoU. OSB's program involved a variety of government entities with multiple technical ministries. Its local NGO partners also had to have the support of an overseeing ministry and these varied too. As a consequence, OSB's licence to operate derived directly from its relationship with Cabinet Secretariat's KTLN (Bureau of Foreign Technical Cooperation). A formal MoU was proposed with KTLN but never negotiated. It was sufficient to occasionally discuss a formal agreement and maintain respectful and cordial relationships at the highest level. Thus both OSB and KTLN could act as if a formal MoU was in force. OSB had learnt this relationship-based way of dealing with the authorities from observing and imitating leaders of Indonesian NGOs.

Laws governing "community organisations" placed further restrictions on Indonesian NGOs. They aimed to control political parties, interest groups, trade unions and grass-roots organisations, obliging all organisations to register with the Department of Home Affairs and listing a broad range of actions or inaction that could lead to an organisation being banned. In addition, sectoral umbrella organisations were to be established to make it easier for government agencies to monitor and supervise NGO activity. Indonesian NGO leaders immediately saw this as a threat to the existence of their organisations. Previous endeavours by NGOs to come together and find common cause had been frustrated by tensions between large and small organisations and a degree of competition between leaders. Suspicions were also raised by the presence of informers and the emergence of government-sponsored NGOs. The NGO leaders collectively agreed that it was safer for them to avoid any umbrella organisation or peak organisation and to take a less structured, more organic approach to networking, thus achieving a more secure strength than any peak body, which could be captured, infiltrated or destroyed, could achieve.

International protection

An opportunity arose for Indonesian NGOs to internationalise and thus protect their networking efforts. The Intergovernmental Group on Indonesia (IGGI) was a group of international donors (including Australian donors) formed in the late 1960s to help coordinate aid flows to Indonesia. In the 1970s and 1980s the annual meetings of IGGI were convened and chaired by The Netherlands. In 1984–85 a parallel non-government group, the Inter-NGO Conference on IGGI Matters (INGI), was set up to foster cooperation among Indonesian NGOs and associated NGOs in IGGI countries. INGI's secretariat operated out of offices in Jakarta and The Hague, which enabled much more concerted and effective lobbying and advocacy on issues of human rights and democracy, as well as social and economic development. For Indonesian NGOs, INGI provided an invaluable opportunity to talk with each other away from the scrutiny and attention of intelligence agencies that prevailed at home.

At the 1986 meeting of INGI in The Netherlands, the ACFOA delegate was approached by Buyung Nasution, a prominent lawyer and human rights activist, about the possibility of a meeting between Indonesian and Australian NGOs. ACFOA was both enthusiastic and cautious. Aswab Mahasin, one of the LP3ES intellectuals, was planning to visit Melbourne and was asked to canvass NGO colleagues in Jakarta to get some insight into the purposes and a possible agenda for such a meeting. Should it be held in Australia or Indonesia? Should it aim to generate maximum public attention, or be low profile? Some in Australia thought that, if the purpose was to build a better base of understanding, it would be important to expose Australian NGOs to the work of Indonesian NGOs in the field.[8]

Anger at Australia

The prospect of building deeper relationships between Australia and Indonesia in the non-government sphere was particularly timely, as the relationship between the two governments was at an extremely low ebb.

In April 1986, not long after the overthrow of President Marcos in the Philippines, the *Sydney Morning Herald* published on its front page an article by David Jenkins with the headline "After Marcos, the Suharto millions". The content exposed the scale of the Suharto family's corruption, which was widely known in Indonesia but could not be discussed in the press. The article also revealed the role played by Suharto's wife in the family's business affairs and let foreign readers in on a joke circulating widely in Indonesia which referred to her as Ibu Tien Persen (Madame Ten Percent), "Tien" being both the popular shortened version of her name, and Dutch for ten.

The Indonesian reaction was fast and furious. Visa-free entry for Australian tourists was suspended, resulting in a jumbo jet en route to Bali being turned back.[9] Indonesia's Minister for Research and Technology cancelled his scheduled trip to Australia; ministerial visits in both directions were stopped and remained so for two years. Military cooperation was suspended overnight after the Head of the Armed Forces, General Murdani, described the *Sydney Morning Herald* article as "an intrusion into domestic Indonesian politics akin to the Dutch paratroop attack on Jogjakarta in the Independence struggle". The Armed Forces' daily newspaper, *Angkatan Bersenjata*, then published a series of six articles on Australia which went beyond a critique of the Jenkins article and Australian media coverage of Indonesia to a "broad and fundamental attack on Australia's motives, its culture, its political system and its place in the region".[10]

It is interesting that two widely read publications in Asia, the *Asian Wall Street Journal* and the *Far Eastern Economic Review*, had both covered in some detail the business dealings of the Suharto family and associates without any repercussions. Soon after the Jenkins article, the *Washington Post* and *New York Times* carried further stories on the same theme that attracted no reaction from Indonesian authorities. There was no doubt that Indonesian outrage was reserved specifically for Australia, with *Angkatan Bersenjata*, for example, describing Australians as "a rich, white race, whose people are arrogant and superior and believe they have the right to impose their views on the coloured Southeast Asians amongst whom they live".[11]

NGO diplomacy

With the relationship between the Australian and Indonesian governments all but severed, there was a clear opportunity for unofficial diplomacy and relationship building, but it has to be said that amongst Australian NGOs at the time there was a very low base of confidence and knowledge about Indonesia. Faith-based groups dealt with their co-religionists in Indonesia, but rarely strayed beyond that level of involvement. AFFHC had supported a single organisation working in family planning. Community Aid Abroad had struggled to develop any programmatic presence in Indonesia and had accepted that its public stance on East Timor made working in Indonesia impossible. OSB had the benefit of knowing first-hand the enduring value of the people-to-people links established through the Volunteer Graduate Scheme and the AVA program. Through its more recent collaborations with significant NGOs in Indonesia, OSB was also unique amongst Australian NGOs in having built personal relationships with Indonesian NGO leaders which gave the Bureau personal knowledge of their aspirations and the constraints that inhibited them.[12]

OSB was asked to consider reversing the volunteer experience by inviting an Indonesian to come to Australia and work at OSB. This had been raised several times and discussed again during Aswab Mahasin's July 1986 visit to Melbourne. It was clear that hosting and employing an Indonesian NGO worker would be a strong demonstration of good faith before any meeting of Indonesian and Australian NGOs took place.

Requests for volunteers from Indonesian NGOs reflected both technical need and a spirit of internationalism. Here was an opportunity to make the arrangement reciprocal, providing an Indonesian with the opportunity to experience Australian civil society and workplaces and making available Indonesian experience to Australians. OSB was increasingly seeking opportunities in many countries to work in the area of community development and recognised that Indonesian NGOs had deep and credible experience in this area of work, albeit in difficult circumstances. Further discussion with LP3ES and others resulted in a recommendation that the opportunity be offered to Arief Mudatsir, a 31-year-old sociologist with a background of youth and student activism in Nahdlatul Ulama. He was a middle-ranking staff member with six years' experience at LP3ES, including in its *pesantren* development program. He had written articles and book reviews based on his community development experience and was also active in environmental circles. It was thought his offering to OSB would be in the areas of cross-cultural adaptation, perspectives on community development, program formulation and implementation, and monitoring and evaluation. Unfortunately an unexpected impediment delayed this exchange.[13]

Volunteer expelled

Graham Habgood, a volunteer working with one of the bigger rural development NGOs, Bina Swadaya, was expelled from Indonesia in October 1986, 14 months into a two-year assignment. OSB contacted the Australian Embassy in Jakarta and the Indonesian Embassy in Canberra to request an explanation, but there was no response. Accordingly, it was decided that Hugh O'Neill, Chair of OSB and a former Volunteer Graduate who had retained strong personal and professional ties in Indonesia, and I would travel to Jakarta in an attempt to discover why Habgood had been expelled and to assess the implications for OSB's activities in Indonesia.

The NGO community in Jakarta was deeply concerned.[14] Bina Swadaya related how they had been approached by Cabinet Secretariat who had told them that Habgood's residence permit would not be extended and asked that he be dismissed. Bina Swadaya refused, explaining that he was a good volunteer, a valued member of staff whom they had no wish to sack. Bambang Ismawan, the head of Bina Swadaya, contacted KTLN Head Widodo Gondowardojo who told him that pressure had come from BAIS (Badan Intelijen Strategis, Armed Forces Strategic Intelligence Agency). With this knowledge, Bina Swadaya knew they could do nothing to help Habgood stay. Aswab Mahasin of LP3ES mentioned other occasions when

Widodo had responded to directions or pressure from outside his agency, including occasions when he had acted on intelligence reports that turned out to be false.

Australian Embassy: No explanation required

The position of ADAB and the Ambassador was that this was an isolated incident; there would be no further repercussions and OSB should immediately continue its program in Indonesia. OSB's position was that it too wished to continue the program but was not prepared to proceed as though nothing had happened and wanted to know why Habgood had been expelled. ADAB's view was that, as Indonesia's sovereignty was involved, it was inappropriate to require an explanation. Reference was made to a letter from Widodo to ADAB, the tone of which was described as apologetic, with Widodo seeming to seek Australia's understanding, but neither ADAB nor the Ambassador would provide OSB with a copy of this letter. ADAB requested that OSB continue without pause the work it was good at – developing people-to-people relations. They argued that to stop doing this would only serve the purposes of those who did not want to encourage further contact with Australia. In this context there was repeated but elliptical reference to the "other agency", the Embassy's in-house term for BAIS.

Abdurrahman Wahid took the issue very seriously commenting that, although little satisfaction would be had from officials in Cabinet Secretariat, it was still important to make formal approaches to them. He confirmed that there was intense rivalry and competition between BAIS and BAKIN and that the pressure attributed to them was not uncharacteristic.[15] Wahid had heard that the Ministry of Home Affairs, which would normally be in the loop if a foreigner was to be expelled, was angry at not being consulted. He undertook to make his own inquiries with people he knew in Home Affairs and Foreign Affairs, as well as the military.

An official "explanation"

Bina Swadaya's top people were angry, as they had lost the services of a particularly productive member of staff who had excellent relationships with his colleagues; they also felt the organisation had been scapegoated by the Government. Habgood, an ADAB official and the Head of Personnel at Bina Swadaya met with the Head of the Ministry of Agriculture's Bureau of International Relations who berated Bina Swadaya for asking Habgood to work outside his job description by visiting Yogyakarta. Bina Swadaya could not understand why the Ministry would choose to make an issue of this or even how they knew that Habgood had visited Yogyakarta. They also could not fathom any reason for the Government to target Bina Swadaya.

Cabinet Secretariat also maintained this "explanation". Pangaribuan, deputy Head of KTLN in Cabinet Secretariat, explained to OSB that Habgood had been expelled at the request of the Ministry of Agriculture because he had worked outside his job description as an English teacher by undertaking research in Yogyakarta. He explained that the error had been Bina Swadaya's and they had been reprimanded. Pangaribuan confirmed there was no issue with Habgood's behaviour and said that he understood OSB did not find this explanation acceptable. When asked if there were other factors in play, he replied that, as far as he knew, there were none, but that Widodo, as Head of KTLN, had a wider view of things and may be able to provide more details.

A convenient "explanation"

Soon after Habgood was informed of the Indonesian government's decision to cancel his visa, he joined ADAB staff at the Embassy in what he thought was to be an informal meeting with sympathetic supporters. In an effort to understand what had happened, Habgood was casting around in his own mind for possible factors and mentioned that he had photocopied the Jenkins *Sydney Morning Herald* article and wondered if it was possible that a copy had ended up in the wrong hands. His comments were duly captured in a record of the discussion. The Embassy seized on this as both the only possible explanation and an acceptable one, as it did not want to entertain any thought that this could be part of any pattern of actions against Australia or Australians. It was convenient to see it as an isolated case in which the victim was also the culprit. This "explanation" quickly spread, as rumours do. It so happened that an Indonesian employee in the ADAB office was the wife of Habgood's supervisor in Bina Swadaya. Another Australian volunteer first heard the story from an Indonesian woman in the ADAB office, while the leaders of Bina Swadaya first heard the rumour within their own office and passed it on to other NGO leaders in LP3ES and elsewhere. An ADAB officer told the Directors of Canadian University Students Overseas (CUSO) and the British Voluntary Service Overseas (VSO) at a party.

No one mentioned hearing the rumour from Cabinet Secretariat or Ministry of Agriculture; its only source was the Australian Embassy. Indeed, in the Ambassador's view it had the status of an admission that was on record. He was not pleased when OSB pointed out that, while it understood why the Embassy had seized on this explanation, it remained one of many and was not seen as plausible by any Indonesian colleagues that OSB had consulted, nor had it even been mentioned by Cabinet Secretariat.

It remained a possibility that this was yet another occasion when Indonesian public servants had been forced to act on flawed intelligence. A European consultant attached to Bina Swadaya in Yogyakarta, who had previously reported his awareness of being under surveillance, was known to have provided copies of the Jenkins newspaper article to friends and colleagues. In the context of relations between Australia and Indonesia, however, it would have made more sense to Indonesian intelligence to assume it was the act of an Australian.

Indonesian NGO leaders supported OSB's efforts to seek an explanation, even though there was no prospect of satisfaction, but they also argued that it was important for OSB's volunteer program to continue its collaboration with Indonesian NGOs, not just because of the technical assistance offered or produced, but because it offered another channel for Indonesian NGOs to maintain links with the world beyond Indonesia. They maintained that Habgood's expulsion was not just Bina Swadaya's problem, but a problem for all of them and even suggested postponing the ACFOA consultation to reinforce this point.

OSB resolved to continue its program in Indonesia and the five volunteers in Indonesia at the time of the Habgood incident continued in their placements. Among them was the first volunteer to live and teach in a *pesantren* – a remote one, approximately 20 kilometres from Pinrang in South Sulawesi.[16] OSB refrained from immediately placing new volunteers in Indonesia and did not recommence until after a full year's hiatus.

Indonesia–Australia Program for Cooperation

Throughout 1987, OSB's Indonesia activities were more focused on helping to bring about the NGO meeting in Australia. The Indonesian group comprised nine representatives of eight organisations, most of which were OSB program partners. They visited Sydney, Canberra and Melbourne in September 1987, meeting with Australian NGOs, government institutions, universities, media and members of Australia's Indonesian community. They also attended the ACFOA council meeting and conferred with its leaders, as well as attending OSB's Annual Reporting to the community. The actual NGO consultation took place in Melbourne and became known as the inaugural consultation of the Indonesia–Australia Program for Cooperation (IAPC). A joint statement reaffirmed the significance of the meeting and agreed on the principles and potential areas of cooperation, and mechanisms and steps for action, including a reciprocal visit by ACFOA members to Indonesia within the next 12 months.

The consultation was a significant undertaking as there had been plenty of tension in its various meetings. Few ACFOA members had a nuanced understanding of the political risks that characterised the Indonesian NGO world. There was an expectation amongst the

Australians that the Indonesians would take the opportunity to publicly share their outrage over Indonesia's actions in East Timor and West Irian, but, even if this had been their position, they would not want to appear unpatriotic. The extent to which the tension impacted the group was revealed in an article written by Aswab Mahasin, the leader of the group, reflecting on the visit and published over two days in one of the major national dailies in Jakarta.[17]

Compared to NGO consultations in Canada and Europe, sensitivities between the two countries made the Indonesian participants in the Australian consultation feel awkward and conscious of the gap in understanding between the communities. At almost every meeting they were challenged and questioned about East Timor, but they refused to make any comment, pointing out that, as its annexation was a political issue and concerned defence and security, it was beyond their area of competence. The group was also aware that they were not well informed about events in East Timor, which was not surprising, given the extent of government control of the media in Indonesia at the time. In any discussion of West Irian the group relied on one of their number who represented an organisation based there; he made it clear he would only speak from the starting point that West Irian was part of Indonesian territory.

Bridge with cracks in it

As the same issues came up again and again, the Indonesian delegation reached a point at which they made it known they were no longer interested in responding, but not before they had attempted to turn the tables by asking about Australia's treatment of its indigenous population, noting that "during the trip we saw for ourselves how miserable these people were, the social class which has almost been deprived of its entire cultural heritage". Aswab Mahasin conceded that the arguments raised by the Australians had been based on concerns for human rights and principles of self-determination, but he felt there was more to it. He sensed that Australians were concerned about a big strong nation to their north and speculated on whether Australians were anxious about their cultural identity reflecting Europe and America while a strong modern culture was rapidly emerging in the Asia-Pacific.

Overall, the outcome of the visit was extremely positive. It was an open exchange which, while inconclusive, produced "a new sense of consciousness in respect of our respective positions and a willingness to learn from one another. This is the beginning of mutual understanding", Aswab Mahasin wrote. He described what had been achieved as a bridge, but a "bridge with cracks in it", the cracks being lack of understanding, suspicion and negative stereotypes on both sides.

Small secretariats were designated in Indonesia (Aswab Mahasin, LP3ES) and Australia (Pat Walsh, ACFOA) to carry on preparations for further dialogue. When OSB resumed placing new volunteers in Indonesia in January 1988, four were placed with organisations that had participated in the consultation meetings: YIS, Bina Desa, LP3ES and Yayasan Annisa Swasti (YASANTI), a relatively new women's worker organisation in Yogyakarta that had received some mentoring and support from LP3ES. The secondment of Arief Mudatsir from LP3ES to OSB also continued successfully through late 1987 with, among other things, his participation in workshops with staff and partner organisations in the Pacific Islands. He returned to Indonesia in August 1988.

IAPC reciprocal visit

After some delays, the second meeting of IAPC took place in May 1989 in Karangasem, Bali. The Indonesians who attended were all senior respected NGO leaders, enough of whom had participated in the previous discussions in Australia to ensure continuity. The same was true of the ACFOA delegation of nine, comprising senior people from the ACFOA Executive Committee and staff and Graham Habgood, who used the opportunity to reconnect with his former Indonesian colleagues who welcomed him warmly. The dialogue in Bali continued from where it had ended in Australia, with a frank acknowledgment that neither side was sure of what the other meant or were thinking. Nevertheless, the importance of working through these difficulties was also acknowledged and a potential program was outlined whereby familiarisation visits would enable personnel exchanges and lead to projects that were jointly planned and managed. Three sectors arose from the discussions as agreed priorities: the environment, labour organisation, and cooperatives.

The IAPC provided a context for ongoing informal meetings and discussions in Indonesia and in Australia about how to progress the relationship. Within ACFOA, it functioned as a sub-committee on Indonesia. The next formal meeting of IAPC was scheduled for June 1993 in Yogyakarta, by which time the situation had become more complex and IAPC was seen by international NGOs and by the Australian and Indonesian governments as an essential partner.

INGI was succeeded in 1993 by the International NGO Forum on Indonesian Development (INFID), which regarded IAPC as an essential member of the broader international grouping. The key Indonesian members in IAPC believed this to be a natural and important alliance, as did ACFOA, which was acknowledged in planning for a joint IAPC/INFID Steering Committee to meet in Jakarta on 15–17 June 1993.

IAPC had encouraged ACFOA to lobby the Australian government to provide funding to Indonesian NGOs and OSB was particularly active in this effort, pointing out that the Indonesian ban on Dutch aid funds continued to have a big impact on Indonesian NGO activity and that the Australian government should target its contributions to organisations working on environmental issues and in Eastern Indonesia.[18] Whether it was due to ACFOA's advocacy or not, the Australian government had started to take providing funds to Indonesian NGOs seriously. Anything proposed by the Australian government in Indonesia had to be approved by, if not planned in conjunction with, Cabinet Secretariat's KTLN.

Indonesian delegation and Australian counterparts at the founding of the IAPC, Melbourne, 1987. L to r, back row: Sutrisno (YIS), Peter Britton (OSB), Pat Walsh (ACFOA), Rustam Ibrahim (LP3ES), Karcono (Bina Desa), Eric Ellem (AUSTCARE), Susan Blackburn (CAA), Abdullah Syarwani (PKBI); middle row: Tony Rehawarin (West Irian), Unknown (FPP), Bill Armstrong (OSB), Christine Wheeler (AFFHC), Aswab Mahasin (LP3ES), Wendy Poussard (WADNA); front row: Russell Rollason (ACFOA), Achmat Rofi'ie (LSP), Graham Alliband (AFFHC), Sri Kusyuniati (Yasanti), Sandra Blamey (ACC). Courtesy AVI

Aswab Mahasin at the IAPC founding meeting with Betty Feith, Melbourne, 1987. Photo Peter Britton

Aswab Mahasin at the IAPC founding meeting with Herb Feith, Melbourne, 1987.
Photo Peter Britton

Graham Habgood joined the staff of OSB, 1988. Courtesy AVI

Peter Britton meets President B.J. Habibie at the opening of the First International Conference of Youth Exchange Programs, with Minister for Cooperatives Adi Sasono and Minister for Education Juwono Sudarsono, State Palace, Jakarta January 1999. Courtesy AVI

Self-propelling growth

As it happened, Cabinet Secretariat had its own agenda and need for a mechanism for NGO consultation. In 1993 Indonesia was mid-way through its term as Chair of the Non-Aligned Movement and its legacy was to be an elaboration of a Self-Propelling Growth Strategy. ACFOA was invited to an Indonesia-Australia NGO/Government Consultation in Yogyakarta entitled "On the Road to Self-Reliance-Strategy for the Development of the People's Economy, Indonesia-Australia Consultative Meeting on People's Economic Development Strategy: The Self-Propelling Growth Scheme", to be held on 16–17 June 1993. Participation was restricted to NGOs active in grassroots economic development and subject to the approval of the governments of both countries.[19] Scheduled for the same dates as the IAPC/ INFID meeting, it presented OSB and ACFOA with a dilemma. Both organisations arranged to be represented at both meetings. If the NGO/ Government consultation was to discuss new modalities for Australian funding of NGO activity in Indonesia, it was essential that they attended the consultation meeting, especially as continued NGO activity depended on the goodwill of Cabinet Secretariat. At the same time, the Australians did not want to neglect INFID friends in favour of organisations selected on the basis of their acceptability to government.

INFID's whole existence was predicated on international solidarity and their international advocacy was based on sound research. OSB and ACFOA continued to participate actively in the INFID network, with activity peaking in 1996 when the 10th INFID conference was hosted by ACFOA in Canberra. More than 50 participants came from Indonesia and a further 30 delegates from Europe and other Asian countries joined 21 Australian participants. The conference was preceded by public forums in Sydney, Canberra and Melbourne on the Freeport mine in Papua, Indonesia's debate regarding nuclear energy, and the plight of organised labour. The increase in Australian activism and interest in Indonesian issues was overtaken by political change in Indonesia, which was hit hard by the Asian financial crisis of 1997. Massive student demonstrations were followed by violent rioting in Jakarta which eventually forced the resignation of Suharto in May 1998 and his replacement as President by B.J. Habibie.

The changed circumstances in Indonesia were reason for OSB to begin in late 1999 to review its program there and determine a new strategy. Despite increased involvement in education, including vocational education, the dominant trend in volunteer assignments had continued to be in Indonesian NGOs. Many of them were with small organisations, often in relatively remote locations. With Indonesia in crisis some of these assignments were not sustainable; security concerns had increased, especially once Australian troops had entered East Timor, and the program shrank. The emphasis on building the program in Eastern Indonesia, which was aligned with AusAID's emphasis on reducing poverty, meant that attention to Java and Sumatra had been reduced. OSB's review referred to an Indonesian critique of Australian aid articulated in the Suharto and Habibie eras. It stemmed from a perception, sometimes genuinely held and sometimes mischievously put about, that Australia's emphasis on Eastern Indonesia represented a preference for working with Christian communities and was, therefore, by extension an anti-Islamic position. In its most extreme form this critique attributed to Australia an interest in seeing a break-up of Indonesian national security.

The review recommended extreme caution regarding any long-term assignments in Eastern Indonesia for at least a year or two and to focus on rebuilding the program in Java, Sumatra, Bali and Lombok. It also observed that civil society, which had largely been secular, was becoming more self-consciously Islamic, as was social and political life. It was further noted that, for all the variety of links (government, NGOs, academic and business) between Australia and Indonesia, Australia's relationships with organised Islam in Indonesia were extremely weak; it predicted that "if, as it is hoped, military power in Indonesia declines this is likely to be replaced by Indonesia's increasingly Islamic character as the focus of Australians' fear and resentments". This analysis pointed to continuing to pro-actively build productive links with Islamic organisations and institutions as an important niche area for AVI to work in.[20]

In subsequent years building these links was a noteworthy, but not exclusive, focus of AVI's program. Collaboration was extended into Islamic tertiary education institutes as well as civil society and included, on the invitation of Islamic scholars and community leaders, multi-year AusAID-funded projects introducing child-centred pedagogy and English language curriculum into rural Islamic boarding schools. This work involved a highly focused professional approach to capacity development, but rested fundamentally on an approach that prioritised building relationships, respect and understanding.

CHAPTER 9

Papua New Guinea and Pacific Islands: A Diversity of Linkages

The context of decolonisation

The Overseas Service Bureau routinely made submissions to parliamentary inquiries relevant to its programs, particularly to those of the Joint Committee on Foreign Affairs and Defence, as they provided valuable opportunities to put the views of OSB on record and to showcase its work to an important group of stakeholders. In 1987 the Joint Committee held an inquiry into Australia's relations with the South Pacific; OSB's submission began with the words of Father Walter Lini, the anti-colonial priest who was Vanuatu's Prime Minister from its independence in 1980 until 1991:

> The success of Australia's relations with the Pacific Island states will be based on the practical and sustained recognition that no one culture is basically superior to another, that each and every culture, together with its social, political and economic ingredients, has a meaning and value to the people who gave birth to it.[1]

In his use of cultural relativism Lini was cautioning Australia about how it projected its power in the South Pacific region. By using Lini's words OSB strategically defined itself as an Australian organisation seeking to prioritise respectful relationships in the region. Compared to Asia, Africa and other regions OSB was later to work in, such as Latin America or the Middle East, the South Pacific presented a different set of social, political and cultural challenges. In those regions, Australians could see the impact of colonialism and identify with and support local decolonisation efforts. In the South Pacific, however, Australia was both a colonial power and the most dominant country, economically and politically. Whereas in Asia and Africa, the volunteer program was imbued with post-colonial solidarity, in the Pacific the volunteer program was for some years a congenial, but inextricably linked component of a colonial undertaking. After all, the initial momentum for Australian government support for OSB had come in part from the Department of Territories. Volunteers to Papua New Guinea (PNG) before it gained independence in 1975 lived and worked predominantly in missionary environments. Mary Considine, a volunteer in 1966 in PNG, an OSB staff member from 1967 to 1970, and one of its management team in the 1980s, later commented that, in the Pacific "Australians [could] see the impact of Australia on other nations. Volunteers in these countries can usually see themselves as 'a piece of aid', and identify issues of dependence, independence and interdependence".[2]

OSB's activities in the Pacific Islands spread beyond the larger countries of PNG, Fiji, Solomon Islands and Vanuatu to the small island states in Polynesia and Micronesia. Its programs maintained assignments in government (at national and sub-national level) and church-run institutions, especially in education and health. Once NGOs began to emerge in greater numbers in the 1980s, they too became a major feature of OSB's work in the social and development space that was not government-run and had differing degrees of connection to the churches. Through the 1980s and 1990s, OSB maintained a dual focus, assisting NGO and government partners with their service delivery and with their own capacity-building and institutional development. It was instrumental and catalytic in developing civil society organisations and their regional networks, while at the same time working within the Australian government's official programs to jointly design and manage technical assistance to improve the machinery of government in most Anglophone countries in the Pacific.

Solomon Islands Development Trust

OSB's engagement with non-government development organisations in the South Pacific is well illustrated by its involvement in the Solomon Islands Development Trust (SIDT), established in Honiara in May 1982 by American John Roughan, a Marist missionary who had married and settled in the Solomon Islands, and Abraham Baeanisea, a young graduate of the University of Papua New Guinea. The two inspirational leaders had a deep conviction that rural people and the villages they lived in were the foundations of development, so their organisation focused on improving village life and strengthening village leadership. Securing foreign aid funds was secondary to working directly with villagers to improve the quality of their life while protecting their environment.[3] SIDT's approach to community development was grounded in informal education, directly engaging villagers and encouraging them to ask questions about assets, processes and behaviours in their own locale. The similarity of their approach to "structural analysis" gave it strong appeal for Bill Armstrong, newly appointed as OSB's Director. He resolved to support SIDT with volunteers who could embrace and contribute to its community development approach, particularly through working with SIDT's mobile teams, which provided information and training in each province for villagers using their community development tools.

OSB began its engagement with SIDT by placing two volunteers, Albert and Janine Barelds, to work in community development for 12 months from January 1983. They stayed with SIDT for two and a half years, managing the development education component of an ADAB-funded national rural water supply and sanitation project and exploring possibilities for further volunteer involvement in SIDT's community development program and its own organisational development. Their proposal called for a further eight volunteers on two-year assignments, the first of whom commenced in January 1984. As Abraham Baeanisea later recalled, they worked in the villages supporting SIDT field workers with planning and organisational skills.[4] The volunteers all had technical skills, but their major contribution arose from their presence in the villages, where they supported community development processes and helped build the confidence and credibility of field workers and villagers. Compared to the more traditional program approach of matching volunteers to assignments where their professional skills were required, such as teachers to schools and doctors to hospitals, SIDT assignments were less clear-cut and regarded by some in OSB as a controversial departure. Community development was not a profession in itself but an approach and a philosophy. In an effort to gain more support and educate OSB staff and Committee members about the nature of community development, an evaluation of the partnership was conducted in 1986. Predictably, it recommended that OSB continue to support the work of SIDT placing volunteers with the Trust, explaining that "Community development is directed towards increasing the community's awareness of itself as subjects in the development process. This awareness takes place as people grow in their perception of the cause of their reality".[5] Australian volunteer involvement in SIDT continued for decades, and SIDT evolved into a pre-eminent Pacific Island NGO renowned for its work in sustainable development and indigenous rights and for its contributions to regional networks.

Pacific Islands Association of NGOs

As established NGOs sought a greater role and new local NGOs emerged in greater numbers in many Pacific Island nations, the idea of a forum for regional dialogue, mutual support and joint advocacy took form. The first steps towards a regional NGO body were taken in 1984 when affiliates of the Foundation of the Peoples of the South Pacific (FSP), an American-led and funded network, met in Tonga to discuss NGO involvement in development programs and how best to support it. They established a secretariat and steering committee to strengthen networking across their movement and, encouraged by SIDT, YWCA Tonga and OSB, agreed to plan a second meeting with broader regional representation in the Solomon

Islands in 1986. The proposed name for the grouping was the Pacific Islands Association of NGOs (PIANGO). Others too were interested in a regional grouping, and in mid-1986 the Commonwealth Foundation hosted a meeting in Western Samoa of NGOs from Commonwealth member countries in the Pacific, who also established a steering committee. The two steering committees met in 1987 and established the basis for PIANGO as a joint regional organisation. Each country was to have a national umbrella group of NGOs, called a National Liaison Unit (NLU), to be strengthened by a series of workshops in preparation for a regional meeting to formally establish PIANGO. The workshops, funded by AIDAB, the New Zealand government, United Nations Development Programme (UNDP) and the Commonwealth Foundation, set about devising strategies for cooperation among small local NGOs, large long-established church-based operations, and members of international organisations and networks, such as Red Cross, YMCA, YWCA, World Vision and service clubs. The networks and workshops were a vital avenue for introducing the small local organisations to a wider world and for giving them access to training and funding. PIANGO was formally launched in 1991.[6]

From the beginning of PIANGO it was understood that the Australian NLU had to be ACFOA, but it was OSB that took the lead in driving support for PIANGO in Australia because its exposure and involvement in the Pacific were wider and deeper than those of any other Australian organisation. Indeed, it was Armstrong and Baeanisia who had championed the idea that NLUs should be both national and local in character to ensure that PIANGO was owned by Pacific Island people. Consequently, it was not surprising that OSB worked hard to get support for PIANGO, applying on its behalf to AIDAB, UNDP and the Commonwealth Foundation for funding. PIANGO brought together two strands in OSB's experience and practice. In the Australian context, OSB had first-hand knowledge of the value of a peak organisation, having been instrumental in the creation of ACFOA in 1965 and having played an active role in its knowledge creation, information sharing and advocacy. In the Pacific context, OSB saw the institutional development of NGOs and their internal and external networks as essential for enabling Pacific Island peoples to participate in developing their own societies, as evidenced by the time OSB staff devoted to PIANGO in its early years. A senior staff member, Diane McDonald, was seconded to Honiara for three months to help establish the first PIANGO secretariat in the Development Services Exchange, the Solomon Islands' NLU.[7] A permanent base for PIANGO, with a fulltime coordinator, was established in 1998 in Fiji, where it continues as an important forum today.

Papua New Guinea

Through its exposure to and involvement in Papua New Guinea affairs from 1964, OSB built considerable knowledge and understanding of PNG. After the country became independent in 1975, Papua New Guineans and Australians participating in and observing the political process and economic life of the new nation had high expectations of progress, but development failed to meet their expectations. Like many who knew PNG, OSB had many reasons to be concerned and outlined them in correspondence with the office of the Minister for Trade and Overseas Development, John Kerin. One of Kerin's advisers, David Hegarty, knew PNG particularly well, having been a lecturer in and subsequently chairman of the Department of Political and Administrative Studies at the University of PNG from 1970 to 1982. Armstrong wrote to him in May 1992 to point out that the approximately 40 Australian volunteers in PNG were meeting only a fraction of the demand, and that a further 109 requested positions, half of them in general and vocational education, had not been filled. OSB would have to double or even treble the size of the program to meet the demand. There were chronic shortages of staff in provincial high schools, teachers' colleges, provincial health departments (doctors, nurses and allied health professionals), and in technical and vocational education. Provincial government departments and authorities made repeated requests for a broad range of professional staff and there were more and more calls for community-based initiatives to address rural poverty and social development which needed time and funding to build the necessary relationships and design appropriate programs. Among many potential foci for such programs were prisoner rehabilitation, rural women's health, and support for landowner groups. For example, there was clear interest in programs to improve maternal and child health and rural water supply and to address the spread of HIV/AIDS. OSB also identified a need to improve the image of PNG in Australia by working with schools, media and community groups to update their knowledge and to present the social and cultural complexity of the peoples of PNG. OSB also advocated for Australian students to undertake practicums in PNG in social work, youth work and community development to strengthen understanding and build closer relationships.[8]

PNG's response to the shortcomings of its education system was a national reform designed to extend the number of years of secondary schooling and improve access to community (primary) schools. In expanding the education system, the Department of Education faced a shortfall of 150 teachers in secondary and vocational schools and asked for more teachers to fill the gaps. AIDAB agreed to fund OSB to manage a project to supply Australian volunteer teachers in partnership arrangements identical to those of the AVA program. The PNG government would pay teachers' salaries at local rates and provide accommodation; other costs, such as recruitment, briefing, logistics and administration, were covered by the AIDAB-funded project. The first two-year phase commenced in January 1994, with a second phase planned through to 2000. OSB undertook to supply Australian secondary teachers to provincial schools, teacher trainers and vocational instructors. Recruiting Australian teachers for many countries had long been a stock-in-trade for OSB, but what had seemed a straightforward request in this project proved to be anything but. In 1994, and again in 1995, 22 teachers, instructors and lecturers took up positions under the Supplementary Teachers Project, but the numbers fell short of the annual target of 37. In 1996 only four additional teachers were mobilised and the project had to be abandoned before the second phase commenced.[9] PNG failed to attract the interest of Australian teachers, partly because of the Australian media's tendency to focus unduly on stories of lawlessness and crime, particularly violent crime against expatriates, in PNG.

Restoring PNG's image

To countervail the media's negative coverage, OSB had a wealth of material in the experience of 800 Australian volunteers who had lived among and worked with Papua New Guineans and appreciated the diversity of experience to be gained there. Despite the difficulties, the rewards were great; 25 per cent of volunteers to PNG extended their assignments – the highest extension rate across the 45 countries where OSB worked. Accordingly, OSB initiated a national community education campaign on PNG in 1995 to promote a more positive and nuanced profile of the country and its people. The campaign did not seek to gloss over negative issues such as crime and violence but sought to provide more context about such things as traditional systems of law and punishment and the overt character of domestic violence. It delved into the dilemmas of young school leavers who not only had little prospect of employment but also were unable to resume subsistence lifestyles in their uprooted communities on town fringes. It was hoped that showing PNG in a better light would encourage Australians to apply for positions there.[10] OSB invested heavily in the campaign, appointing a former PNG volunteer, Maddy Harford, as a fulltime coordinator and providing a staff working group led by Deborah Rhodes, OSB's Pacific Director, to give ongoing attention to the campaign.[11]

The national launch of "PNG Profile: Diversity Next Door" on 13 June 1995 coincided with the opening of an exhibition of photos of PNG and OSB personnel working there that travelled to all Australian states, publication of a booklet on development issues in PNG and a resource kit for use in schools. Realising the importance of having a credible PNG voice during the campaign, OSB arranged a speaking tour for Simon

Pentanu, PNG's Chief Ombudsman.[12] In Canberra, the Parliamentary Library hosted a major speaking event and he spoke separately with officials from the Department of Foreign Affairs and Trade, AusAID and other agencies before addressing groups of business people, parliamentarians and journalists in Brisbane, Sydney and Melbourne. The campaign aimed to inform decision-makers and the broader community through a variety of activities. PNG community worker Dorothy Budiara visited Adelaide and Sydney to meet with community organisations. A team of former PNG volunteers toured a roadshow through rural Western Australia, conducting community information sessions and exhibiting their own photographs of PNG. OSB was also the major sponsor of PNG performance groups Drum Drum and Sanguma who performed at the Adelaide Fringe Festival and the South Australian Youth Education Program. It commissioned a film about PNG for Australian television, securing a grant from AusAID for this purpose and selecting documentary-maker Don Parham to direct a docu-comedy featuring Melbourne comic Mary Coustas, in her well-known Effie character, on tour in PNG. *Big Hair Woman* screened on Channel 10 on 17 December 1996 to an estimated audience of a million viewers.[13] Given the demographic profile of Channel 10 viewers at the time, it can be assumed that the film reached many with no previous exposure to recent material about PNG. Against spectacular scenery, the film totally humanised Papua New Guineans as warm, intelligent and funny, highlighting the role of women in PNG society and speaking with young people about their aspirations.[14]

The year-long campaign succeeded in presenting a more nuanced and more positive picture of PNG to many Australians in diverse settings, but it is more difficult to measure the success of the campaign in recruiting volunteers. In 1997, the year after the campaign, 45 volunteers went to PNG – double the number of volunteers who went in the preceding year. Although this highpoint was never achieved again in ensuing years, the numbers remained higher than they had been previously.

Technical assistance to Pacific Island governments

Technical assistance to the governments of the Pacific Islands was a significant component of Australia's overall aid program through the 1980s. Australia, because of its proximity and prior involvement, understood that it occupied a position of natural leadership amongst international donors in the region. With this understanding came the perception of a responsibility to provide professional administrators and other specialists to contribute leadership and advice and fill gaps in departments and agencies of Pacific Island governments. The major mechanism for delivering this technical assistance, the Australian Staffing Assistance Scheme (ASAS), was a direct descendant of Australia's colonial practice. It was modelled on a British equivalent and operated on a smaller scale in parts of Africa. ASAS was able to deliver highly skilled personnel, informed advice and expertise, but it exhibited and perpetuated the elitist and privileged excesses of expatriate living made possible by generous allowances in addition to local salaries. The scheme ran on the assumption that assistance would always be required and did little to assist local people to take professional responsibility or develop organisational capacity. Some local and foreign critics sometimes referred to ASAS personnel as "long socks", alluding to the tropical dress code of the British Empire. Many ASAS officers developed deep knowledge and understanding of the people they worked with and their culture, but they did so as individuals rather than as a result of the scheme.

Sometimes AVA volunteers worked in government departments where ASAS personnel were also engaged, living in similar government housing and with similar qualifications and experience. The differences were in philosophy, motivation and dollars. In the 1980s, OSB had attracted ADAB funds to support a relatively small Development Worker Scheme (DWS) in Pacific Island countries, which enabled allowances to be paid to personnel who had previously been volunteers. The DWS was based on the idea that returned volunteers who volunteered again were perpetuating their financial disadvantage. The additional allowances paid under DWSs recognised that volunteers had financial commitments in Australia and were paid in Australia.

Apart from this, DWS assignments were like other volunteer placements, with the employing authority in the host countries providing local housing and salary, thus maintaining the volunteer program philosophy.

In the 1990s, AIDAB occasionally requested OSB to consider recruiting for particular fields where a skill shortage had been identified. Several such requests in 1994 triggered discussion about enhanced remuneration levels for volunteers and the payment of fees to OSB for the service. The first positions requested were for subject department heads at Vanuatu's Matevulu College, followed by requests for people to fill senior public service roles in Tonga. To ensure that the roles were quickly filled, AIDAB was prepared to pay additional allowances up to $21,000 and a 14 per cent management fee to OSB. The OSB management team was gratified by AIDAB's recognition that OSB routinely recruited people with the skills and experience required for these positions. It gave them a sense that OSB was in a strong position because, even with the additional allowances and management fees, OSB offered substantial savings compared to the ASAS recruiting process.[15] Because responding to unscheduled requests, sometimes for different countries at the same time and always with a sense of urgency and priority, was potentially disruptive to OSB staff and workflows OSB's Pacific Director, Deborah Rhodes, undertook to explore with AIDAB the possibility of an umbrella agreement between AIDAB and OSB that set out how such positions would be filled and funded and drew on the experience of other technical assistance projects funded by AIDAB in Swaziland, Cambodia, Laos and Vanuatu.[16]

AIDAB welcomed the opportunity to work towards a Pacific Personnel Recruitment Service, and the prospect of this new approach caused OSB's management group to discuss and analyse some key issues and questions. They recognised that, while personnel recruited by OSB may well have the mindset of volunteers, their remuneration would be a departure from traditional volunteer norms. OSB had to guarantee to fill the roles as requested by AIDAB officers in Australian High Commissions in Pacific Island nations, and the arrangements had the potential to change the relationships between OSB, AIDAB, local employers and the "volunteers". The OSB needed AIDAB to understand that such a service would be separate from arrangements for AVA volunteers and would need to be fully funded. Should the arrangement be global or restricted to the Pacific? As the independence of OSB's programming had been sacrosanct for so long and OSB did not want AVA to be directed by AIDAB, it wanted to deal with AIDAB on technical assistance issues region by region. Would this mean separate recruitment processes? Would it require dedicated staff? Would it take higher priority over AVA?[17]

AusAID too had been discussing the prospect and informed OSB in July 1995 that circumstances had changed and that a Pacific Personnel Recruitment Service might have to be put out to tender.[18] Nevertheless, OSB continued its efforts to influence the nature of the arrangement by suggesting that it be seen as an extension of the AVA program or at least informed by AVA practice, a suggestion that AusAID people were receptive to. OSB was particularly keen that the scheme would not involve employment contracts between individuals and OSB, but would involve people participating in a scheme of service. The expectation was that if issues arose between employers and personnel, both OSB and AusAID would be involved in negotiating and trouble-shooting.

A draft synopsis of the proposed Pacific Personnel Recruitment Service (PPRS) was finalised for Rhodes to present to the AusAID Executive on 7 September 1995. The Service was described as a response to ongoing needs for technical assistance expressed by Pacific Island countries, specifically for positions in middle and senior levels of public service. Countries like Australia, it was argued, would continue to be asked for technical assistance because of ongoing shortages in expertise created by continuous migration of qualified people from countries with small populations to neighbouring countries. AusAID's procurement processes were such that, for PPRS to be funded without a competitive tender, it had to be demonstrated that it was a natural extension of the AVA program and, consequently, that OSB was a sole provider. OSB's programs would operate at three levels: recent graduates in roles that suited their recently acquired knowledge but relative inexperience; the AVA program in which the average age of volunteers was approximately 40; and the PPRS comprising people with substantial experience who were highly skilled, happy to be placed in senior roles and needing to cover financial commitments in Australia. It was proposed that those appointed be paid salaries similar to local personnel in similar roles with a supplement of between $15,000 and $20,000 per year and further adjustments for cost of living variations and dependants. OSB would be paid a fee for each appointment, with the amount to be determined country by country. Even with these supplements and fees, it was clear that the proposed arrangements would be cheaper than ASAS appointments arranged through commercial contractors.[19]

Pacific Technical Assistance Facility

Some OSB staff and Committee members were reluctant to pursue a scheme they thought had the potential to undermine the traditional volunteer model. Following the Committee's policy discussion in August 1995, they were largely persuaded that, by incorporating features from the volunteer program into the new arrangement, it would provide additional validation of the volunteer idea and acknowledgment of OSB's expertise. In AusAID also differing agendas and interests of individuals ensured that it took many months to negotiate a way forward. Rhodes kept the dialogue going and stood by OSB's proposed scheme, eventually prevailing. By the end of June 1996 it was intimated that a contract would soon be available to make $50,000 available for set-up costs, placing an initial limit of 30 appointments. The new AusAID facility would be called Pacific Technical Advisory Facility (PACTAF), and it would be managed by OSB.[20] A four-year contract to July 2000 was extended to July 2001, after which it was revised and renewed as PACTAF Phase Two through to July 2004 and further extended to November 2006.

PACTAF became AusAID's primary channel to supply technical assistance to Pacific Island governments and grew rapidly beyond its initial limit to 30–40 appointments each year. While the facility was used for short-term inputs when required, most assignments were for more than two years. PACTAF became OSB's most substantial and enduring activity apart from the AVA program. As it grew, the PACTAF continued to be based on and exhibit features derived from OSB's volunteer program experience and, consequently, was widely appreciated across the region. In no sense were Australian experts foisted on aid recipients; all assignments were requested by the employing department in the host country. Personnel were understood to work for that department and within its structures, often signing an agreement to that effect, and to receive a local salary and housing. Supplementary allowances were paid, some standardised and others based on particular circumstances. In large measure the character and reputation of PACTAF stemmed from OSB's approaches to selection and pre-departure briefing. Clearly it was essential to examine carefully candidates' experience and professional standing in their respective fields, but OSB staff knew that it was just as critical to select candidates with the personal attributes to enable connection and communication in cross-cultural settings. Openness, curiosity and empathy were as important as expertise. Inevitably some PACTAF positions existed to fill gaps and deliver professional services, such as positions for medical specialists in hospitals, but the program as a whole was framed to engender capacity development that impacted not only an individual's colleagues, but also the organisations they worked in and the ways the organisations related to others.

Building Australian connections with the Pacific

While many OSB projects were necessarily implemented in one or more of the Pacific countries, others were more about bringing Pacific Islanders to Australia to showcase the realities of their life and the efforts, particularly of local community organisations in the Pacific, to improve their lives. The Melanesian Women's Tour in 1994 was an innovative example, whereby seven Melanesian women were invited to spend one month touring five Australian states with public and media engagements in the towns and cities they visited. In part it was a celebration of OSB's 30 years work in

Melanesia, but, more significantly, it was an endeavour to promote greater understanding in the Australian community of Melanesian cultures and of the ways in which Melanesian communities were facing up to contemporary challenges, highlighting the crucial leadership roles played by women. In determining the composition of the group, OSB consciously adopted the Melanesian view that, as a cultural grouping and an ethno-geographic area, Melanesia extended beyond the Melanesian states of PNG, Solomon Islands, Vanuatu and Fiji to include Indonesian Papua (Irian Jaya) and Kanaky in New Caledonia. The women were proposed by organisations that knew OSB, mainly through the AVA program. They revelled in the opportunity to get to know each other and to experience and demonstrate a pan-Melanesian solidarity. All had stories to tell reflecting their diverse involvements in their own communities: one was a radio journalist with an indigenous radio station; one trained young rural women through a church program; others ran their own business, promoted nutritious food processing, and worked in domestic violence and women's literacy programs. The tour involved a mix of speaking engagements, informal interactions and media interviews, concluding with a seminar in Parliament House, Canberra and a meeting with Gordon Bilney, Minister for Development Co-operation and Pacific Island Affairs.[21]

In the following year another set of linkages was promoted through an Aboriginal women's tour to the Solomon Islands, which enabled OSB to connect its relationships in the Solomon Islands with its work in Aboriginal Australia. Julalikari Council Aboriginal Corporation in Tennant Creek, a strong supporter of the OSB's recruitment services for Aboriginal communities, was a natural partner for this activity, which was an extension of the Tennant Creek women's activities in health promotion, nutrition, domestic violence, alcohol abuse and the arts in their community. Five women involved in Julalikari Council's community work travelled to Solomon Islands to spend time with community and women's organisations known well to OSB in the capital Honiara and the Western Province towns of Munda and Gizo. Their interaction generated recognition of the strength and power of each other's cultures and the

Solomon Islands women showcased their role as community leaders, spokespersons and organisers.[22]

Among others in a diverse range of projects that OSB managed outside Australia for the Australian government was a project with the Western Samoa Department of Public Works Building Inspection Unit from 1992 to 1996 to upgrade building practices to cyclone-proof standard. The practical demonstration of the standard involved retrofitting 95 schools, in collaboration with work teams recruited through Rotary Australia. Because natural disasters occur regularly in the Pacific Islands, there was sustained interest in improving community readiness. In 1993 OSB, in collaboration with the Australian Red Cross, won a tender for an Australian government-funded project to increase disaster preparedness across the Pacific Islands. As well as collaboration with national Red Cross societies, this project also involved close cooperation with PIANGO in coordinating the delivery of NGO training workshops.

Bougainville

Bougainville was the site for several projects that attracted Australian government funding and built on OSB's history of assigning Australian volunteers to Bougainville since 1968. Twenty-five volunteers worked in the health and education sectors in what was then PNG's North Solomons Province, until the program had to be suspended at the height of the civil war in 1988. It resumed again in 1994, long before the 1997 ceasefire and the four-year peace process leading to the 2001 Bougainville Autonomy Agreement. Volunteer community development workers trained Bougainvilleans in conflict resolution and helped facilitate traditional reconciliation meetings; doctors provided emergency medical assistance; and financial advisers helped develop micro-enterprise and micro-finance schemes. The presence of the volunteers – 40 between 1994 and 2002 – together with the Peace Monitoring Group sent by the Australian Government, was instrumental in rebuilding relations between Australians and Bougainvilleans.

AVI worked hard to build relationships with the communities and with the leaders of both the Bougainville Transitional Government and the Bougainville Revolutionary Army (BRA), thus emphasising its transparent commitment to peacebuilding. The program was not without risk and there were occasions when the volunteers comprising the Medical Support Team had to be temporarily evacuated when hostilities resumed between the PNG Defence Force and the BRA in Bougainville and Buka. AVI had worked in post-conflict situations in several countries in Africa, Asia, and the Pacific and had developed from these experiences a coherent view of what was involved:

> In post-conflict situations, Australian Volunteers International recognises that peacebuilding is not only about implementing peace agreements, repairing damaged infrastructure and rebuilding an economy. It's about working with communities to rebuild or strengthen grassroots institutions that have been shattered in conflict, connecting communities that have been divided, and facilitating the development of structures that support good governance. It's also about restoring trust, rebuilding dignity and faith, repairing relationships and developing confidence.[23]

AVI's activities in Pacific countries and the linkages forged between communities were undoubtedly the most varied and complex of any region. Here was a full spectrum of initiatives: plugging gaps in service delivery especially in health and education; assisting community development in both peacetime and post-conflict situations; assisting NGOs to build institutional networks; capacity development in government agencies; linking active women across the region; and endeavouring to change perceptions and stereotypes in the Australian community. The richness of these multi-dimensional relationships arose in large measure from the continuous significance of the region in the organisation's programs from the early 1960s.

OSB staff member Kate Greaves encounters a small pig on one of many trips to PNG, 1994. Courtesy AVI

The Melanesian Women's Tour participants meet Gordon Bilney, Minister for Development Cooperation and Pacific Island Affairs, Parliament House, Canberra, 11 March 1994. Courtesy AVI

Vocational instructor Robert Green with students in the carpentry workshop of the Education Division, Manus Island, PNG, 1994–95. Courtesy AVI

Valeska Wood, community worker for the Simbu Provincial Council of Women, Kundiawa, PNG, 1994–95. Photo Brian Gilkes. Courtesy AVI

Mary Coustas as Effie, during the filming of *Big Hair Woman,* 1995. Photo Dennis Wisken. Courtesy AVI

Cartographer/survey draftsperson David Llewellyn with colleagues at the Kiribati Ministry of Home Affairs and Decentralisation, 1997. Photo Brian Gilkes. Courtesy AVI

Carolyn Barnes, primary school teacher on Efate, Vanuatu, with friends Lina and Leimet at a Port Vila market, October 2000. Photo Will Salter. Courtesy AVI

CHAPTER 10

East Timor: Supporting Self-determination

Indonesia's occupation of East Timor began in December 1975, eight months after the fall of Saigon. Internationally there was a conservative view that an independent East Timor could also fall to Communism and become the region's Cuba. Consequently, Indonesia's annexation of East Timor had broad international support, including from successive Australian governments. Despite this, large sections of the Australian community had a different view. The deaths of Australian TV journalists, who came to be known as the Balibo Five, produced a visceral reaction among those who were outraged that Indonesian forces had killed them to hide evidence of the impending invasion. There was strong sentiment in favour of self-determination, particularly among church circles (progressive Catholics being the most active), trade unionists and veterans of the Second World War with grateful memories of the assistance they received from the people of East Timor. A significant community of Timorese exiles in Australia circulated what information they had about events in East Timor.

Defining issue in human rights advocacy

ACFOA played an important role in advocating for the right of the East Timorese to determine their own future, particularly through its East Timor Sub-Committee, chaired by Bill Armstrong and driven mainly by Pat Walsh. By the mid-1980s, ACFOA's enthusiasm for such advocacy had waned, but Armstrong, as Vice-President of ACFOA, provided crucial support to establish ACFOA's Human Rights Office in Melbourne with Walsh as the ACFOA staff member responsible for its leadership. By placing East Timor in a broader human rights agenda they had made it possible to continue to campaign for self-determination. OSB actively participated in the ACFOA Human Rights Committee and supported the work of the Human Rights Office, which, along with advocacy for the rights of people in Sri Lanka and Burma, continued to focus on East Timor.[1] OSB had a strong reputation for activism on the East Timor issue, even though it was not a component of its organisational policy, as a number of key staff had been involved in East Timorese advocacy in organisations such as Action for World Development and the Australia–East Timor Association (AETA) in the 1970s, years before they worked at OSB.[2]

The Indonesian occupation was characterised by systematic violence and human rights abuse, and at least until the late 1980s it effectively isolated East Timor and prevented informed reporting about incidents there.[3] Indonesia insisted that East Timor was prospering from its integration into Indonesia, a message that circulated particularly successfully within Indonesia where the press was tightly controlled, but also internationally, thus concealing or at least preventing much attention to the reality of the situation in East Timor. The actual state of affairs was revealed in 1991 with coverage of the Santa Cruz massacre, when 250 unarmed Timorese were killed at a demonstration filmed by foreign journalists. This film grabbed media attention worldwide and brought to life international concern for East Timor's self-determination. It also revealed the real situation to politically aware Indonesians as film clips of the massacre circulated informally. Because of the attention it received, the Santa Cruz massacre was an iconic moment in East Timor's struggle for independence and the OSB Committee discussed it at length, describing it as "not only an outrage against the East Timorese people but also against the people of Indonesia".[4] In a statement to all staff Armstrong passed on the Committee's recognition and support for the efforts of many Bureau staff in support of the rights of the people of East Timor.[5]

Support in Australia

Beginning in the 1980s OSB provided informal and discreet support to the East Timor campaign in Australia, especially in Melbourne. Abel Guterres* was a bus driver well known to Armstrong, Chris Dureau and others involved in the East Timor solidarity movement.[6] His bus depot was close to OSB's office and, through the 1980s, he would occasionally visit the office after his shift, knowing that he could talk about his concerns and get a supportive hearing. He also was able to use a photocopier, fax machine and telephone. Over time his visits gradually became more frequent, until they were almost daily in the 1990s when OSB became his de facto operational base until the East Timor Development Office was established in mid-1999. Guterres had become a key figure in the Timorese independence movement in Australia and his access to OSB's telephone and fax facilities enabled him to liaise with colleagues in the movement in other states and, more importantly, with others in Indonesia, Portugal and Mozambique. The support he received in the OSB office may well be the Bureau's most significant contribution to the East Timorese struggle for self-determination.

Because East Timor had remained on the agenda of the United Nations' Decolonisation Committee, it had always received a measure of diplomatic attention. By the 1990s it was also receiving much greater attention from the international media. By this time there were significant numbers of East Timorese students at schools and universities in Java and other parts of Indonesia who adeptly maintained a momentum of activism and publicity. It was understood that, while Suharto was Indonesia's President and the military retained its power, Indonesian policy on East Timor would not change. The Asian financial crisis of 1997–98 introduced an unexpected instability that led to Suharto's forced resignation. His successor B.J. Habibie introduced the notion of a higher degree of autonomy for the province of East Timor, to which Australian Prime Minister John Howard responded by writing to Habibie to suggest that a period of autonomy be followed by an act of self-determination. Habibie, conscious of the high cost of Indonesia's

* Guterres later became East Timor's diplomatic representative in Australia.

presence in East Timor and the ingratitude of the East Timorese, elected to go straight to a choice between autonomy and independence.[7] The Indonesian military were determined that Indonesia hold onto East Timor, but Habibie's government included fellow members of the Indonesian Association of Muslim Intellectuals, such as Adi Sasono and Dewi Fortuna Anwar, who were fully aware of the diplomatic cost to Indonesia and highly critical of Indonesia's occupation. In January 1999 Habibie declared that if the East Timorese chose independence Indonesia would let the province go.

It was at this point that OSB's Melbourne-based Program Officer for Thailand and Malaysia, Kirsty Sword resigned to return to Jakarta to join Xanana Gusmão on his release from prison to a prison-service house in Central Jakarta. After his capture in 1992 Gusmão had continued to lead the liberation movement from prison in Jakarta and had achieved international standing as its leader. Sword had previously lived in Jakarta, supporting the liberation movement while holding a number of temporary part-time jobs, one of which involved administration and liaison work for OSB's Indonesia program in 1993–95, but it was not until she returned to Jakarta on Gusmão's release that OSB learned of the depth of the relationship that had developed between them.[8] Anticipating the heavy workload that would descend on Gusmão, Sword helped plan a support office for him. He was responding daily to requests for meetings from diplomats, visiting world leaders such as Madeleine Albright and Jimmy Carter, politicians such as Alexander Downer, journalists from around the world, and Timorese youth in Jakarta, as well as keeping abreast of developments in Timor. Once agreement had been reached in New York that the popular consultation would take the form of a direct ballot, Gusmão also had to respond to senior United Nations officials needing to consult with him.[9]

CNRT's Planning Conference

In April 1998, at a meeting in Portugal, all Timorese parties agreed to join a single national umbrella group or peak council, the Conselho Nacional de

Resistência Timorense (CNRT, National Council of Timorese Resistance) under the leadership of Xanana Gusmão. In Australia, one of CNRT's major undertakings was to organise a Strategic Development Planning Conference in Melbourne in April 1999. Leading the effort was Emília Pires, a public servant in the Victorian Department of Human Services, who brought together a group to help plan the event.* The Australian government provided funding support and senior AusAID staff participated in conference sessions, as well as meeting with ACFOA's East Timor Working Group, including OSB, as part of their preparation for a programming mission to East Timor, previously agreed with Indonesia, which they were intent on carrying through with as soon as the changing political environment allowed.[10] The mission's Terms of Reference specifically anticipated the need for a volunteer program component in the assistance package.

The conference brought together Timorese and other academics with specialised knowledge of the country from around the world, policy makers, aid administrators, and staff from development NGOs. OSB used its participation in the conference to garner support for its intention to prepare for a special recruitment initiative once a political resolution had been reached. It was evident that the lack of skilled and trained East Timorese was looming as a significant constraint to development in all areas of public life and private enterprise. Some believed that East Timorese living in Australia would be interested in returning to an independent East Timor, but there was no real evidence of this interest or knowledge of their skills. To assist in planning future technical assistance it was important to ascertain the numbers and skills of those considering a return to East Timor once circumstances permitted. The total number of East Timorese in Australia was estimated at between 15,000 and 20,000, but it was possible that only a relatively small number of these would have professional skills and be available. OSB put a proposal to AusAID on 22 April 1999 for funding to conduct a skills survey of the East Timor diaspora in Australia. Given the political sensitivities and suspicion that the East Timorese community was accustomed to, OSB insisted that the

* Emília Pires was East Timor's Minister for Finance from 2007 to 2015.

survey be conducted in partnership with CNRT and worked closely with Pires to develop the proposal.

Diaspora survey

AusAID accepted that CNRT's involvement was essential and contracted OSB (AVI after May 1999) to undertake the survey in May and June. Pires was engaged as a consultant along with Filomeno Tilman de Andrade, another well-credentialed CNRT member who was a Sydney-based engineer. The project organised 17 public meetings of the East Timorese community (five in Darwin, three in Sydney and Melbourne, two in Perth and Cairns, one in Brisbane and Adelaide) at which people were invited to register their interest and provide personal details. Either Pires or de Andrade or another CNRT colleague attended each of the meetings to explain the purpose of the survey and assuage any fear or suspicion community members might have about providing personal details; AVI staff attended all meetings to introduce the organisation and explain its role. The survey instrument and an accompanying explanatory letter were available in English, Portuguese, Tetum and Hakka.

The meetings were advertised through the East Timor community as CNRT meetings and followed a set agenda that began with an information update on the situation in East Timor and on negotiations with the United Nations, discussion of the human resources project explaining what AVI was and why it was involved, and why the Australian government was interested in funding the project. This was followed by more CNRT business, including distribution of CNRT's census forms, an update on the Strategic Development Planning Conference, fundraising and an explanation of CNRT's regional structures (in the states that had no regional structure).[11] Despite the large attendance at the meetings – a total of 659 attended across the country – the project was not without controversy. In Darwin, although 70 East Timorese attended one of the meetings, some chose to boycott them because they had no reason to trust AVI, forcing Pires to clarify that AVI was involved at her request and with Gusmão's support.[12] From the survey data a database of the personal details and CVs of 108 skilled East Timorese, 40 of whom were women, was compiled.[13]

Preparing for the ballot

Negotiations at the United Nations concluded in May, with Indonesia's agreement that the popular consultation would be a simple ballot. The United Nations Security Council resolved in June to establish the United Nations Mission in East Timor (UNAMET), with a mandate to conduct a ballot in which East Timorese would choose to accept Indonesia's offer of special autonomy or to reject it and thus vote for independence in effect. UNAMET had little more than two months to make administrative and logistical arrangements, including the registration of voters. In order to mobilise skilled people rapidly it turned to the United Nations' volunteer program (UNV), which had demonstrated its capacity in the Cambodian elections of 1993 by mobilising 450 electoral officers and other specialists in support of UNTAC. UNV's Program Manager in Cambodia, Kevin Gilroy, was to coordinate the East Timor operation. Aware of AVI's reputation from his time in Cambodia, he requested AVI's cooperation to help recruit the district electoral officers he needed. Within six weeks UNV mobilised 500 volunteers from 79 countries; the largest contingent was the 29 Australians recruited by AVI.[14] In addition to its Cambodia experience, AVI brought to UNV its experience in Indonesia and its ability to recruit Australian volunteers who understood the Indonesian language.

The international volunteers were marshalled in Darwin at the Royal Australian Air Force base, with most of the Australians in the first group. UNV welcomed AVI's request to brief the volunteers.[15] AVI was conscious that if something was to go amiss, as an Australian organisation it was exposed to recriminations that would not apply to countries that were not neighbours. The briefing on 18 June 1999 in part addressed the need for volunteers to maintain an official neutrality, irrespective of their own sentiments but, following strong representations from AVI, UNV also took advantage of expertise in AVI to brief the volunteers on the Indonesian army's background and likely reaction if the ballot supported independence.

Support in Jakarta

AVI was now being asked to help send people to both East Timor and Jakarta. As there was no program framework within which it could do so, AVI decided to use its own resources to support a few people well-known to AVI as one of several avenues to support CNRT. The first was João Gonçalves, who contacted Armstrong when Gusmão requested his presence in Jakarta. Gonçalves and Armstrong had previously collaborated in lobbying for the recognition and resettlement of Timorese exiles and their access to protection and services.* He was joined in Jakarta on 9 August by Pires, who wrote

> Poor Xanana really needs all the help he can get. People of all sorts, from individuals to organisations to countries representations just bombard him and I am not sure how he gets his head around on all the issues. That's why we are trying to get a team up behind him so we can get a bit of this pressure off him in some of the matters. Joe [João] has been helping him with some of the important matters like security and other things.

Pires had also been liaising with small organisations in East Timor and fielding requests for assistance from them. One was an orphanage in Dare that had extended its work into assisting internally displaced persons in places that neither Caritas nor UNAMET could get into because of militia activity. Her idea was to send East Timorese volunteers for periods up to two months to provide and build additional organisational capacity. The person she identified was Melbourne-based Vicky Tchong, known to

* Gonçalves was Minister of Economy and Development from 2007 to 2012 before becoming Head of Mission Unit for the Timor-Leste–Indonesia–Australia Growth Triangle.

AVI as the woman who had translated the Diaspora Skills Audit materials into Hakka while leaning on the counter next to the cash register in her family's Kensington supermarket. Pires asked if Tchong could be routed via Jakarta so she could meet Gusmão.[16] Thus, instead of proceeding to Dili, she became a key person in the Jakarta team that focused on arranging for East Timorese students to return home.

The team supporting Gusmão in Jakarta was to a large extent from Australia. He had identified particular CNRT people whose advice and assistance he wanted, and AVI responded. Pires was required because of her leadership role in the Strategic Development Conference, after which she took leave from the Victorian Public Service to manage full-time the East Timor Development Office she had established with some financial support from AVI. The office was located with ACFOA's Human Rights Office, enabling a close working relationship with Pat Walsh. She was in contact with a wide range of people with development experience and expertise and could help Gusmão think about what independence would look like and assist him in discussions with Sarah Cliffe, Chief of Mission for the World Bank's program in East Timor.[17] Cliffe and her colleague, Klaus Rohland, had begun working on East Timor in early 1999 and, unlike United Nations agencies' insistence that CNRT be regarded as a political party, the World Bank saw CNRT as a necessary and constructive partner in making East Timorese views known.[18]

At the beginning of September, Armstrong wrote to Graham Barrett, a former foreign correspondent and foreign editor for *The Age* newspaper who was then working for the World Bank, to explore further assistance for CNRT. Armstrong applauded the World Bank's interest in holding further discussions with East Timor's political leadership and planning professionals, but pointed out that the President of CNRT and his ad-hoc advisory team were operating without financial resources. Armstrong stressed their urgent need for funds, explaining that $50,000 could immediately be spent on airfares, office equipment and communications. If it was difficult for the Bank to release funds from Jakarta, CNRT was happy for any funding to be channelled through AVI. The World Bank responded that it was aware of the situation and would do what it could once the outcome of the ballot was known.[19]

The ballot and the aftermath

East Timorese overwhelmingly voted for independence in the 30 August 1999 referendum. Within hours of the announcement of the result on 4 September, the Indonesian military and the militias it had created and trained launched revanchist attacks across East Timor, razing towns and massacring their inhabitants. They implemented a scorched earth policy, using arson and looting, as well as killing and forcibly relocating people. There was no surprise about this among informed observers and people close to the situation in East Timor as there was no semblance of Indonesian civilian control over the military, which was never going to enable a peaceful transition. Tragically, the international community could do nothing to prevent the disaster. International assessors estimated that 75% of the population was displaced and almost 70% of the infrastructure destroyed.[20]

The UNVs were forced to take sanctuary in the crowded United Nations compound until all were evacuated to Darwin. The evacuation of United Nations staff, other foreign nationals, and refugees began on 6 September, taking over a week to complete. About 100 UNVs remained in Darwin to help UNAMET with nearly 2,000 refugees. In mid-September the United Nations Security Council mandated Australia to organise and lead a peacekeeping mission, the International Force East Timor (INTERFET). Once Dili had been secured the UNVs who had kept working in Darwin were able to return to East Timor, although some were stationed in areas where militias were still active, so they established close working relationships with INTERFET troops in their locale. Among the UNVs to return were 11 Australians attached to the United Nations Transitional Administration in East Timor (UNTAET) when it was established in late October 1999. Four of them acted as District Administrators – the highest rank in the civilian administration at district level; others left UNV to take up ongoing positions in UNTAET.

Gusmão was finally released on 7 September 1999. The Indonesian plan was to fly Gusmão to Dili, but nobody in his team thought this a safe option. Looking for an alternative, they asked the British Ambassador for refuge and a makeshift residence and office was set up in the British compound.[21] This respite was temporary, however, as the increased pressure on the Indonesian government to allow an international force to restore order in Timor led to increasingly violent demonstrations in Jakarta against foreign targets. There were also rumours that the military might launch a coup against Habibie and the militias were a constant threat. The Portuguese Ambassador agreed to pay for a number of rooms in the Mandarin Hotel for Gusmão and some of his team. Gusmão, Sword and a small group of colleagues flew to Darwin on 18 September, the day before INTERFET landed in Dili. This move also had to be negotiated as Gusmão did not want to abandon the Timorese in Indonesia, who were increasingly at risk of attacks by militia. Before leaving Jakarta he insisted that some of his team stay there to ensure their evacuation to East Timor.

East Timor Humanitarian Response Group

The repatriation of the East Timorese in Jakarta and other parts of Indonesia became the responsibility of Tchong, assisted by Pires, Gonçalves and Mike Parsons, a newly arrived team member, known as the East Timor Humanitarian Response Group. Parsons had a long involvement in the East Timor independence campaign and substantial experience in the Pacific Islands.[22] Earlier in 1999, Walsh had arranged for him to work with Pires and Guterres in the East Timor Development Organisation. In the period after the ballot, they decided he was needed in Jakarta and AVI agreed to support him.

Their urgent task was to find, register and assist in the repatriation of East Timorese students and others who were increasingly frightened by the activities of militia groups in Indonesia. Initially this group largely consisted of students at universities and colleges in Jakarta, Java and other parts of Indonesia, but their numbers were swollen by thousands who had fled East Timor, many to Bali and Javanese cities. Parsons followed up Pires' visits to embassies in Jakarta, drafting formal submissions for funding and liaising with Dureau in Bali where he and Christine Perkins were coordinating a group to identify, register and support East Timorese.[23] Parsons also made domestic airline bookings. Once the United Nations High Commissioner for Refugees, Sadako Ogata, had intervened, UNHCR and the International Organization for Migration (IOM) cooperated more readily with facilitating direct flights from Indonesia to Timor for the returning Timorese. It has been estimated that the Response Group managed to get more than 15,000 people back to East Timor from various parts of Indonesia on flights, ships and trucks.[24]

The Response Group's operations were hampered by the constant threat of the militias. With around 20 CNRT people working with them, they stayed in cheap hotels in Central Jakarta, moving almost daily to keep one step ahead of the militias. Fortunately, once Gusmão's group had left Jakarta, more of them could live and work, albeit in crowded circumstances, in the Mandarin Hotel. Even there they were not immune from the militias' menace; when militia booked a room on the floor below them, they decided it was time to leave. Gonçalves arranged for people from the Brazilian Embassy to escort him and Parsons to the airport and they flew to Darwin via Singapore. Tchong moved to the Hyatt.[25]

Planning to provide appropriate human resources

AVI had remained in frequent contact with CNRT at its Darwin base, with AusAID in Canberra, and with the World Bank and UNDP to discuss how best to ensure that appropriate human resources were available for reconstruction. All parties agreed that AVI's plan to open a register of interested people was worthwhile and it was launched on 21 September, providing a way of dealing with the large number of unsolicited calls from people around Australia wanting to help. As Armstrong pointed out, it was a response to "Xanana Gusmão who has requested a team of Australian volunteers to support the longer-term reconstruction and rehabilitation of his country once the emergency relief effort has subsided".[26]

AusAID responded quickly to the urgency of the need and informed AVI that it wanted to respond to requests for personnel through AVI.[27] AusAID proposed to contract OSB to deliver a Staffing Assistance Program to East Timor (SAPET), largely based on the PACTAF contract. AusAID flagged that, while in the longer term another program would be required to provide people with a range of skills in a capacity-building framework, SAPET would be the rapid-response mechanism for requests for personnel made to AusAID by the United Nations, NGOs, international organisations and the East Timorese community.[28] AusAID also informed CNRT that AVI would be their contractor for staffing assistance and asked CNRT to tell interested East Timorese to register with OSB. Accordingly, in a letter Pires circulated throughout the East Timorese community in Australia, she encouraged people interested in returning to register with AVI – "an organisation that we have chosen to help us find jobs for Timorese who want to go back".[29]

The violence that followed the ballot changed assumptions about how planning might proceed, so the World Bank took the lead in organising a Joint Assessment Mission in late October and early November. The Mission included the major financial institutions and donor countries and equal numbers of Timorese and other experts. As the World Bank had no way of directly funding the Timorese participation, and no channels were available through the United Nations or bilateral donors, AVI agreed to receive the funds to pay the costs for the East Timor Technical Group for one month.[30] A similar request followed in January 2000 for AVI to receive World Bank funds to support East Timorese "sector technicians" to advise the National Consultative Council which was established to convey East Timorese advice and views to UNTAET.[31]

AVI's East Timor Task Force

Because of the variety and volume of AVI's activity relating to East Timor, an internal Task Force was established for three months under the management of Megs Alston, who initiated a weekly bulletin to keep all staff informed. AVI's communication with the World Bank and the United Nations was ongoing, as was the mobilisation of people. By 11 November 1999, 14 volunteers were in East Timor working with the United Nations and the Jesuit Refugee Service, in addition to a group with CNRT, including Tchong, who continued to work with refugees and displaced people,* Emília Pires in the East Timor Development Agency (ETDA), and Alfredo Pires supporting CNRT's office functioning in Dili.† CNRT suggested it was now possible for AVI to directly investigate further requests for volunteers and, accordingly, the writer travelled to Dili on 11 November where he joined the others camping in the house requisitioned for CNRT. This was an important opportunity to build relationships with officials already in Dili from AusAID, the United Nations administration and the World Bank, as well as with church and educational institutions and other Timorese groups. In addition to the specialist professionals that UNTAET needed, it was evident that, with English a prerequisite for working in UNTAET, there was an immediate demand for teachers of English in a variety of educational settings. There was also a demand for people to work in public health and to build confidence and competence in new and fragile organisations.

AVI's register of interest had grown to include details of over 400 skilled people, which placed it in good stead as personnel requests were finalised and formalised. In mid-November AVI launched a public appeal for funds to send more Australian volunteers to East Timor. Armstrong made it clear that AVI would focus on long-term needs, emphasising that "rebuilding the community, rebuilding people's spirits, lives and culture are emerging as an important aspect of the work. All volunteers who go there will need the ability to work with people whose lives have been shattered, and who have lived through years of conflict".[32]

* Vicky Tchong later served as a senior official in East Timor's Department of Foreign Affairs before being posted as Ambassador to China from 2011 to 2015.

† Alfredo Pires was a geology graduate from the University of Ballarat. In 2007 he became Secretary of State for Natural Resources and subsequently Minister for Petroleum and Mineral Resources until 2017.

In a wide-ranging telephone conference between AusAID and AVI, the potential role of SAPET in assisting UNTAET was discussed, especially as it was clear that UNTAET was encountering difficulties in recruiting enough appropriately skilled people. AusAID conveyed its respect for AVI's recruitment expertise, mentioning the 600 CVs they received from people within the public service interested in working for UNTAET and restating their preference for AVI as the recruiter for any UNTAET positions that Australia was to sponsor. To this end AVI had already forwarded 44 CVs to AusAID for consideration. AusAID was enthusiastic about a proposal from AVI that it focus on the sectors identified by the World Bank mission for which it had applicants: shelter, education, translating/interpreting and counselling. AVI explained the nature and extent of the direct assistance it was providing to CNRT and CNRT's need for additional and ongoing assistance. AVI also alerted AusAID to its urgent need for additional funds for volunteers in addition to the OVTA allocation, clarifying that sending volunteers to East Timor was jeopardising AVI's ability to meet its contractual obligations under OVTA.[33] The costs associated with sending volunteers to East Timor, including the 30 Australian UNVs to date, were all unplanned and unbudgeted costs against the OVTA budget. AVI was under pressure from CNRT, the United Nations and AusAID to provide more volunteers, but the funds were not available. AVI pushed hard for more financial support from AusAID, with Armstrong travelling to Adelaide to meet with Downer in his electoral office who made it quite clear that he would not provide further specific support.[34] Consequently, much of AVI's response was unfunded.

For AVI, the lack of funds had become the constraining factor. There was substantial interest amongst local governments in Victoria that wanted to be involved in East Timor's development. The cities of Melbourne, Port Philip and Darebin had all committed to providing some assistance and wanted to develop long-term relationships with particular towns. They saw AVI as an honest broker who could connect them to East Timorese communities and ensure their responses were appropriate and, recognising that AVI was well connected to CNRT, wanted agreements with AVI. For

AVI, the appeal in working with local government was twofold: it offered the potential for community involvement in advocacy and community education, and it was the level of government that had expertise in so many of the services required in East Timor. The Australian Local Government Association (ALGA) put on the agenda of its 1999 General Assembly in Canberra a resolution asking that ALGA engage in dialogue with aid agencies and CNRT on the most appropriate way to facilitate assistance to East Timor. By June 2002, active partnerships had been developed with the cities of Moreland, Yarra, and Mornington, with more to come. This did not require large amounts of cash, but staff time and travel costs were certainly an issue for AVI.

Building the volunteer program

Alston undertook a follow-up field trip to East Timor in late December returning with 30 confirmed requests for volunteers, including teachers of English and teacher trainers, building supervisors, lawyers, midwives, translators/interpreters, administrators and psycho-social and grief counsellors. She also confirmed that AusAID would not support using AusAID funds for volunteer positions with CNRT unless they were with either the Commission for Emergency or the ETDA.[35] AusAID was not alone in this stance, as no international donors, whether government or NGO, would provide any support to CNRT. They were acting on and thus perpetuating a misapprehension originating in UNTAET that CNRT was a political party and, therefore, not to be endorsed.[36]

During her travel to East Timor, Alston recognised that an AVI staff position in Darwin was needed from January 2000 to manage the volunteer program in East Timor. Living and working conditions were tough for volunteers in East Timor as housing, power, water and food supplies were inadequate. Prices were naturally impacted by the scarcity of essential commodities, but were dramatically inflated by the distorting impact of the United Nations and other expatriates. By basing the Country Manager in Darwin, that person could work in a fully resourced office with an adequate communications infrastructure and could travel easily to monitor and support volunteers and liaise with individuals and organisations in East Timor. Christine Perkins, who had long been involved in the solidarity movement supporting the Timorese struggle for self-determination and identified with AVI's approach to development, was appointed to the role in January 2000. She worked out of AVI's Remote Recruiting office in Darwin for a full year before relocating to the national office in Melbourne where she continued to manage the volunteer program in East Timor until 2004.

SAPET

The contract for SAPET was finally signed in late December 1999, thus opening another channel for AVI in East Timor. In early March 2000, AVI was supporting, to varying extents, 26 volunteers with UNV, CNRT, other Timorese organisations and the Jesuit Refugee Service and was about to mobilise the first 13 Advisers under SAPET, which grew quickly to 28 by October. SAPET and the volunteer program were separately managed within AVI and had quite different profiles. The volunteer program continued to work closely with CNRT and assigned volunteers in Timorese civil society and educational institutions; it was also able to arrange some assignments in areas away from Dili. SAPET positions were all approved by AusAID and exclusively in the Administration, notably in the Land and Property Commission, Office of Water and Sanitation, the courts, Civil Service Academy and the ETDA. In July 2000, several positions in ETDA were shifted from the volunteer program into SAPET, thus enabling Emília Pires, Tchong, Alfredo Pires and others to be better remunerated. One position that was approved in CNRT was that of General Secretary, International Relations, which was filled by Gonçalves.

In August, the recently married Kirsty Sword also became a volunteer, first in her role as Executive Assistant in Gusmão's office and then, in

June 2001, as head of the Alola Foundation she had established to raise awareness of and campaign against sexual and gender-based violence. AVI supported her as a volunteer from August 2000 to March 2002, when the support was brought to an end after Armstrong was telephoned by an Australian Government official relaying "what was believed to be the wishes of the Foreign Minister's Office",[37] in response to the screening in February 2002 of the ABC's "Australian Story" featuring Kirsty Sword Gusmão's work for East Timor's independence. A year later, Gusmão himself divulged to Armstrong that the allowances she had been receiving from AVI (approximately $10,000 a year) were the household's only income at that time.[38]

East Timor became independent in May 2002. In the two and a half years to June 2002, AVI had recruited people for 255 placements in East Timor in response to both emergency and longer-term needs. Of these, 167 were through the core volunteer program, including 39 as UNVs; seven were attached to small projects and 81 were mobilised through SAPET.[39]

AVI was able to continue to build a strong program in East Timor because of its remarkable and unique foundations. Initially, East Timor was a major focus of the organisation's human rights advocacy, principally in the name of ACFOA. This led to opportunities to work with the Timorese diaspora in Australia, building confidence and showing that AVI's style of development was to respond to needs expressed by the community rather than through its own planned interventions. When opportunities arose to move beyond advocacy with practical and tangible actions, AVI did not hesitate to use its own resources. As a result, the Timorese leadership trusted AVI and saw it in a different light to other NGOs; the relationship was transparent and there for the United Nations, the World Bank and AusAID to see. They all held in high esteem AVI's professionalism and capacity to recruit and mobilise appropriate people for the circumstances, and it was this credibility that lay behind the success with which AVI was able to keep building its program of support to the new nation.

Kirsty Sword with Xanana Gusmão and fellow inmate João Freitas da Câmara, at the Salemba prison house, Jakarta, 1999. Courtesy Kirsty Sword Gusmão

CNRT meeting, Salemba prison house, Jakarta, 1999. L to r: Emília Pires, Xanana Gusmão, Lucas da Costa, and one of their Indonesian lawyers. Courtesy Kirsty Sword Gusmão

Some of the East Timor Humanitarian Response Group in the British Embassy, Jakarta, 1999. L to r: Mike Parsons, João Gonçalves, Cesar Dias Quintas (bodyguard of Xanana Gusmão during his house arrest), Vicky Tchong.
Courtesy Mike Parsons

Mike Parsons with Xanana Gusmão in the British Embassy, Jakarta, 1999.
Courtesy Mike Parsons

Xanana Gusmão reveals his AVI T-shirt, c.2000. Photo Kirsty Sword Gusmão

Melanie Stevens, a project development mentor with Organização Mulher Timor (Organisation of East Timorese Women) from 2000. Photo Mathias Heng. Courtesy AVI

Postscript

In writing this book, the task I set myself was to research and document the institutional history of OSB/AVI from its origins to 2002, a period of more than 50 years. Of course history has no end; AVI continues to exist and is now managing larger volunteer programs than ever. So the task remains for others to continue the research and present the path taken by the organisation since then in response to challenges and opportunities.

Throughout its history, OSB (and then AVI) has been remarkably successful in adapting to changes in its social, political and financial environments and to new opportunities in both the domestic and international arenas. It pioneered a respectful approach to providing professional recruitment services to indigenous communities; it developed partnerships to promote international opportunities for young Australians (most often in youth-to-youth programs) and it provided cross-cultural training and briefing programs to corporate Australia. AVI also successfully managed Australia's most significant technical assistance program to the Pacific Islands (through the Pacific Technical Assistance Facility/Mechanism (PACTAF/PACTAM)) and a diverse portfolio of other projects.

AVI's key achievement, however, was in keeping alive a vision and a practice, embodied in the volunteer program, which recognised that development was not something that outsiders could impose, direct or manage. This is not to say that the application of foreign expertise was irrelevant; it had to be locally managed and directed, and required thoughtful and respectful behaviour by volunteers who through their exposure to local realities and interactions with local colleagues became more attuned to issues of justice and injustice. These characteristics may not feature in official descriptions of the volunteer program but inevitably remain to some extent part of the motivation and the learning of individual volunteers and the local people they work with.

For much of its history AVI has displayed intriguing and at times contradictory personality traits such as would be found in an activist's concern for justice, an educator's focus on experiential learning, and a professional's attachment to performance and credibility. For decades the balance of these traits has shifted in response to the demands, opportunities and constraints of the specific era and to express the priorities and values of the organisation's Board and Executive. And so may it continue.

Abbreviations

ACIAR	Australian Centre for Agricultural Research
ACC	Australian Council of Churches
ACFOA	Australian Council for Overseas Aid
ACR	Australian Catholic Relief
ACTU	Australian Council of Trade Unions
ADAA	Australian Development Assistance Agency
ADAB	Australian Development Assistance Bureau
AESOP	Australian Executive Service Overseas Program
AETA	Australia-East Timor Association
AFFHC	Australian Freedom from Hunger Campaign
AIDAB	Australian International Development Assistance Bureau
ALGA	Australian Local Government Association
AMC	Australian Managing Contractor
ANC	African National Congress
ANU	Australian National University
AODRO	Australian Organisation for Disaster Relief Operations
APHEDA	Australian People for Health, Education and Development Abroad
APY	Anangu Pitjantjatjara Yankunytjatjara
ASAS	Australian Staffing Assistance Scheme
ASCM	Australian Student Christian Movement
ASEAN	Association of Southeast Asian Nations
ASIO	Australian Security Intelligence Organisation
ATBC	Australia Thailand Business Council

ATCC	Australia Thailand Chamber of Commerce
ATSIC	Aboriginal and Torres Strait Islander Commission
AusAID	Australian Agency for International Development
AustCare	Australians Caring for Refugees
AVA	Australian Volunteers Abroad
AVI	Australian Volunteers International
AVID	Australian Volunteers in International Development
AVTAP	Australian Voluntary Technical Assistance Program
AWD	Action for World Development
AYAD	Australian Youth Ambassadors for Development
BAIS	Badan Intelijen Strategis (Armed Forces Strategic Intelligence Agency)
BAKIN	Badan Koordinasi Intelijen Negara (State Intelligence Coordinating Agency)
BBYT	Beyond Borders Youth Tour
BRA	Bougainville Revolutionary Army
CAA	Community Aid Abroad
CARE	Campaign Against Racial Exploitation
CCC	Cooperation Committee for Cambodia
CDC	Committee for Development Cooperation
CIDSE	Coopération Internationale pour le Développement et la Solidarité (International Cooperation for Development and Solidarity)
CNRT	Conselho Nacional de Resistência Timorense (National Council of Timorese Resistance)
CUSO	Canadian University Service Overseas
DEET	Department of Employment, Education and Training
DFAT	Department of Foreign Affairs and Trade
DIFF	Development Import Finance Facility
DWS	Development Worker Scheme
ECPAT	End Child Prostitution in Asian Tourism
ELT	English Language Training
EOL	Exchange of Letters

ETDA	East Timor Development Agency
FAO	Food and Agricultural Organization
FNS	Friedrich-Naumann-Stiftung
FPP	Foster Parents Plan
FSP	Foundation of the Peoples of the South Pacific
GMKI	Gerakan Mahasiswa Kristen Indonesia (Indonesian Student Christian Movement)
IAPC	Indonesia Australia Program of Cooperation
IDP	International Development Program
IGGI	Intergovernmental Group on Indonesia
INFID	International NGO Forum on Indonesian Development
INGGI	Inter-NGO Conference on IGGI Matters
INTERFET	International Force East Timor
JANGOO	Joint Australian NGO Office
JAWG	Joint Agency Working Group
JCAC	Julalikari Council Aboriginal Corporation
KTLN	Kerjasama Teknik Luar Negeri (Foreign Technical Cooperation)
LDC	Least Developed Countries
LGANT	Local Government Association of Northern Territory
LP3ES	Lembaga Penelitian, Pendidikan dan Penerangan Ekonomi dan Sosial (Institute for Social and Economic Research, Education and Information)
LSP	Lembaga Studi Pembangunan (Development Studies Institute)
LWF	Lutheran World Federation
Manipol-USDEK	Manifes Politik-Undang-undang Dasar 1945, Sosialisme Indonesia, Demokrasi Terpimpin, Ekonomi Terpimpin, Kepribadian Nasional (Political Manifesto: 1945 Constitution, Indonesian Socialism, Guided Democracy, Guided Economy, National Identity)
MOU	Memorandum of Understanding

NCDS	National Centre for Development Studies
NLU	National Liaison Unit
NU	Nahdlatul Ulama
NUAUS	National Union of Australian University Students
OSB	Overseas Service Bureau
OVTA	Overseas Voluntary Technical Assistance
P3M	Perhimpunan Pengembangan Pesantren dan Masyarakat (Centre for Pesantren and Community Development)
PACTAF	Pacific Technical Assistance Facility
PACTAM	Pacific Technical Assistance Mechanism
Palms	Paulian Lay Missionary Society
PIANGO	Pacific Islands Association of NGOs
PDA	Population and Community Development Association
PPRS	Pacific Personnel Recruitment Service
RAVAA	Returned Australian Volunteers Abroad Association
RENAMO	Resistência Nacional Moçambicana (Mozambique National Resistance)
ROVA	Returned Overseas Volunteers of Australia
SADC	Southern African Development Community
SADCC	Southern African Development Co-ordination Conference
SAPET	Staffing Assistance Program for East Timor
SAPSAN	Special Assistance Program for South Africa and Namibia
SCFA	Save the Children Fund Australia
SCM	Student Christian Movement
SIDT	Solomon Islands Development Trust
SWAPO	South West African Peoples' Organisation
TAA	Trans Australian Airlines
TAYAP	Thailand Australia Youth Ambassadors Program
TEFL	Teaching of English as a Foreign Language
UNAMET	United Nations Mission in East Timor

UNAMIC	United Nations Advance Mission in Cambodia
UNDP	United Nations Development Program
UNESCO	United Nations Educational, Scientific and Cultural Organization
UNHCR	United Nations High Commissioner for Refugees
UNTAC	United Nations Transitional Authority in Cambodia
UNTAET	United Nations Transitional Administration in East Timor
UNV	United Nations Volunteers
VGA	Volunteer Graduate Association
VGS	Volunteer Graduate Scheme to Indonesia
VSA	Volunteer Service Abroad
VSO	Voluntary Service Overseas
WADNA	Women and Development Network of Australia
YASANTI	Yayasan Annisa Swasti (Annisa Swasti Foundation)
YCW	Young Christian Workers
YIS	Yayasan Indonesia Sejahtera (Indonesian Welfare Foundation)
ZANU	Zimbabwe African National Union
ZAPU	Zimbabwe African People's Union
ZIMFEP	Zimbabwean Foundation for Education and Production

Notes

Introduction

1 Peter Britton, "The Light, Powder and Construction Works", in *Breaking Out: Memories of Melbourne in the 1970s*, Susan Blackburn (ed.) (Willoughby: Hale and Iremonger, 2015), 294–310.

2 Examples include Susan Engel and Nichole Georgeou, "The Impact of Neoliberalism and New Managerialism on Development Volunteering: An Australian Case Study", *Australian Journal of Political Science* 46, No. 2 (June 2011), 297–311; Agnieszka Sobocinska, "How to Win Friends and Influence Nations: The International History of Development Volunteering", *Journal of Global History* 12, No. 1 (2017), 49–73; Benjamin J. Lough, *The Evolution of International Volunteering* (Bonn: United Nations Volunteers, 2016); Anthony Fee, Helena Heizmann and Sidney Gray, "Towards a Theory of Effective Cross-cultural Capacity Development: The Experiences of Australian International NGO Expatriates in Vietnam", *International Journal of Human Resource Management* 28, No. 14 (2017), 2036–61.

3 Australian Volunteers International, *A Place in the World: Stories from Australian Volunteers International* (Melbourne: Melbourne Books, 2007).

4 Australian Volunteers International, "Finding a Window to Reach In: An Evaluation of the Volunteer Program in the Middle East; 2001–2011" (Melbourne, 2012); Australian Volunteers International, "It's the Invisible Things: An Evaluation of the Volunteer Program in China 1988–2013" (Melbourne, 2013).

5 Betty Feith, "An Episode in Education for International Understanding: The Volunteer Graduate Scheme in Indonesia, 1950–1963: 'Putting in a Stitch or Two'", in *Bridges of Friendship: Reflections on Indonesia's Early Independence and Australia's Volunteer Graduate Scheme*, Ann McCarthy and Ailsa Thomson Zainuddin (eds.) (Melbourne: Monash University Publishing, 2017), 11–88.

Chapter 1: Volunteer Graduate Scheme to Indonesia (1951–69)

1 Renate Howe, *A Century of Influence: The Australian Student Christian Movement, 1896–1996* (Sydney: UNSW Press, 2009), 144–5.

2 Chris Waters, "The Macmahon Ball Mission to East Asia 1948", *Australian Journal of Politics and History* 40, No. 3 (1994), 361. For more about Ball's contribution to Australian policy and scholarship, see Rex Mortimer, "From Ball to Arndt: The Liberal Impasse in Australian Scholarship on Southeast Asia", in *Showcase State: The Illusion of Indonesia's Accelerated Modernization*,

Rex Mortimer (ed.) (Sydney: Angus and Robertson, 1973), 101–30, and Ai Kobayashi, *W. Macmahon Ball: Politics for the People* (North Melbourne: Australian Scholarly Publishing, 2013).

3 For details of Feith's life, see Jemma Purdey, *From Vienna to Yogyakarta: The Life of Herb Feith* (Kensington, NSW: UNSW Press, 2011).

4 Herb Feith, interview by Tim Bowden, 8 April 1991, ABC Social History Unit (unpublished transcript in AVI archives).

5 Jamie Mackie, "After the Revolusi: Indonesia 1956–58", in *Half a Century of Indonesian–Australian Interaction*, A. Lucas (ed.) (Adelaide: Flinders University, 1996).

6 Howe, *A Century of Influence*, 275–6.

7 Feith, interview by Bowden.

8 Frank Engel, Talk to AVA briefing on origins of the Overseas Service Bureau, 18 January 1983, AVI archives.

9 Betty Feith, "An Episode in Education for International Understanding", 17.

10 Frank Engel, "A Changing World", in "Six Stories from the Overseas Service Bureau", an unpublished collection, Wendy Poussard (ed.), June 1988, in AVI archives.

11 For more on the extraordinary activism and service of Molly and Bondan, see Ivan Southall, *Indonesia Face to Face* (Melbourne: Lansdowne Press, 1964), and Molly Bondan, *In Love with a Nation: Molly Bondan and Indonesia, Her Own Story in Her Own Words*, Joan Hardjono and Charles Warner (eds.) (Picton, NSW: C. Warner, 1995).

12 Purdey, *From Vienna to Yogyakarta, 77.*

13 The ASCM sustained a strong relationship with GMKI built around support for the Sukarno government (see Howe, *A Century of Influence*, 331).

14 Engel, "A Changing World".

15 Jim Webb, interview by Tim Bowden at Corinella, 25 May 1992, ABC Social History Unit (unpublished transcript in AVI archives).

16 NUAUS, "Volunteer Graduate Scheme", 8 July 1954, Union House, University of Melbourne.

17 NUAUS Committee for Graduate Employment in Indonesia, "Some Suggestions for Future 'Pegawais'". Union House, University of Melbourne, October 1954.

18 The full name of VGA was the National Committee of the Volunteer Graduate Association for Indonesia. It was established in 1957 to administer VGS and maintained an inclusive and entirely voluntary ethic (Feith, "An Episode in Education for international Understanding", 13).

19 Feith, "An Episode in Education for International Understanding", 32.

20 Jo Kurnianingrat, "An Indonesian Opinion on the VGS", in *Bridges of Friendship*, Ann McCarthy and Ailsa Thomson Zainuddin (eds.), 91–4.

21 Jo Kurnianingrat, "Other Worlds in the Past", in *Bridges of Friendship*, 105–69.

22 Feith, "An Episode in Education for International Understanding", 25.

23 Minutes of VGA Committee Meeting No.7, 25 July 1959, AVI archives.

24 Bondan, *In Love with a Nation*, 220.

25 Webb, interview by Bowden, 8.

26 Minutes of VGA Committee Meeting No.7, 25 July 1959, AVI archives.

27 Minutes of Special Meeting, VGA Committee, 9 August 1959, AVI archives.

28 Don Anderson, Confidential Notes on Visit to Sydney and Canberra 15–16 July 1959, dated 22.7.59, AVI archives.

29 Ibid.

30 Ailsa Zainu'ddin, *A Short History of Indonesia*, (Melbourne: Cassell Australia, 1968), 262. For an analysis of the rampant inflation, see Douglas S. Paauw, "From Colonial to Guided Economy", in *Indonesia*, Ruth T. McVey (ed.) (New Haven: Yale University Press, 1963), 204–5

31 Feith, "An Episode in Education for International Understanding", 43.

32 Lance Castles (Bendungan Jago, Jakarta), letter to VGA Committee, 7 March 1960 (written as his contribution to the Review), AVI archives.

33 Acting Secretary, Department of External Affairs, to Jim Webb, 14 August 1962, AVI archives.

34 Acting Secretary, Department of External Affairs, to Jim Webb, 23 July 1963, AVI archives.

35 Minutes of VGA Committee Meeting, 10 July 1963, AVI archives.

36 Don Anderson, Melbourne, to H. O'Neill, Melbourne, 22 October 1964, AVI archives.

37 Anderson to O'Neill, 22 October 1964.

38 For a brief discussion of this period, see Jamie Mackie, *Australia and Indonesia: Current Problems, Future Propects* (Sydney: Lowy Institute, 2007), 49.

39 Lyn Erickson, Melbourne, to Harold Crouch and Joan Hardjono, Indonesia, 7 May 1969 (copied to all VGA Committee, Hugh O'Neill and David Scott and located in AVI archives).

40 Erickson to Crouch and Hardjono, 7 May 1969.

41 David Mitchell, Djakarta, to VGA Committee, 30 May 1969, AVI archives.

42 Australian Volunteers Abroad (AVA) was the broader international volunteer program developed by OSB which had attracted Australian Government support. For details of its emergence, see Chapter 2.

43 The advice from Shann is contained in the circulated letter from Erickson to Harold Crouch and Joan Hardjono, 7 May 1969.

44 Less directly, VGS influenced the formation of the United States Peace Corps and the UK's Voluntary Service Overseas, as discussed in Agnieszka Sobocinska, "A New Kind of Mission: The Volunteer Graduate Scheme and the Cultural History of International Development", *Australian Journal of Politics and History* 62, No. 3 (September 2016), 369–87.

45 Herb Feith, "Mary Johnston", *Inside Indonesia* 30 (March 1992): 20–1.

Chapter 2: Overseas Service Bureau: The Early Years (1961–68)

1 Jim Webb to Herb Feith, 14 September 1961, J. Webb correspondence file, AVI archives.

2 For more on this association of Catholic students, see Val Noone et al., *Golden Years, Grounds for Hope: Father Golden and the Newman Society 1950–1966* (Melbourne: Golden Project, 2008).

3 Webb to Feith, 14 September 1961.

4 Overseas Service Bureau, *Bulletin*, February 1962, AVI archives.

5 Garnett's life and achievements are explored in Andrew Lemon, *The Master Gardener* (Melbourne: Hardie Grant Books, 2018).

6 Minutes of OSB Committee Meeting, 7 November 1962, OSB Meeting Papers and Minutes, 1962–65, AVI archives.

7 Minutes of OSB Committee Meeting, 13 December 1962, OSB Meeting Papers and Minutes, 1962–65, AVI archives.

8 Minutes of OSB Committee Meeting, 24 April 1963, OSB Meeting Papers and Minutes, 1962–65, AVI archives. Clemens and his scouts worked closely with US Marines, raiding Japanese supplies and gathering intelligence on Japanese activities ("Martin Clemens", Wikipedia: https://en.wikipedia.org/wiki/Martin_Clemens, accessed 23 October 2017).

9 Overseas Service Bureau, *Bulletin of Overseas Vacancies* No. 4, May 1963, AVI archives.

10 Minutes of OSB Committee Meeting, 24 April 1963.

11 Renate Howe, *A Century of Influence: The Australian Student Christian Movement, 1896–1996* (Sydney: UNSW Press, 2009), 330.

12 Jim Webb, in "Six Stories from the Overseas Service Bureau".

13 Minutes of Committee Meeting, 5 July 1963, OSB Meeting Papers and Minutes, 1962–65, AVI archives.

14 Ibid.

15 Major General Sir Walter Cawthorn to Sir Garfield Barwick, 23 July 1963, AVI archives.

16 Sir Garfield Barwick to J. Webb, 15 August 1963, J. Webb Correspondence File, AVI archives.

17 Jim Webb, Memo to OSB Committee, 23 July 1963, OSB Meeting Papers and Minutes, 1962–65, AVI archives.

18 Minutes of OSB Committee Meeting, 11 October 1963, OSB Meeting Papers and Minutes, 1962–65, AVI archives.

19 Jim Webb, Report on Visit to Canberra, October 15th 1963, 18 October 1963, AVI archives.

20 Crawford became Professor of Economics and Director of the Research School of Pacific Studies at the Australian National University in 1960 after a distinguished public service career. He continued to advise the government ministers and officials on economic, trade and aid matters.

21 Minutes of OSB Committee Meeting, 10 December 1963, OSB Meeting Papers

and Minutes, 1962–65, AVI archives.

22 Jim Webb, Memo to OSB Committee, 30 October 1963, OSB Meeting Papers and Minutes, 1962–65, AVI archives.

23 Minutes of OSB Committee Meeting, 13 March 1964, OSB Meeting Papers and Minutes, 1962–65, AVI archives.

24 Webb, Memo to OSB Committee.

25 Minutes OSB Committee, 10 December 1963.

26 Minutes of OSB Committee Meeting, 13 March 1964.

27 Minutes of OSB Committee Meeting, 12 June 1964, OSB Meeting Papers and Minutes, 1962–65, AVI archives.

28 Ibid.

29 Patrick Kilby, *NGOs and Political Change: A History of the Australian Council for International Development* (Acton, ACT: ANU Press, 2015), 34.

30 Quoted in David Marr, *Barwick* (Sydney: George Allen and Unwin, 1980), 193.

31 Jim Webb, interview by Tim Bowden at Corinella, 25 May 1992, ABC Social History Unit (unpublished transcript in AVI archives).

32 Ibid.

33 On the list were Professor Fred Alexander, Miss Betty Archdale, Lady Bailey, Sir Macfarlane Burnet, Dr J.F. Cairns MHR, Mr Martin Clemens, Lady Clunies Ross, Sir John Crawford, Rt. Hon. Sir Owen Dixon, Mr Vincent Fairfax, Mr Peter Howson MHR, Sir Robert Jackson, Mr Alan Marshall, Rt. Rev. J.S. Moyes, Col. J.K. Murray, Mr W.N. Oats, Most Rev. Eris O'Brien, Mr John O'Grady, Mr S.L. Prescott, Sir Grenfell Price, Professor Sir Fred Schonell, Mr David Scott, Very Rev. Michael Scott, Very Rev. Dr Alan Watson and Mr E.G. Whitlam. Later Sir Garfield Barwick and Most Rev. Frank Woods were added to the list.

34 Minutes of OSB Committee Meeting, 31 July 1964, OSB Meeting Papers and Minutes, 1962–65, AVI archives.

35 Kilby, *NGOs and Political Change,* 36–9.

36 Minutes of OSB Committee Meeting, 29 October 1964, OSB Meeting Papers and Minutes, 1962–65, AVI archives.

37 Jim Webb, Memo to OSB Committee on Bureau Finance, 25 November 1964, OSB Meeting Papers and Minutes, 1962–65, AVI archives.

38 Kilby, *NGOs and Political Change*, 37. The Australian Council for Overseas Aid (ACFOA) was formed in April 1965, with OSB, Australian Council of Aid to Refugees, Australian Council of Churches (ACC), Catholic Overseas Relief, Community Aid Abroad, Federation of Australian Jewish Welfare Societies and World University Service as founding members.

39 Webb, Memo to OSB Committee on Bureau Finance.

40 Minutes of OSB Committee Meeting, 3 December 1964, OSB Meeting Papers and Minutes, 1962–65, AVI archives.

41 Jim Webb to David Derham, 12 May 1965, Prof. D.P. Derham Correspondence File, AVI archives.

42 Overseas Service Bureau, *AVA Newsletter* No. 1 (26 February 1965).

43 Overseas Service Bureau, *AVA Newsletter* No. 2 (12 April 1965).

44 Overseas Service Bureau, *AVA Newsletter* No. 3 (24 June 1965).

45 Webb, in "Six Stories from the Overseas Service Bureau", 15–16.

46 Webb, interview with Bowden.

47 Minutes of OSB Committee Meeting, 12 August 1965, OSB Meeting Papers and Minutes, 1962–65, AVI archives.

48 Overseas Service Bureau, Statement for Discussion with the Government, 16 August 1965, AVI archives.

49 Jim Webb, Memo to OSB Committee, 21 October 1965, OSB Meeting Papers and Minutes, 1962–65, AVI archives.

50 P. Hasluck, Minister for External Affairs, to David Derham, Chairman OSB Committee, 5 November 1965, AVI archives.

51 Department of External Affairs, Outward Cablegram to All Posts, 9 December 1965. National Archives of Australia: A4250, 1988/2591.

52 Department of External Affairs, Submission to the Minister (Hasluck), 4 August 1965. National Archives of Australia: A4250, 1988/2591.

53 Hasluck to Derham.

54 Government Assisted Voluntary Overseas Service Scheme, Minutes of Meeting of Representatives of Department of External Affairs and Overseas Service Bureau, 4 November 1965. J.B.W. Committee Meetings 1962–65, AVI archives.

55 Overseas Service Bureau, *AVA Newsletter* No. 5 (6 December 1965).

56 Overseas Service Bureau, *AVA Newsletter* No. 1 (March 1966).

57 Overseas Service Bureau, *AVA Newsletter* No. 2 (August 1966).

58 Overseas Service Bureau, *AVA Newsletter* No. 1 (7 February 1967).

59 David Derham, Fundraising letter to companies, June 1968, Prof. D.P. Derham Correspondence File, AVI archives.

60 Overseas Service Bureau, *AVA Newsletter* No. 3 (28 August 1967).

61 Ron Crocombe, "Wot, No Volunteers?", *New Guinea and Australia, the Pacific and South-East Asia* 2, No. 4 (January 1968), 32.

62 Ibid., 29.

63 David Derham, "Letter to the Editor", *New Guinea and Australia, the Pacific and South-East Asia* 3, No. 1 (April 1968).

64 Ibid.

65 Overseas Service Bureau, *AVA Newsletter* No. 3 (July 1968).

66 Overseas Service Bureau, *AVA Newsletter* No. 1 (February 1969).

Chapter 3: Preservation, Defence and Crisis (1969–82)

1 Allen Martin to David Derham, 29 May 1969, Prof. D.P. Derham Correspondence File, AVI archives.

2 Memo from Colombo Plan Attache to Ambassador, Australian Embassy, Jakarta, 23 October 1969. National Archives of Australia: A4359; 221/4/28A (Jakarta-

Overseas Service Bureau, 1965–1971).

3 Overseas Service Bureau, *AVA Newsletter* No. 3 (October 1977).

4 Overseas Service Bureau, *Newsletter to Returned Volunteers*, 1 March 1973. Newsletters 1969–1982, AVI archives.

5 Overseas Service Bureau, *AVA Newsletter* No. 1 (March 1973).

6 Committee of Review into the Australian Volunteers Abroad Program, *Report to the Minister for Foreign Affairs* (Canberra, 1981), 40. AVI archives.

7 Overseas Service Bureau, *AVA Newsletter* No. 3 (August 1976).

8 Committee of Review into the Australian Volunteers Abroad Program, *Report to the Minister for Foreign Affairs*, 107.

9 Roger King, "Why Join?" *ROVA Magazine* No. 1, December 1983.

10 David Derham to R. King, 13 September 1974, Prof. D.P. Derham Correspondence File, AVI archives.

11 Committee of Review into the Australian Volunteers Abroad Program, *Report to the Minister for Foreign Affairs*, 105.

12 Ibid., 104–5.

13 Bill Armstrong, personal communication, 24 June 2016.

14 NGO and Information Section, Notes of Annual Meeting ADAB-OSB 1980, 26 May 1980. National Archives of Australia: A4250, 1988/2591 (Non Government Organisation History. Government Support for Scheme and meeting with Overseas Service Bureau, 5823233, 1965–1980).

15 Allen Martin to D. Derham, 22 July 1974, Prof. D.P. Derham Correspondence File, AVI archives.

16 Allen Martin to D. Derham, 25 September 1974, Prof. D.P. Derham Correspondence File, AVI archives.

17 Allen Martin to D. Derham, 9 October 1974, Prof. D.P. Derham Correspondence File, AVI archives.

18 Allen Martin to D. Derham, 25 October 1974, Prof. D.P. Derham Correspondence File, AVI archives.

19 NGO and Information Section, Notes of Annual Meeting ADAB-OSB 1980.

20 Neville Ross, Matters for Consideration before Meeting with OSB. National Archives of Australia: A4250; 1977/1252 (Overseas Service Bureau-Annual Reports and Meetings; 1977–1978).

21 ADAB, Record of Annual Meeting with Mr A.A.B. Martin, Director OSB, 31 May 1977. National Archives of Australia: A4250; 1977/1252.

22 Allen Martin to J. Ingram, 15 August 1977. National Archives of Australia: A4250; 1977/1274 (Overseas Service Bureau: Australian Volunteers Abroad; 1977–78).

23 Cavan Hogue, Australian Embassy, Jakarta, to Secretary Department of Foreign Affairs, 23 January 1978. National Archives of Australia: A4250; 1977/1274

24 Neville Ross, Memo to K. Detto, ADAB, Canberra, 27 February 1978. National Archives of Australia: A4250; 1977/1274.

25 Ross, Memo to Detto, 1978.

26 P. Flood, Australian Embassy, Washington, Record of Conversation with S. Brown (US Peace Corps), 7 June 1977. National Archives of Australia: A4250; 1977/1274.

27 Ross, Memo to Detto, 1978.

28 Neville Ross, Notes for ADAB Meeting with A. Martin, 4 May 1978. National Archives of Australia: A4250; 1977/1274.

29 Neville Ross, Memo to Ingevics, Branch Head, 21 March 1979, National Archives of Australia: A4250; 1977/1274.

30 E. Ingevics, Notes on discussions with A. Martin, 29 March 1979. National Archives of Australia: A4250; 1977/1274.

31 Neville Ross, Briefing note for Director ADAB, 13 July 1979. National Archives of Australia: A4250; 1977/1274.

32 NGO and Information Section, ADAB, Meeting with Overseas Service Bureau, Position Paper, May 1979. National Archives of Australia: A4250; 1977/1274.

33 Ross, Briefing Note for Director ADAB.

34 Ibid.

35 Elizabeth Britten to D. Derham, 20 March 1981, Prof. D.P. Derham Correspondence File, AVI archives.

36 NGO and Information Section, Notes of Annual Meeting ADAB-OSB 1980.

37 Martin to D. Derham, 29 May 1969.

38 Luxton took up rowing at Melbourne Grammar School, made his mark rowing for Pembroke College at the University of Cambridge, and represented Britain at the 1932 Olympics. As a member of the International Olympic Committee he played a significant role in organising the 1956 Olympic Games in Melbourne. Most of his business life was with Shell, and he eventually became the first Chairman of Shell Australia.

39 Overseas Service Bureau, *Newsletter to Returned Volunteers*, 1 March 1973.

40 Allen Martin to D. Derham, 14 May 1972, Prof. D.P. Derham Correspondence File, AVI archives.

41 Overseas Service Bureau, *Bulletin* No. 18 (April 1976), AVI archives.

42 Elizabeth Britten, personal communication, 15 September 2016.

43 At the time of her appointment she was known as Jeannine Mills. Soon after she reverted to her maiden name, Paton, which is used for her in this book.

44 Allen Martin to D. Derham, 14 May 1976, Prof. D. P. Derham Correspondence File, AVI archives.

45 Overseas Service Bureau, *Bulletin* No. 20 (April 1978), AVI archives.

46 Committee of Review into the Australian Volunteers Abroad Program, *Report to the Minister for Foreign Affairs,* 104.

47 Hugh O'Neill, personal communication, 27 June 2016. R.A. Simpson was a prominent Adelaide businessman whose company manufactured washing machines and other household appliances. He was a long-standing member of the

Committee, presumably invited by Derham.

48 Chris Fogarty to D. Derham, 7 January 1980, Prof. D.P. Derham Correspondence File, AVI archives.

49 Chris Fogarty, personal communication, 13 December 2016.

50 Allen Martin to D. Derham, 14 March 1980, Prof. D.P. Derham Correspondence File, AVI archives.

51 Chris Fogarty, personal communication, 13 December 2016.

52 Garry Bargh (Botswana 1972–73 and staff), Jeff Atkinson (Malaysia 1969–72; staff from 1973–76), Athol Brewster (India 1968–71 and former staff), Lyn Kane (staff), Jennifer Keys (staff) and Geoffrey Clarke (Indonesia 1976–77).

53 David Derham to B. Preston, R. King, G. Bargh, J. Atkinson, A. Brewster, L. Kane, J. Keys, G. Clarke, 23 October 1980, Prof. D.P. Derham Correspondence File, AVI archives.

54 Barry Preston to Chairman and OSB Committee, 1 December 1980, Prof. D.P. Derham Correspondence File, AVI archives.

55 Minutes of OSB Committee Meeting No.1, 9 April 1981, OSB Papers, AVI archives.

56 Britten to Derham, 20 March 1981.

57 Senator Baden Teague, personal communication, 17 June 2016.

58 Hugh O'Neill, personal communication, 27 June 2016.

59 Senator Baden Teague, personal communication, 17 June 2016.

60 Committee of Review into the Australian Volunteers Abroad Program, *Report to the Minister for Foreign Affairs*, 3.

61 Allen Martin to D. Derham, 22 February 1981, Prof. D.P. Derham Correspondence File, AVI archives.

62 Senator Baden Teague, personal communication, 17 June 2016.

63 Committee of Review into the Australian Volunteers Abroad Program, *Report to the Minister for Foreign Affairs,* 13.

64 Ibid., 80.

65 Minutes of OSB Committee Meeting No.2, 21 May 1981, OSB Papers, AVI archives.

66 Chris Fogarty, personal communication, 13 December 2016.

67 Frank Engel to B. Callinan, 6 July 1981, Sir Bernard Callinan Correspondence File, AVI archives.

68 Elizabeth Britten to R. Chancellor, 27 July 1981, R. Chancellor Correspondence File, AVI archives.

69 Elizabeth Britten to R. Chancellor, 5 August 1981, R. Chancellor Correspondence File, AVI archives.

70 Elizabeth Britten to R. Chancellor, 8 August 1981, R. Chancellor Correspondence File, AVI archives.

71 Elizabeth Britten to F. Engel, 10 August 1981, Elizabeth Britten Correspondence File, AVI archives.

72 Notes of Informal Committee Discussion, 12 August 1981 (Abridged). AVI archives.

73 Memo, Director to Chairman, 24 August 1981, R. Chancellor Correspondence File, AVI archives.

74 Memo, Chairman to Committee, 4 September 1981, Elizabeth Britten Correspondence File, AVI archives.

75 Memo, Director to Chairman, 31 August 1981, R. Chancellor Correspondence File, AVI archives.

76 Memo, R. Chancellor to Committee, 29 September 1981, AVI archives.

77 David Derham, Memo to R. Chancellor, B. Callinan, L. Luxton, A. Martin, 14 October 1981, AVI archives.

78 Hugh O'Neill, personal communication, 27 June 2016.

79 Minutes of OSB Committee Meeting No. 4, 13 October 1981, Elizabeth Britten Correspondence File, AVI archives.

80 Memo, Director to Chairman, 14 October 1981, Elizabeth Britten Correspondence File, AVI archives.

81 R. Chancellor to Committee, 14 October 1981, R. Chancellor Correspondence File, AVI archives.

82 E. Britten to R. Chancellor, 14 October 1981, Elizabeth Britten Correspondence File, AVI archives.

83 Elizabeth Britten to Foreign Minister A. Street, 26 October 1981, Elizabeth Britten Correspondence File, AVI archives.

84 Elizabeth Britten to R. Simpson, 12 November 1981, Elizabeth Britten Correspondence File, AVI archives.

85 Bill Armstrong, personal communication, 24 June 2016.

86 Hugh O'Neill, personal communication, 27 June 2016.

87 Memo Acting Chairman to Committee, Minister for Foreign Affairs, ADAB and B. Armstrong, 19 January 1982, R. Chancellor Correspondence File, AVI archives.

88 Russell Chancellor, Notes for Committee Meeting, 25 January 1982, R. Chancellor Correspondence File, AVI archives.

Chapter 4: Organisational Renewal (1982–90)

1 Barry Mitchell, "Action for World Development: From Charity to Justice", in *Breaking Out: Memories of Melbourne in the 1970s*, Susan Blackburn (ed.) (Sydney: Hale and Iremonger, 2015), 272–93.

2 Bill Armstrong, *The Aid Debate* (Melbourne: Action for World Development, 1982), 16.

3 Overseas Service Bureau, *AVA Newsletter* No. 3 (26 July 1982).

4 Roger King, to Former Volunteers in Victoria, 10 December 1982, AVI archives.

5 Elizabeth Britten, Letter from the Chairman, 26 October 1982, AVI archives.

6 Overseas Service Bureau, Minutes of Extraordinary General Meeting (by

Telephone), 31 March 1983, AVI archives.

7 Australian Catholic Relief to Director, OSB, 27 May 1983, AVI archives.

8 Bill Armstrong, Director's Report to OSB Committee, 1982–83, August 1983, AVI archives.

9 Ibid.

10 Overseas Service Bureau, *AVA Newsletter* No. 1, September 1983.

11 Bill Armstrong, Notes for Meeting with Richard Manning, December 1983, AVI archives.

12 Overseas Service Bureau, Three Year Plan, July 1984–June 1987, 1 February 1984, AVI archives.

13 Tam Lynden-Bell, Memorandum to Bill Armstrong Regarding Development Worker Scheme, 28 May 1984, AVI archives.

14 Record of OSB Committee Discussion at Indented Head, 6 July 1984, AVI archives.

15 See Chapter 7, Africa: Working in the Frontline States.

16 Committee to Review the Australian Aid Program, *Report* (Canberra: Australian Government Publishing Service, 1984), 100. Referred to as the Jackson Report.

17 Bill Armstrong to Dr Dun, 27 July 1984, AVI archives.

18 Bill Armstrong to OSB Committee, 20 August 1984, AVI archives.

19 Bill Armstrong to Minister for Foreign Affairs, 10 December 1984, AVI archives.

20 Richard Manning to Bill Armstrong, 7 March 1985, AVI archives.

21 Overseas Service Bureau, Minutes of OSB Committee Meeting, 22 March 1985.

22 Overseas Service Bureau, Three Year Plan Revised July 1985–June 1988, May 1985, AVI archives.

23 Committee of Review into the Australian Volunteers Abroad Program, *Report to the Minister for Foreign Affairs* (Canberra: The Committee, 1981).

24 Senator Baden Teague to Bill Armstrong and OSB Committee, 27 November 1985, AVI archives.

25 Overseas Service Bureau, OSB Committee Response to the Minister Re Recommendations of the Committee of Review, 3 February 1986, AVI archives.

26 Bill Armstrong, VGS-AVA-DWS The Evolution of an Ideal. Discussion Paper – OSB Committee and Staff, 28 November 1984, AVI archives.

27 Discussion Paper Prepared by Promotion and Recruitment Section for OSB Committee Meeting, 22 March 1985, AVI archives.

28 Discussion Paper Prepared by Promotion and Recruitment Section, 22 March 1985.

29 Ibid.

30 Tam Lynden-Bell, Towards a Communication Policy – Discussion Paper for OSB Committee and Staff, July 1985, AVI archives.

31 Mary Considine, Development and the Involvement and Placement of Development Workers – Discussion Paper for Staff Workshop, July 1985, AVI archives.

32 Overseas Service Bureau, Minutes of OSB Committee Meeting, 27 August 1983.

33 Overseas Service Bureau, Revised Staff Manual, September 1987, AVI archives.

34 Susan Blackburn, *Practical Visionaries: A Study of Community Aid Abroad* (Melbourne: Melbourne University Press, 1993), 311.

35 Graham Alliband, Mozambique: The Anatomy of a Joint Project, 24 February 1987, AVI archives.

36 See Chapter 7, Africa: Working in the Frontline States.

37 See Chapter 6, Indochina: Working in Times of Transition.

38 Minutes of Meeting of Joint Agency Working Group, 2 August 1984, AVI archives.

39 ACFOA, Memo to Member Agencies, 24 July 1986, AVI archives.

40 Overseas Service Bureau, *OSB Newsletter* No. 11, November 1986.

41 For 1987/88, OSB requested $2.37 million to maintain about 200 volunteers in the field; supporting 250 volunteers would have required an additional $250,000.

42 Notes of OSB Managers' Meeting at Tobin Bros., 11 February 1987.

43 Bill Armstrong, Paper for the OSB Committee Re Future Funding and Status of the OSB, March 1987, AVI archives

44 Bill Armstrong, Report on Visit to Canberra March 1987 to Discuss Funding and OSB Relationship to Government, 25 March 1987, AVI archives.

45 ADAB, Variation of Understanding Relating to Development Worker Scheme (Original Agreed 30 May 1985), 15 June 1987, AVI archives.

46 Minutes of Meeting of OSB Executive Committee Including Bill Armstrong's Report on His Meeting with R. Manning, Deputy DG, ADAB on 29 July 1987, 4 August 1987.

47 In August 1987, the Australian Development Assistance Bureau (ADAB) became the Australian International Development Assistance Bureau (AIDAB).

48 Bill Armstrong, Report of Discussion with Tony Vale, AIDAB, 24 November 1987.

49 Draft Terms of Reference for Joint Review (for Agreement by 20 May 1988), 8 April 1988, AVI archives.

50 Diane McDonald, Notes Taken at Meeting with Dr Dun, 14 April 1988, AVI archives.

51 Bill Armstrong to Bob Dun, DG AIDAB, 30 August 1988, AVI archives.

52 Overseas Service Bureau, Response to the AIDAB Questionnaire, November 1988, 3, AVI archives.

53 Ibid., 28.

54 Ibid., 43.

55 Mary Considine, Notes of Meeting between OSB and AIDAB, 7 December 1988, AVI archives.

56 AIDAB Policy Branch, NGOs and AIDAB: A Diverse Relationship. Draft Discussion Paper, 31 March 1989, AVI archives.

57 Minutes from a Meeting to Discuss the Location and Management of Voluntary Technical Assistance Programs Administered by OSB and AESOP, 10 May 1989, AVI archives.

58 Ibid.

59 Minutes of OSB Committee Policy Weekend Meeting, 12 May 1989, AVI archives.

60 Bill Armstrong to John Holloway, 18 May 1989, AVI archives.

61 Record of Meeting Between Members of the OSB Committee and Representatives of AIDAB, 2 June 1989, AVI archives.

62 Bill Armstrong to John Holloway, 14 June 1989, AVI archives.

63 Overseas Service Bureau, Minutes of OSB Committee Meeting, 15 July 1989.

64 Bill Armstrong to Bob Dun (DG AIDAB), 11 September 1989, AVI archives.

65 Bill Armstrong, Notes of Telephone Conversation with John Holloway, 13 September 1989, AVI archives.

66 R.B. Dun to Bill Armstrong, 11 October 1989, AVI archives.

67 Douglas Carter, Australian Government Solicitor, Agreement between Commonwealth of Australia and Overseas Service Bureau Regarding the Provision of Grants to the Latter's Voluntary Technical Assistance Program, 6 July 1990, AVI archives.

68 Bill Armstrong to Bob Dun (DG AIDAB), 30 August 1990, AVI archives.

69 Bill Armstrong to Bob Dun, 6 September 1990, AVI archives.

70 Bill Armstrong to all Committee members, 10 October 1990, AVI archives

71 Bill Armstrong, Notes of Second Annual High Level Meeting between OSB and AIDAB, 27 June 1991, AVI archives.

Chapter 5: Diversification and Dependence (1991–2002)

1 Stephen Sherlock, *A Guide to the Australian Aid Program and Issues in Development Assistance*: *Background Paper* (Canberra: Parliamentary Research Service, 1991).

2 Overseas Service Bureau, *Future Directions* (Fitzroy, Vic., 1991), 2.

3 Minutes of OSB Committee Meeting, 7–8 February 1992, AVI archives.

4 Bill Armstrong, Executive Director's Report to Committee, 2 May 1992, AVI archives.

5 Overseas Service Bureau, Public Information and Education Report to Executive Director, January 1992, AVI archives.

6 Bill Armstrong to Treasurer (John Dawkins), 17 July 1992, AVI archives.

7 Kieran Donaghue (AIDAB) to Bill Armstrong, 22 September 1992, AVI archives

8 Overseas Service Bureau, *Annual Report 1992–93*, 2.

9 Bill Armstrong to Dr Bob Dun, Director-General AIDAB, 13 October 1992, AVI archives.

10 Diane McDonald, An Evaluation of the Participation of Young People in the AVA Program 1989–92, 23, AVI archives.

11 Program Development and Training Unit, OSB Processes for Project Design, Implementation, Monitoring and Evaluation, January 1993, AVI archives.

12 Overseas Service Bureau, *Annual Report 1992–93*, 15.

13 Roger Peacock, FAS International Division, DEET, to Secretaries of State Education Departments, August 1994, AVI archives

14 Minutes of OSB Committee Meeting, 24–25 July 1992, AVI archives.

15 He first approached OSB in a letter, to Bill Armstrong on 26 October 1984, AVI archives.

16 Bill Armstrong, Executive Director's Report to Committee, 18–19 June 1993, AVI archives.

17 BBYT began in 1991 as a project of ACFOA and involved several member agencies led by OSB, who provided the project's coordinator and engaged networks of returned volunteers, Committee members and supporters.

18 Overseas Service Bureau, Beyond Borders Youth Tour 13 October–12 November 1993, AVI archives.

19 Further details of the Melanesian Women's Tour can be found in Chapter 9.

20 Overseas Service Bureau, *Annual Report 1993–94*, 16.

21 Overseas Service Bureau, OSB Operational Plan 1993/94, AVI archives.

22 Minutes OSB Committee Policy and Evaluation Weekend, 6–8 August 1993, AVI archives.

23 Philip Flood, Commercial Benefits from Development Cooperation, Address to National Trade and Investment Forum, Canberra, 13 July 1993, AVI archives.

24 Notes of OSB Managers Meeting, 16 December 1993, AVI archives.

25 *Australia's Development Cooperation Program 1994–1995* (Budget Related Paper No. 2) (Canberra: AGPS, 1994), 45.

26 Overseas Service Bureau, OSB Operational Plan 1994–95, June 1994, AVI archives.

27 Bill Armstrong, Executive Director's Report to Committee, 10–11 February 1995, AVI archives.

28 Minutes of OSB Directors Meeting, 15 December 1994, AVI archives

29 Minutes of OSB Committee Meeting, 10–11 February 1995, AVI archives.

30 Bill Armstrong, Briefing notes for meeting with Philip Flood, 30 March 1995, AVI archives.

31 In March 1995, the Australian International Development Assistance Bureau (AIDAB) became the Australian Agency for International Development (AusAID).

32 Philip Flood to Bill Armstrong, 29 March 1995, AVI archives.

33 Bill Armstrong, Briefing notes for meeting with Directors, 11 April 1995, AVI archives.

34 Bill Armstrong, Notes of meeting between OSB (Chris Fogarty, Sally-Anne Watts, Bill Armstrong) and AusAID (Philip Flood, Angus McDonald, Chris Kennar), 18 April 1995, AVI archives.

35 Chris Fogarty to Bruce Davis, 26 April 1995, AVI archives.

36 Gordon Bilney to Chris Fogarty, 1 June 1995, AVI archives.

37 MediaWise Pty Ltd, Communications Strategy for Overseas Service Bureau's Public Affairs Unit, May 1995, AVI archives.

38 Overseas Service Bureau, Policy, Program Development and Public Affairs Quarterly Report to Executive Director, January 1996, AVI archives.

39 Minutes of OSB Committee meeting, 18–20 August 1995, AVI archives.

40 Overseas Service Bureau, OSB Strategic Directions 1995–96 to 1998–99, AVI archives.

41 Committee to Review the Australian Overseas Aid Program, *One Clear Objective: Poverty Reduction Through Sustainable Development* (Canberra: AusAID, 1997); known as the Simons Review, the Committee reported in April 1997.

42 David Penman, Notes of Meeting with Alexander Downer (Greg Hunt, Ali Gillies and Andrew Thomson) by Bill Armstrong, Margaret Christie and David Penman, 29 May 1996, AVI archives.

43 Alexander Downer to Bill Armstrong, 17 June 1996, AVI archives.

44 Minute from Jeremy Wilson, AusAID, to Greg Hunt, Senior Adviser, Office of the Minister for Foreign Affairs, 21 May 1996, AVI archives.

45 AusAID, Unclassified cable from Barge, Bangkok, 9 August 1996, AVI archives.

46 AusAID had allocated $250,000 for TAYAP; of this $19,000 paid for the project design.

47 OSB Director, Policy and Public Affairs, Notes for Australia-Thailand Ministerial Economic Commission, Canberra Youth Ambassadors Program, 26–27 February 1997, AVI archives.

48 Alexander Downer, Minister for Foreign Affairs, Speech to OSB Private Sector Launch Fundraising for the Thailand-Australia Youth Ambassadors Program, NAB, Sydney 22 October 1997, AVI archives.

49 Minutes OSB Committee Policy Weekend, 23–25 August 1996, AVI archives.

50 AusAID's Risk Management and Audit Section engaged BDO Australia to conduct audits of CARE, AESOP and OSB during 1995 (Minutes of OSB Directors meeting, 26 October 1995, AVI archives).

51 Minutes of OSB Directors meeting, 24 October 1996, AVI archives

52 Minutes of OSB Directors meeting, 21 November 1996, AVI archives.

53 Widin Williams, Audit Report: Overseas Service Bureau, 28 April 1997.

54 "1997: The Year of Living Carelessly", ACFOA press release, 15 May 1997. AVI archives.

55 Bill Armstrong, to Andrew Thomson, 6 June 1997, AVI archives.

56 Bill Armstrong, OSB Position Paper May 1997, AVI archives.

57 Bill Armstrong, OSB Financial Management. Confidential, 16 June 1997, AVI archives.

58 Audit of the Overseas Service Bureau: Points of Agreement, signed Armstrong and Mick Cummins, Assistant Director-General, AusAID Sectoral Policy and Review Branch, following meeting on 17 June, 20 June 1997, AVI archives.

59 Peter McCawley, Deputy Director-General AusAID Asia, Africa and

Community Programs Division, to Bill Armstrong, 21 February 1997, AVI archives.

60 AusAID, Umbrella Contract in Relation to Periodic Funding, 30 May 1997, AVI archives.

61 Audit of the Overseas Service Bureau: Points of Agreement, 20 June 1997.

62 Peter McCawley to Bill Armstrong, 18 August 1997, AVI archives.

63 Memorandum of Understanding between Overseas Service Bureau and Julalikari Council Aboriginal Corporation, Signed 4 and 8 August 1997, AVI archives.

64 Overseas Service Bureau, Policy, Program Development and Public Affairs Quarterly Report, July 1997, AVI archives.

65 Bill Armstrong, CEO Report to Committee, 5–6 December 1997, AVI archives.

66 Minutes of OSB Committee Policy Weekend 22–24 August 1997, AVI archives.

67 Overseas Service Bureau, Draft Strategic Plan, 15 August 1997, AVI archives.

68 Bill Armstrong, Submission Relating to Agreement between the Commonwealth of Australia and Overseas Service Bureau for the Australian Volunteers Abroad Program, 23 December 1997, AVI archives.

69 Minutes of OSB Executive Committee, 11 February 1998, AVI archives.

70 Notes of Business Planning Workshop, 22 May 1998, AVI archives.

71 Bill Armstrong, CEO Report to Committee, 22–23 May 1998, AVI archives.

72 AusAID, Agreement for OVTA, 7 August 1998, AVI archives.

73 Minutes of OSB Governance Sub-Committee, 16 April 1998, AVI archives.

74 Andria Hutchins, Public Affairs Manager, Briefing Paper to the OSB Committee, Rebranding of the Overseas Service Bureau, 3 November 1998, AVI archives.

75 Kerr Walsh Communications, Communications Audit for the Overseas Service Bureau, August 1998, AVI archives.

76 Overseas Service Bureau, People Prepared Quarterly Report, 30 December 1998, AVI archives.

77 Keith England, Manager NGO Programs, AusAID, to David Penman, Executive Director AVA, 16 April 1999, AVI archives.

78 AusAID, Amendment No 1 to OVTA Agreement, 2 June 1999, AVI archives.

79 AusAID, Exchange of Letters Number 2 in Accordance with Deed of Agreement 07519 Amendment No 1 for 1 July 1999 to 30 June 2000, 19 July 1999, AVI archives.

80 David Penman, Proposals for Variation to the Agreement 23 March 2001, AVI archives.

81 Minutes of AVI Board Meeting, 5 February 2000, AVI archives.

82 Bill Armstrong, Australia's International Volunteer Program: The Way Forward (Private and Confidential), 30 August 2001, AVI archives.

83 See Chapters 9 and 10.

84 Bill Armstrong, to Board and senior management re meeting to be held with Bruce Davis, Charles Tapp, Ellen Shipley, 29 November 2001, AVI archives.

85 Notes of meeting between AusAID (Charles Tapp, Dep D/G, Ellen Shipley) and AVI (Bill Armstrong, David Penman, Chris Dougherty (in part)), 17 December 2001, AVI archives.

86 Bill Armstrong, How Are We Travelling?, 22 February 2002, AVI archives.

87 David Penman, to AusAID, 3 June 2002, AVI archives.

Chapter 6: Indochina: Working in Times of Transition

1 Moreen Dee and Frank Frost, "Indochina", in *Facing North: A Century of Australian Engagement with Asia. Volume Two: 1970s to 2000*, Peter Edwards and David Goldsworthy (eds.) (Carlton: Melbourne University Press, 2003), 199.

2 Minutes of meeting of ACFOA Indo-China Sub-Committee, 1 August 1983, AVI archives.

3 Patrick Kilby, *NGOs and Political Change: A History of the Australian Council for International Development* (Acton, ACT: ANU Press, 2015), 100.

4 Record of discussion between Mr Hun Sen, Prime Minister and Foreign Minister of the People's Republic of Kampuchea and the ACFOA Delegation, 22 June 1985, AVI archives.

5 Peter Britton, Record of telephone discussion with Graham Alliband, 1 November 1985, AVI archives.

6 Jennifer Ashton, to Peter Britton, 24 November 1987, AVI archives.

7 Minutes of meeting of JANGOO Management Committee, 2 June 1987, AVI archives.

8 Bill Armstrong, OSB and Geoffrey Leach, AIDAB, Project Review Visit to Vietnam, AIDAB/NGO Cooperation Program, Committee for Development Cooperation, October 1987, AVI archives.

9 Dee and Frost, "Indochina", 199.

10 Minutes of meeting of JANGOO Management Committee, 13 April 1988, AVI archives.

11 Minutes of meeting of ACFOA Indo-China Sub-Committee, 21 February 1989.

12 Darryl Bullen, Memo to Bill Armstrong on NGO Office, Phnom Penh, 11 May 1989, AVI archives.

13 Bill Armstrong, Letter to the Editor, *The Age*, 28 July 1989.

14 Bill Armstrong, News Release, 2 August 1989, AVI archives.

15 Minutes of OSB managers' meeting, 6 December 1989. AVI archives.

16 Bill Armstrong, Director's Report to OSB Committee, January 1990, AVI archives.

17 Bob Debus, AFFHC, to Bill Armstrong (OSB), Wendy Rose (SCFA), and Helen McCue (APHEDA), 1 June 1990, AVI archives.

18 Bill Armstrong, to Bob Debus, AFFHC, 7 June 1990, AVI archives

19 AIDAB Indochina and Burma Section, to Bill Armstrong, 20 December 1990, AVI archives.

20 Graham Alliband, Australian Ambassador, Hanoi, telex to Bill Armstrong, 20 December 1990, AVI archives.

21 AIDAB Indochina and Burma Section, to Bill Armstrong, 15 January 1991, AVI archives.

22 Minutes of meeting of OSB Committee, 2 August 1991, AVI archives.

23 Kilby, *NGOs and Political Change*, 17.

24 David Horner and John Connor, *The Good International Citizen: Australian Peacekeeping in Asia, Africa and Europe 1991–93. Volume Three of the Official History of Australian Peacekeeping, Humanitarian and Post-Cold War Operations* (Port Melbourne, Vic: Cambridge University Press, 2014), 114–15.

25 Meas Nee with Joan Healy, *Towards Restoring Life* (Melbourne: Overseas Service Bureau, 1995).

26 Joan Healy, *Writing for Raksmey. A Story of Cambodia* (Clayton, Vic.: Monash University Publishing, 2016), 128–31.

Chapter 7: Africa: Working in the Frontline States

1 Bill Armstrong, Director's Report to OSB Committee, 1982–83, August 1983, AVI archives.

2 Peter Limb, "The Anti-Apartheid Movements in Australia and Aotearoa/New Zealand", in *The Road to Democracy in South Africa, Volume 3, International Solidarity, Part II* (Pretoria: South African Democracy Education Trust, 2015), 922.

3 Patrick Kilby, *NGOs and Political Change: A History of the Australian Council for International Development* (Acton, ACT: ANU Press, 2015), 61.

4 Limb, "The Anti-Apartheid Movements", 929.

5 Kilby, *NGOs and Political Change*, 53–4. Sekai Holland was appointed in 2009 Zimbabwe's Co-Minister of State for National Healing, Reconciliation and Integration in the Cabinet of President Robert Mugabe and Prime Minister Morgan Tsvangirai. Holland came to Australia as a student in the mid-1960s and played a major role in galvanising support across the country for non-violent resistance in the campaign against the Springboks in 1971. She was a founding member of the Southern Africa Liberation Centre in Sydney (1971–80) and from 1974 to 1976 was the representative of Zimbabwe African National Union (ZANU) in Australasia, Southeast Asia and the Far East.

6 Tanya Lyons and Elizabeth Dimock, "The State of African Studies in Australia", in *The Study of Africa – Vol. II: Global and Transnational Engagements*, Paul Tiyambe Zeleza (ed.) (Dakar: Council for the Development of Social Science Research in Africa, 2007), 317.

7 Eddie Funde became chairman of the Board of the South African Broadcasting Corporation (2004–07) and Ambassador to Germany (2008–12).

8 Limb, "The Anti-Apartheid Movements", 948.

9 At a later meeting with her in 1987 in Zambia, possibilities for volunteers to work at Nyango refugee settlement in Zambia were discussed.

10 Hishongwa went on to become a Member of Namibia's National Assembly from 1990 to 2005, when he served as Deputy Minister in several portfolios.

11 Limb, "The Anti-Apartheid Movements", 971.

12 OSB in Africa, Staff Development Seminar, 28 August 1985.

13 Diane McDonald, (Preliminary Report) Evaluation Report of the Participation of OSB in the Botswana Teachers Program, October 1997, AVI archives.

14 Minutes of Meeting of OSB Executive Committee, 21 August 1985, AVI archives.

15 McDonald, Preliminary Report, 12.

16 Graeme Bruce, Memo to Volunteer Development Workers in Botswana, 9 July 1986, AVI archives.

17 Stuart Doran, "Massacre in Matabeleland", *The Guardian*, 19 May 2015, https://www.theguardian.com/world/2015/may/19/mugabe-zimbabwe-gukurahundi-massacre-matabeleland.

18 Minutes of Meeting of OSB Committee, 20 July 1985, AVI archives.

19 Susan Blackburn, *Practical Visionaries: A Study of Community Aid Abroad* (Melbourne: Melbourne University Press, 1993), 314–17.

20 Bill Armstrong, Memo to JAWG, 1 October 1986, AVI archives.

21 W.J. Armstrong, OSB and A.M. Vale, ADAB, Review of the Inhambane Rehabilitation and Rural Development Project, Mozambique, Vol. 1, September 1986, AVI archives.

22 Graham Alliband, Mozambique, the Anatomy of a Joint Project, 24 February 1987, AVI archives.

23 Hadino Hishongwa, SWAPO Chief Representative, to Bill Armstrong, 20 February 1987, AVI archives.

24 Tor Sellstrom, *Sweden and National Liberation in Southern Africa, Volume II: Solidarity and Assistance 1970–1994* (Uppsala: Nordiska Afrikainstitutet, 2002), 357–8.

25 Christopher Dureau, Report on Visit to Namibian Secondary Technical School, 12 June 1989.

Chapter 8: Indonesia: Working with Civil Society

1 Ken Ward, "Indonesia's Modernisation: Ideology and Practice", in *Showcase State*, 73.

2 For further exploration of the dilemmas Indonesian NGOs faced, see Philip J. Eldridge, *Non-Government Organizations and Democratic Participation in Indonesia* (New York: Oxford University Press, 1995).

3 Jemma Purdey, *From Vienna to Yoyakarta: The Life of Herb Feith* (Sydney: UNSW Press, 2011), 400.

4 Greg Barton, *Abdurrachman Wahid, Muslim Democrat, Indonesian President* (Sydney: UNSW Press, 2002).

5 Eldridge, *Non-Government Organizations and Democratic Participation in Indonesia*, 5–16.

6 Peter Britton, "The Indonesian Army: 'Stabiliser and Dynamiser'", in *Showcase State*.

7 Peter Britton, *Profesionalisme dan Ideologi Militer Indonesia* (Jakarta: LP3ES, 1996).

8 Peter Britton, to Aswab Mahasin, 13 June 1986, AVI archives.

9 This decision was soon overturned in response to lobbying by Indonesia's tourism industry.

10 Richard Robison, "Explaining Indonesia's Response to the Jenkins' Article: Implications for Australian-Indonesian Relations" *Australian Outlook* 40, No. 3 (December 1986), 132.

11 Ibid., 135.

12 These included: Abdurrahman Wahid, Aswab Mahasin, Dawam Rahardjo, and Daniel Dhakidae of LP3ES; Mulya Lubis and Buyung Nasution of LBH (Lembaga Bantuan Hukum, (Legal Aid Institute)); Adi Sasono of LSP; Bambang Ismawan of Bina Swadaya; Karcono of Bina Desa; Erna Witoelar of WALHI (Wahana Lingkungan Hidup Indonesia (Indonesian Forum for the Environment)); Sutrisno of YIS; Hardaputranto of LPPS (Lembaga Penelitian dan Pengembangan Sosial (Institute for Social Research and Development) and Anton Sujarwo of Dian Desa.

13 He was eventually welcomed to OSB in August 1987 for a 12-month appointment as a project officer in the field of community development and training.

14 The account in the following paragraphs is based on my records of discussions held 15–18 December 1986 in Jakarta with Aswab Mahasin (LP3ES), Abdurrahman Wahid, Jatikusumo (Bina Swadaya), Adi Sasono (LSP), Karcono (Bina Desa), Nasihin Hasan (P3M), Australian Embassy officials, and with Australian and other international volunteers.

15 Later correspondence from the Cabinet Secretariat allowing Habgood to stay a further two weeks to finalise his affairs was copied to a limited list of four officials. One was the Foreign Affairs officer responsible for restamping Habgood's passport; another was in the Taxation Directorate. The first two copies went to the Head of BAKIN and the Deputy Head of BAIS. Not only were the two intelligence agencies involved in the case; they were involved at the highest levels.

16 The volunteer was Robert Kingham and this assignment marked the beginning of his engagement with Indonesia over more than 30 years, mostly supporting a variety of Australian projects concerned with Islamic education in Indonesia and creating opportunities for Muslim scholars to study in Australia.

17 "For Every Action an Equal, but Opposite Reaction", *Kompas*, 12–13 October 1987, English translation by Australian Embassy, Jakarta, ACFOA Human Rights Office Archives, Clearing House for Archival Records on Timor, Columban Mission Centre, Essendon.

18 Overseas Service Bureau, A Brief Contribution to the Production of a Development Assistance Strategy for Indonesia, 20 July 1992, AVI archives.

19 The meeting was part of preparations for the Joint Meeting of Experts and Decision Makers on the Self-Propelling Growth Strategy, Jakarta, 12–16 June 1995.

20 Peter Britton, Australian Volunteers International's Indonesia Program, March 2000, AVI archives.

Chapter 9: Papua New Guinea and Pacific Islands: A Diversity of Linkages

1 Walter Lini, "Keynote Address", in *Australia and the South Pacific: Proceedings of the Conference held at the Australian National University from 18–19 February 1982*, Brendan O'Dwyer (ed.) (Canberra: Centre for Continuing Education, Australian National University, 1983), 11.

2 Mary Considine, Exploring the Meaning of a Development Worker Program, February 1987, AVI archives.

3 "Solomon Island Development Trust: History", https://solomonislandsdevelopmenttrust.wordpress.com/history-2/, accessed 18 September 2018.

4 Overseas Service Bureau, *Annual Report 1996–97*.

5 Diane McDonald, Chris Dureau, Lyn Creek, An Evaluation of OSB Involvement in the SIDT Community Development/Education, Rural Water Supply and Sanitation Project, July 1986, AVI archives.

6 PIANGO. A Background Paper Prepared for the Steering Committee of the Pacific Island Association of NGOs, July 1991, AVI archives.

7 Overseas Service Bureau, Minutes of Committee Meeting, 2 May 1992, AVI archives.

8 Bill Armstrong to David Hegarty, 25 May 1992, AVI archives.

9 Overseas Service Bureau, Policy, Program Development and Public Affairs Quarterly Report to Executive Director, January 1996, AVI archives.

10 Overseas Service Bureau, Notes of OSB Directors Meeting, 2 March 1995, AVI archives.

11 Deborah Rhodes, Executive Summary of PNG Profile: Diversity Next Door, Report to OSB Committee, 18 July 1996, AVI archives.

12 Following the 2015 elections for the Autonomous Bougainville Government, Pentanu was elected Speaker of the House.

13 *Big Hair Woman*, Parham Media Productions, http://www.parham-media.com/docos/bhwoman/bhw_index.htm, accessed 6 May 2018.

14 Overseas Service Bureau, Policy, Program Development and Public Affairs Quarterly Report, January 1997, AVI archives.

15 Overseas Service Bureau, Notes of OSB Directors Meeting, 19 January 1995, AVI archives.

16 Overseas Service Bureau, Minutes of OSB Committee Meeting, 10–11 February 1995, AVI archives.

17 Overseas Service Bureau, Notes of OSB Directors Meeting, 9 March 1995, AVI archives.

18 Overseas Service Bureau, Notes of OSB Directors Meeting, 27 July 1995, AVI archives.

19 Deborah Rhodes, Proposed Pacific Personnel Recruitment Service – Draft Synopsis Presented at OSB Committee Policy Weekend, 19–20 August 1995, AVI archives.

20 Overseas Service Bureau, Notes of OSB Directors Meeting, 27 June 1996, AVI archives.

21 Overseas Service Bureau, Melanesian Women's Tour, 14 February–11 March 1994, AVI archives.

22 Overseas Service Bureau, *Annual Report 1994–95*, 13.

23 Australian Volunteers International, *Year in Review 2001–02*.

Chapter 10: East Timor: Supporting Self-determination

1 ACFOA's human rights work is discussed in Patrick Kilby, *NGOs and Political Change: A History of the Australian Council for International Development* (Acton, ACT: ANU Press, 2015), 113–28.

2 As well as Armstrong, they included Mary Considine, Christopher Dureau, Diane McDonald and Julia Wyrsch.

3 The human rights violations from 1974–99 are well documented and summarised in *Chega!: The Report of the Commission for Reception, Truth and Reconciliation in Timor-Leste. Executive Summary* (CAVR, 2005).

4 Minutes of OSB Committee Meeting, 22–23 November 1991, AVI archives.

5 Bill Armstrong, Statement to All Staff 6 December 1991, AVI Archives. OSB made one attempt to establish a volunteer presence in occupied East Timor. In 1995 a volunteer was placed in a vocational education institution where the situation was so polarised that he was suspected by both the Indonesians and East Timorese. The assignment ended abruptly with no consideration of a repeat.

6 For more about his career, see Carolyn Webb, "Timor's Son Heeds the Call Via Oxford and a City Tram", *The Age*, 15 August 2001.

7 Richard Woolcott, "Howard's 'Noble Act' Was Folly", *The Age*, 7 March 2003.

8 For Sword's story, see her autobiography, Kirsty Sword Gusmão, *A Woman of Independence* (Sydney: Pan Macmillan, 2003).

9 These included Tamrat Samuel, the Secretary-General's focal point on the East Timor question, Francesc Vendrell, Pacific Director of the Department of Political Affairs, and Ian Martin, Special Representative of the Secretary-General for the East Timor Popular Consultation, who also consulted with and briefed interested Australian NGOs. OSB met with Francesc Vendrell on 25 March 1999.

10 M. Shepherdson (AusAID) to Pat Walsh (ACFOA) email 26 March 1999, forwarded by Pat Walsh to Peter Britton (AVI), 1 April 1999.

11 Emília Pires to Peter Britton (AVI), email 10 May 1999.

12 Martin Lynzaat (AVI staff, Darwin) to Peter Britton (AVI), email 25 May 1999.

13 AVI, East Timor Diaspora Skills Survey, July 1999, AVI archives.

14 Sharon Capeling-Alakija, Executive Coordinator UNV, "Volunteerism: You Can't Measure Courage", address to National Press Club of Australia, Canberra, 2 November 2000.

15 Claude Belleau (UNV) to Bill Armstrong, email 11 June 1999.

16 Emília Pires to Peter Britton (AVI), email 13 August 1999.

17 Gusmão later recorded his gratitude to Pires in an "Open Letter to Emília Pires", 25 January 2017, http://timorlestebele.blogspot.com.au/2017/01/xananas-open-letter-to-emilia-pires.html.

18 Klaus Rohland and Sarah Cliffe, *The East Timor Reconstruction Program: Successes, Problems and Tradeoffs* (Working Paper No. 2), (World Bank Conflict Prevention and Reconstruction Unit, 2002), 5–6.

19 Bill Armstrong and Graham Barrett, email exchange, 2 and 3 September 1999.

20 Draft Summary Report of the Joint Assessment Mission to East Timor, 15 November 1999 (coordinated by World Bank), AVI archives.

21 Gusmão, *A Woman of Independence*, 240–7.

22 Working as an adviser to Vanuatu's Prime Minister, Walter Lini, in the early 1980s, Parsons helped coordinate Vanuatu's support for East Timor at the United Nations.

23 After leaving OSB in 1996, Chris Dureau had been living and working in Indonesia.

24 Before the decision was made to return the people to East Timor, the group had registered groups of 5,000 to go to Australia and Portugal, with smaller groups to Macau, Thailand and Philippines. Vicky Tchong, to the author, email 22 August 2018.

25 Mike Parsons to the author, email 23 May 2018.

26 AVI Press Release, "East Timor Register Established", 21 September 1999, AVI archives.

27 Reena Ghelani (AusAID) to David Penman (AVI), email 20 September 1999.

28 Reena Ghelani (AusAID) to David Penman (AVI), email 12 October 1999.

29 Emília Pires, circular letter, 13 December 1999, AVI archives.

30 M. Proctor (World Bank) to Bill Armstrong, emails 8 October 1999 and 21 October 1999.

31 L. Campeau (World Bank) to Bill Armstrong and Peter Britton (AVI), email 6 January 2000.

32 AVI, Bill's talking points, 11 November 1999, AVI archives.

33 Megs Alston, Record of Discussion of Meeting with AusAID, 19 November 1999, 23 November 1999, AVI archives.

34 Bill Armstrong, personal communication, 23 July 2018.

35 Megs Alston, Field Trip Report, 10–19 December 1999, 22 December 1999, AVI archives.

36 Rohland and Cliffe (*The East Timor Reconstruction Program*, 6) attribute this stance to the United Nations' experiences in the Balkans.

37 Kirsty Sword Gusmão, "Spies, Lies, Trade and Aid: What Are Friends for?", *Sydney Morning Herald*, 28 December 2013.

38 Bill Armstrong, personal communication, 26 April 2018.

39 AVI, *2001–2002 Year in Review*.

Index

www.ingramcontent.com/pod-product-compliance
Ingram Content Group UK Ltd.
Pitfield, Milton Keynes, MK11 3LW, UK
UKHW041633190726
13854UKWH00006B/2468